Why we dream tells the remarkable story of Joe Griffin's successful quest to solve the question of why we dream, and vividly describes the practical uses his discoveries are being put to. His easily testable theory is not only consistent with neuroscientific findings from current sleep research, but also reveals important new psychological insights into the causes of depression, psychosis and the role that the state in which most dreams occur (the REM state) plays in developing each person's view of reality.

How we dream, it turns out, is vital both to our mental health and how we each fulfil our potential. Reading this remarkable book could easily change your life.

* * *

REVIEWS FOR _DREAMING REALITY_, THE EARLIER EDITION OF THIS BOOK

"The conclusions arrived at in *Dreaming Reality* are breathtaking, and given the freedom that the reader has to apply them to his or herself, they prove to be astonishing. This book gives such rational explanations that the cumulative effect is like turning on a light in a room full of shadows. Read it for yourself, without prejudice, and try it out – just feel those dark shadows withdraw." *Mental Health Practice*

"*Dreaming Reality* exquisitely scythes through the Gordian knot created by past dream theories. Even better, like all the very best explanations, its central theme is as far-reaching as it is intuitive. Through a fascinating combination of dream examples and scientific findings, it provides lucid and compelling evidence for how our night and daydreams not only mould our personalities but also lie at the very heart of being human." *Dr Clive Bromhall, author of 'The Eternal Child'*

"This book is revolutionary in more than one way. Past and sometimes over-looked research is re-evaluated, and a persuasive theory emerges... long overdue to my mind... an intriguing guidebook." *Doris Lessing*

"Compelling reading. Griffin and Tyrrell's adroitly written text challenges traditional views on our knowledge and understanding of the mystifying covert world of human dreams." *Professor Tony Charlton, Professor of Behaviour Studies, University of Gloucestershire*

"For anyone who has speculated on the meaning and purpose of dreaming, Griffin and Tyrrell's astounding insights light up the dark corners of the mind. Not since 1964 when Carl Jung's book *Man and his Symbols* was published has anyone set out to write so conclusively on dreaming for a wide audience.

Griffin and Tyrrell [propose] that dreaming functions to cleanse the undischarged emotional arousals of the day and they explain how this happens through metaphorical pattern-matching. From this one sets off on the journey to understanding the true causes of (and routes to healing) depression.

This book is revolutionary in thought, revelatory in content and will be established as the most important twenty-first century milestone on the road to accessible mental health treatment for all. It's a must for all who live with mental illness or work for its relief." *Ian Hunter* OBE

"Tells the remarkable story of Joe Griffin's twelve-year quest to solve the question of why we dream, and vividly describes the practical uses this knowledge brings to us all... Compelling reading for all dreamers." *The Alternative*

"The authors propose a purpose and function of dreaming that is rather enticing ... and sets the imagination going." *The Irish Psychologist*

"This is a book which is scientific and understandable, practical as well as theoretical and which brings clarity to a subject which has intrigued the human race for millennia." *Footnotes Journal*

"Joe Griffin's key insight... [means that] weekly excavation of your painful past in an attempt to understand your present depression has never seemed so foolish. There is a new king in the sacred grove [of psychology]." *Financial Times*

WHY WE DREAM

The definitive answer

ALSO BY THE AUTHORS

Human Givens: the new approach to emotional health and clear thinking
Joe Griffin and Ivan Tyrrell

How to lift depression – fast
Joe Griffin and Ivan Tyrrell

Freedom from Addiction: the secret behind successful addiction busting
Joe Griffin and Ivan Tyrrell

How to Master Anxiety
Joe Griffin and Ivan Tyrrell

Godhead – The Brain's Big Bang: the explosive origin of creativity, mysticism and mental illness
Joe Griffin and Ivan Tyrrell

*Learning from Nature: solving the mysteries of human behaviour and consciousness**
Joe Griffin and Ivan Tyrrell

The Origin of Dreams
Joe Griffin

The Survival Option
Ivan Tyrrell

*** E book available on Amazon***

WHY WE DREAM

The definitive answer

How dreaming keeps us sane,
or can drive us mad

JOE GRIFFIN & IVAN TYRRELL

PUBLISHING

Parts of this work were first published in Great Britain in 2004,
followed by a paperback edition published in 2006

Published by HG Publishing, an imprint of Human Givens Publishing Ltd,
Chalvington, East Sussex, BN27 3TD, United Kingdom.
www.humangivens.com

A catalogue record for this book is available from the British Library.

ISBN 978-1899398-42-3

Typeset in Sabon and Twentieth Century MT.
Printed and bound by CPI Group (UK) Ltd, Croydon, CR0 4YY

Cover illustration: © Michael Renouf 2014
Cover design: Bronwen Jarman

Dedicated to dreamers
everywhere

CONTENTS

"Travellers repose and dream among my leaves."

WILLIAM BLAKE

FOREWORD

"The effort to strive for truth has to precede all other efforts."

ATTRIBUTED TO ALBERT EINSTEIN

No product of human thought and ingenuity exists in isolation. Every project is built on earlier efforts and the new findings set out in this book are no exception. Significant portions of the material content of *Why we dream: the definitive answer* originally appeared in a monograph that described Joe Griffin's absorbing twelve-year research project, which he undertook with the aim of finding out why we dream. It was published in book form under the title *The Origin of Dreams: how and why we evolved to dream* and in *Dreaming Reality*

In it, Joe wrote up his key experiment, which he was the first dream researcher ever to think of carrying out. The experiment eventually led him to solve one of nature's most enduring mysteries and to go on to unravel some of its implications. Reviewers who understood his achievement were effusive in their praise: "A major key to the nature of all psychic states", "A giant leap forward" and "A watershed in our exploration of the evolution of mental processes" were typical reactions.

Although written for a scientific audience, *The Origin of Dreams* sold many thousands of copies to interested members of the general public, many of whom, as we know from numerous letters and conversations, were delighted to find that they could easily confirm Joe's findings by studying their own emotional life and dreams. This was surprising to us because the requirements of scientific writing, and the necessary use of technically correct terms rather than plain English, made it not a particularly easy book to read.

Dreaming Reality, this book's predecessor, was deliberately written in a style that was easier to follow. However, it was much more than a rewrite of the original; it was a fresh presentation, greatly extended, incorporating new research findings and more dream examples. It explored some of the practical applications, previously only hinted at, for what is now known as 'the expectation fulfilment theory of dreams', particularly in relation to improvements in psychotherapy and the treatment of depression and psychosis. The rewriting was done, then, not to dumb down the ideas but to take them further and, by using non-technical language as far as possible, to make them clearer and thus more accessible to a wider readership. *Why we dream: the definitive answer* has kept all these valuable changes but added yet more material to bring the content up to date, including work from other researchers that support the theory, and more dreams selected from the countless examples that people continually report to us, confirming its explanatory power.

We hope these ideas inspire you, and thereby enrich your life as much as they have ours.

Joe Griffin and Ivan Tyrrell

ACKNOWLEDGEMENTS

We have discussed the findings in this book with hundreds of individuals over the last few years and would like to thank them all for listening, thinking and commenting. We would also like to thank Val Baker, Andrew Boden, Abigail Darling, Dan Jones, Dr James Tapper, Jane Tyrrell and Juliette Young for permission to use their dreams.

Thanks are also due to our families (for their tolerance of our preoccupations) and our editors, Denise Winn and Jane Tyrrell, for their guidance and attention to detail – and, again, to Denise for all her work on this revised edition.

1

AN ANCIENT PUZZLE

"Such fantastic images give us great delight, and, since they are created by us, they undoubtedly have a symbolic relation to our lives and destinies."

GOETHE

One bright morning, long ago in Greece, perhaps after pondering the meaning of a particularly vivid dream, the brilliant polymath Aristotle gave voice to a scientific challenge that has echoed down the ages: "We must inquire what dreams are, and from what cause sleepers sometimes dream, and sometimes not; or whether the truth is that sleepers always dream but do not always remember; and if this occurs, what its explanation is." In the shade of sun-drenched olive trees at the Lyceum in Athens, where he and his brilliant band of thinkers used to meet, the father of natural sciences urged them to "obtain a scientific nature of dreaming and the manner in which it originates".

Since those seminal times, 23 centuries have come and gone but, despite the best efforts of many of the world's greatest minds, no satisfactory explanation was found. The answer to the question of what dreams are for, and their evolutionary cause, remained tantalisingly out of reach – a baffling mystery. In the 20th century, one of the pioneers of modern scientific dream research, Dr David Foulkes, reminded our own scientific community of why the central issue raised by Aristotle was still so important. "Dreaming," he wrote, "needs once again to be recognised as a problem so central to the study of the mind that its resolution can help to reveal the fundamental structures of human thought."[1]

We are going to make the case that, since he wrote those words, the problem of what dreaming is, and why we evolved to dream, has at last been solved. And, as a result, a richer mental landscape is revealed to us, one that provides new opportunities to expand human understanding – not only for scientists, but for every curious individual. We can now view a scene quite different from what might have been expected by modern neuroscience and psychology, but one that is full of psychobiological explanatory power. This is the territory that Aristotle had the prescience to know was vital for us to explore and understand.

The breakthrough discovery of why we dream was made by Joe Griffin, one of the authors of this book, and offers a truly significant 'organising idea'. All good scientists recognise that the devil is in the detail but that real understanding comes from the type of thinking that produces organising ideas that are big enough to make sense of that detail.[2] An organising idea is always needed to shape our perception and our thinking. This is because we organise what we see through what we believe we know. Thus an organising idea determines where we look and will guide our research endeavours. A new organising idea is always bigger than earlier ideas because it has to explain the anomalies that previously caused confusion. All progress comes from this type of thinking, a fact that is in tune with the recent recognition that understanding human nature requires an open-minded, holistic approach – in this case, a recognition of the interdependence of the biological and the psychological. What is now commonly referred to as 'mind-body' research has developed rapidly in recent decades and has produced enormous advances in our knowledge of the relationship between the brain, immunity and disease, for example, as well as in psychology and behaviour.

Joe's breakthrough occurred because accumulated research data about dreaming and new technologies to facilitate sleep research had made it possible.[3] It is truly an organising idea, in that the discovery of why we dream could only be made by integrating the findings of many disciplines, and thinking deeply through the implications until new insight occurred.

In the 20th century, the theories that arose to explain why we dream were divided into two broad categories – psychological and biological. Psychological theories, mostly of the psychodynamic type (such as those of Sigmund Freud and Carl Jung, which we describe in the next chapter), held sway during the first half of the century until, in 1953, Eugene Aserinsky and Nathaniel Kleitman made a groundbreaking discovery. They identified a special brain arousal state, occurring periodically during sleep, that became known as 'rapid eye movement', or 'REM' sleep, because of the darting, swivelling action of the eyes during these times. REM sleep was found to have a close relationship with dreaming.[4] (Further research soon showed that, during REM sleep, breathing became more rapid, irregular, and shallow; heart rate increased; blood pressure rose; and genital engorgement occurred in both males and females.) All this gave a great boost to the search for biological explanations for dreaming.

However, for any theory to account for the full complexity of human dreaming, there was clearly a need to integrate its biological and psychological aspects, as psychologist Dr Liam Hudson foresaw when he wrote: "This evolutionary puzzle [dreaming and REM sleep] and the question of the brain's operating principles are tied together, as [scientists] correctly assume. What they do not entertain is the possibility of an altogether more sweeping synthesis, and at the same time more rigorous explanation, in which these biological considerations are gathered together with another more strictly psychological one: the question of the formal properties implicit in the meaning of dreams themselves. In such a synthesis 'bottom up' and 'top down' theorising about the sleeping brain and its products would knit together, and the conceptual gap within psychology between mechanistic and interpretative modes of explanation would close ... Such a synthesis is as exciting a prospect as any psychology now offers, and eminently achievable – although at present it hovers in mid-distance, still out of reach."[5]

It was the realisation that Hudson was right that prompted Joe to set off on a research programme of his own (after reading all the available literature on the subject that he could lay his hands on). It became his passion. But it took 12 years before the full fruits of his work were realised. Since his theory was published as *The Origin of Dreams*,[3] an academic monograph in book form, no scientist has disproved it and even more evidence has emerged to support it.

When Joe first published his answer to Aristotle's challenge, he had no idea of the wider significance of his findings. However, as a result of ongoing work over the ensuing years, remarkable new connections have emerged. For example, the relationships between dreaming and how we learn, dreaming and daydreaming, dreaming and creativity, and dreaming and problem solving, have made an important practical difference to the work of educationalists, whose attention has been drawn in increasing numbers. Many psychologists have realised that Joe's insight provides a unified theory of hypnosis and a new way to think about the nature of consciousness. Furthermore, the relationship between dreaming and emotional distress – depression, anger, addiction, anxiety and psychosis – has had such a direct bearing on psychological treatment that it has produced a new school of scientifically grounded, effective psychotherapy known as the human givens approach. This has had a powerful impact on thousands of lives in the UK, Ireland and beyond.

From the speed with which practical applications have arisen from this discovery about why we dream, it is clear that the synthesis Hudson looked forward to is no longer "hovering in mid-distance"; it has been made. And the story of how it was done, and what more it may mean for us all, you now hold in your hands.

2

EARLIER EXPLANATIONS EXAMINED

"Time is but the stream I go a-fishing in."

THOREAU

It is a human given that we dream. Every night when we sleep we enter a magical world where the normal rules of physics, propriety and logic no longer reign: a world where, one night, we can dine with royalty, converse with famous poets or sportsmen, or walk naked down the street and, on another, we might have the ability to fly or talk with animals. Dreams inhabit a mysterious place, saturated with intense meaning, where experiences range from the prosaic to the wondrous and bizarre, from blind terror to sweet sensual delights. It is hardly surprising, then, that from the earliest times in every culture humankind has had its theories to explain the strange happenings in the land of dreams. And it is hardly surprising, either, that dreams were first thought to be inhabited by gods and devils.

The ancient civilisations of Babylon, Assyria, Egypt, Greece, India and China took dreams very seriously, believing they were messages from the gods which often foretold future events. The Ancient Greeks, however, although still believing that the gods communicated human destiny through dreams, observed that not all dreams came true. Homer, Plato and also the Roman poet Virgil subsequently made the discrimination that true dreams came from the 'Gate of Horn' and false dreams from the 'Gate of Ivory', probably building on earlier ideas from Egypt and Mesopotamia, which also had a 'Gate of the Horns'.[1] Interestingly, as puns can often be found in dreams, the names of these gates also contain puns – the Greek for ivory is *elephas*, also meaning ‘to cheat’, and the Greek for horn is *karanoo*, which also means ‘to accomplish’. Temples were erected throughout Greece to encourage, under the guidance of a special priesthood, ‘healing dreams’ which would indicate which medicine or activity was appropriate for the dreamer’s ailment. Hippocrates placed great emphasis upon symbolism in dreams that he thought indicated particular ailments; for example, dreaming of overflowing rivers meant an excess of blood.

Aristotle, however, rejected notions of the divine origin of dreams. How could it be so, he reasoned, since animals could also be seen to dream? Instead, he saw dreams as residual sensory impressions left over from waking experience. Plato pointed out that, since our higher reasoning faculties were absent in dreams, this left the way open to the expression of unbridled passion. In all people, he claimed, there was a lawless wild beast whose presence is glimpsed in dreams of passion and anger. He also thought it possible to have morally superior dreams when reasoning is appropriately stimulated.

The most comprehensive work on dreams to come to us from ancient times are the five books of dream interpretation written by Artemidorus, who lived in Italy in the second century AD. He held a sophisticated view of dream interpretation, believing that the same dream could have a different meaning depending on the character and circumstances of the individual dreamer. But the idea that dreams contained divine messages persisted.

The Bible has many examples of God advising people by means of dreams, perhaps the most famous in the Old Testament being Pharaoh’s dream of seven fat cows followed by seven lean ones. This Joseph interpreted as seven years of plenty followed by seven years of famine. And the New Testament, too, is full of dream references, particularly around the story of the birth and life of Jesus.

Dreams also played a major role in Islamic cultures. The Koran was said largely to have been revealed to Mohammed in a series of dream visions, each of which appeared to him “like the break of dawn”. Ramadan, the ninth month of the Moslem year, celebrates the days leading up to the night when Mohammed received his first revelations. Each day of Ramadan, Moslems fast from sunrise to sunset until the date of Mohammed's 'Night of Power' when, according to tradition, Gabriel first told him of his mission in a dream in which he ascended to heaven on a winged horse and met Abraham and Jesus. He was then given instructions, and he and his followers returned to Mecca before dawn. It is said that on this 'Night of Power' the gates of Paradise are open, the gates of Hell shut and the devils are in chains. (Gates were clearly a powerful metaphor in ancient times, perhaps because they were such a useful invention.)

Records show that Mohammed frequently interpreted the dreams of his disciples. Following his example, dream interpretation became a widespread feature of Islamic culture. An Arabian dream book of the eleventh century makes mention of several thousand dream interpreters operating at that time.[2]

The great Arab historian, traveller, statesman and Sufi, Ibn Khaldûn, in his 1377 introduction to his monumental history of the world, *The Muqaddimah*, described three types of dream. There are 'clean' dream visions that come from God, 'allegorical' dream visions that are inspired by 'angels' (higher human faculties of perception according to Sufis) and 'confused' dreams which are inspired by 'Satan' (the material world). He noted that, "When the spirit withdraws from the external senses during sleep, it can activate forms from memory which can then become clothed by the imagination in the form of sensory images". He also described a technique for inducing spiritual dreams which involved focusing a clear desire to have such dreams and the repetition of certain phrases, indicative of the "perfection of human nature", before falling asleep. He pointed out that this technique could only create a state of preparedness for such dream visions, it provided no guarantee of receiving them.[3]

Whilst Khaldûn was writing within the accepted religious orthodoxy of his day, this approach does hint at a sophisticated use of the potential of the dream state. From the research evidence explored later in this book in regard to creativity and dreams, it will become clear that the technique which Khaldûn describes would certainly facilitate the expression of a solution to – or knowledge of – a problem, arrived at unconsciously.

Whilst dreams remained important in the Islamic world up to modern times, in Europe during the Middle Ages studying them fell into disrepute and was progressively identified with 'the devil', sin and sources of temptation. This only started to change during the Renaissance, when artists like Giotto used dreaming as a metaphor for prophetic inspiration. To indicate this, he painted the saints asleep within pictures that portrayed the subject matter of the visions inspired by their dreams.

It was not until the nineteenth century, when writers such as Alfred Maury[4] and Ludwig Strumpell[5] emphasised the role played by waking experiences and emotions that were insufficiently inhibited during sleep in instigating dreams, that a more scientific approach to the topic began in the West. Ideas about the role of unconscious processes were also widely circulating by this time and it was Freud who famously pulled some of these ideas together, combined them with his theory of neurosis, and produced the first attempt at a systematic theory of dreaming.

Freud's censor

Sigmund Freud's theory of dreams grew out of his theory of neurosis. He saw a neurotic symptom as being a solution to conflict between a conscious wish and an unconscious repressed wish.[6] Each neurotic symptom was, he believed, an attempt at simultaneously satisfying both wishes.

Freud noticed that patients often talked about dreams during therapy sessions. He saw dreams as the product of a conflict between the wish to sleep and unconscious repressed wishes from early childhood. He believed that, while we are awake, these repressed wishes are active in the unconscious but are held in check or restrained from entering consciousness by what he termed a 'censor'. He posited that, during sleep, however, this censor was not as alert as during our waking hours, and that repressed wishes, if sufficiently disguised, could sometimes get past it and be expressed in a dream. Freud believed dreams to be very similar to neurotic symptoms and that they acted as the guardian of sleep, performing a protective role by allowing the expression of unconscious wishes that would otherwise disturb sleep.

He believed that the fact that we sometimes wake up from a nightmare was the result of the failure of a particular dream to sufficiently disguise the unconscious wishes being expressed. As a consequence, the censor was suddenly aroused to full waking alertness. Freud saw the disguise taken in the dream by the unconscious wish as the product of 'dream work'. (This is where Freud's theory becomes incredibly complicated. We contend that, if even our very brief outline generates a degree of cognitive indigestion, this is intrinsic to Freud's theory rather than our explanation of it!) Dream work was deemed to involve the condensing of material, so that a particular element of the obvious content represented several dream thoughts. It might also involve displacement, where a dream element's clear and obvious significance was far less than the disguised, concealed significance. It also involved representation – primarily the translation of a thought into visual images. The final process involved the replacing of a particular character or action with symbols. This happened, Freud thought, because of the need to disguise the salacious, largely sexual, nature of the hidden content.

Freud described the day's residue of problems, worries, unsatisfied wishes or purely indifferent material, as acting as, in his words, the 'entrepreneur' for a dream, and stated that the 'psychical capital' which made the dream possible was invariably a repressed infantile wish contained in the subconscious to which the daytime residue became linked. The images from waking experiences that were usually contained in the clear content of dreams came from a repressed infantile wish that saw an affinity with the waking experience and which used these images, and others from memory, as a sort of disguise to slip past the half-asleep censor and thereby gain a degree of expression for itself.

By now you are probably thinking that it must be well nigh impossible to discover the meaning of a dream with all this convoluted distortion ... yet more is to come. The waking mind, according to

Freud, gave a secondary revision to the obvious content of the dream story in order to give it a more logical façade. Freud declared that the real meaning of a dream could be uncovered by getting a patient to 'free associate' to each element in the dream that they had described. This free association process, he believed, unravelled the dream work and revealed the hidden wish or wishes that caused the dream. This random, open-ended interpretive technique adopted by Freud, where any dream symbol could be given a meaning associated with sexual desires or repressions of any kind, was what enabled the hermetic world of psychoanalysis to grow into the massive cult that it did.

Nowhere in Freud's self-declared masterpiece, *The Interpretation of Dreams*, did he actually give an example of an analysed dream showing an infantile wish as its source, although he did elsewhere. For the most part, he seemed to have been satisfied with his own confident interpretation of a repressed wish of recent origin, usually sexual in nature, being the source of any dream he 'analysed'. Many people have commented on the singular oddness of Freud's ideas and how they crumble when faced with empirical evidence (that is to say, facts). Ludwig Wittgenstein, for example, pointed out that, "Freud very commonly gives what we might call a sexual interpretation. But it is interesting that among all the reports of dreams that he gives, there is not a single example of a straightforward sexual dream. Yet these are as common as rain."

Jung's myths and legends

Carl Jung was a colleague of Freud who became increasingly disaffected with what he felt to be Freud's doctrinaire approach to the investigation of dreams and neurotic symptoms. He came to believe that, while Freud's free association method of dream interpretation might lead to the identification of the dreamer's psychological complexes, it nonetheless led away from the real meaning of the dream. He could not accept that the meaning was hidden or disguised to get past a censor so that it could enter consciousness. For him, the symbols in a dream were the natural form in which the unconscious expressed itself. He saw dreams as the unconscious mind's way of correcting distortions and imbalances in the conscious mind. He also saw the unconscious mind as the repository of the 'collective unconscious', which he described as the archaic consciousness of primitive man, from which the consciousness of modern man developed – just as our body still conforms to a basic pattern that was typical of primitive mammals. He believed these archaic elements of the unconscious were sometimes expressed in dreams, and called them 'archetypes'. To identify these archetypes, according to Jung, a wide knowledge of ancient myths and legends was necessary.[7]

Jung developed, and encouraged, a cult around himself and his ideas, and many of his followers came to believe that dreams provided evidence of life after death. This meant that implicit in Jungian analysis was the idea that it was an initiatory preparation for the afterlife.[8]

Although few of Jung's ideas achieved the same degree of popular acceptance that was conferred on Freud's sex-obsessed theories, the increasingly widespread view among dream theorists – that dreams in some way help us come to a more balanced view of our emotional problems – owes more to Jung than Freud.

The multiplicity of modern theories

From the 1950s onwards, scientists generated a host of theories to explain dreaming. 'Dreams as problem solving' was one such, strongly put forward by a researcher called Thomas French.[9,10] He suggested that recent interpersonal conflict was the focus of problem solving in dreams but that dreams substituted analogous problems to 'solve' which were more suited to the nonverbal-thinking characteristic of sleep. He thought that, when making interpretations, it was more meaningful to work with a series of dreams rather than just one.

In 1953 a dream researcher called Calvin Hall proposed a cognitive theory in which dreaming was an extension of 'ego psychology'.[11] Dreams, according to this theory, are a continuation of normal thinking processes carried on through the medium of pictures or visual images. His research showed that the subjects of dreams were the personal concerns of the dreamer rather than the great political issues of the day. For instance, in the numerous dreams he collected from his students during the last days of the Second World War, when the first atomic bomb was dropped on Hiroshima in Japan, he noted that this catastrophic event did not feature in a single one. Therefore, he deduced, dreams were primarily to do with reflecting the dreamer's self-image, and he likened them to a work of art. An artist expresses his or her ideas through some medium, be it writing, pictures, sculpture, music or dance. The essence of the endeavour is that the artist succeeds in communicating inner conceptions by translating them into a medium perceptible to others. In the same way, according to Hall, the dreamer translated his conceptions about his own personal concerns into pictures and thus made them perceptible to himself. When a thought was made perceptible, Hall said, it was communicated. Unlike the communications of waking life, which, he noted, might have an audience of millions, the dream was a private communication with an audience of one, rather like the ancient Talmudic idea of a dream being 'a letter to oneself'. Dreams could thus reveal an honest and undistorted view of the dreamer's self-conceptions. Hall suggested that this report to oneself was unlikely to be as superficial or distorted as reports of dreams collected during waking.

Hall developed his theory of dreaming by collecting a large number of wide-ranging dreams and meticulously analysing their content.[12] On reading the dream accounts he collected, and comparing the dreams with the known concerns of each dreamer, it is difficult not to be impressed with his theory. Yet the theory did not receive the attention it deserved. Most recent books about dreaming do not even mention Hall's name.

One reason for this neglect might be that the theory seems incomplete. The idea that dreamers send themselves communications in pictures several times a night, which for the most part are forgotten on waking, seems rather wasteful. And the idea that nature evolved and preserved intricate biological mechanisms for the purpose of creating works of art to be seen only by one person who then, on most occasions, instantly forgets them, makes little intuitive sense. Yet one cannot deny the strength of Hall's empirical findings.

In fact, the strength of his empirical approach was also its weakness. The missing vital part of the dream process that could, potentially, have completed Hall's theory only becomes available initially through inspection of one's own dreams and one's own waking concerns, in the manner Hall used so brilliantly for other people's dreams. We will come back to this shortly. We need to look at some representative examples of other dream theories first.

In 1977, the 'activation synthesis theory' was put forward by J. Allan Hobson and Robert McCarley.[13] Hobson developed it further in work published in 1988.[14] They suggested that dreaming was the result of the attempt by the neocortex – *the higher brain* – to make sense of the random barrage of signals sent from the lower brain, and that the synthesis of material in the dreams we create may reveal something of how one's personality habitually operates. They thought that running out these random dream patterns might also serve a maintenance and developmental function. However, it quickly became clear, from the research of Hobson, McCarley and others, that the REM state is controlled by mechanisms in *the lower brain* and that dreaming in the REM state is more intense during bursts of activity such as rapid eye movements, fine muscle twitching, and breathing and heart rate changes.

According to Hobson and McCarley's original theory, a barrage of random stimulation was coming up periodically from the brainstem and being synthesised by the frontal cortex into dreams. But, once PET scanning of the brain was developed, scans of the brain in the REM state showed that the cortex was very selectively activated. The emotional brain (the limbic system) and the visual brain were highly activated but the pre-frontal cortex was excluded from this stimulation (the very part supposed to be doing the synthesising).[15] Hobson now concedes that, instead of global forebrain activation being responsible for dream synthesis, it is the emotional brain that is responsible for dream plot formation.[16]

Hobson and McCarley also theorised that REM sleep served to 'rest' the cells in the brainstem which produce serotonin and noradrenalin, because in REM sleep these particular neurotransmitters are not used by the brain. Their idea was that these neuronal pathways were being rested so that we would wake up the next day, refreshed by REM sleep. Consequently, then, the more REM sleep people had, the more refreshed they should be. But researchers looking at the sleep patterns of depressed patients found that they had massive amounts of REM sleep in proportion to slow-wave sleep and yet, far from waking up refreshed, they were waking up exhausted![17] How did Hobson account for this? He just said, "It is a paradox." (The amount of REM sleep experienced by depressed patients is very important for our understanding of the role of dreaming and we shall come back to it later.)

Yet another problem with their theory, which Hobson admits, is that it can't explain why certain dreams have positive aspects and some have negative aspects.[18] But the final nail in the activation synthesis theory's coffin is the finding that deep brainstem lesions do not generally stop dreaming, whereas certain lesions in the cortex do, despite the existence of brainstem-initiated REM sleep.[19]

Another possibility, the 'we dream in order to forget' theory, was put forward by Francis Crick and Graeme Mitchison in 1983.[20] Their idea came from studying work done on computer programs that simulated neural intelligence. An overload of incoming information could trigger "parasitical connections" between unrelated bits of information – leading to the association of purely tangential or weak connections to the original learning (for instance, something one just happened to be thinking about at the time, when learning how to change a flat tyre). To stop the brain from getting overburdened by storing such remote connections to new material, it would make sense, Crick claimed, if there were a way to knock out such unhelpful associations. He saw REM sleep as providing this service, by delivering a series of bangs to the neocortex that would break the weaker links in the neural network. The clear implication of this idea is that dream material is essentially meaningless and without coherent structure. As, at that time, most dreams were thought to be bizarre in content, this was taken as evidence for the existence of these parasitical connections. Crick and Mitchison theorised that, if we didn't have dreaming, we would go on making more and more bizarre connections, which would imply that, if we block REM sleep, our memories should become more confused. If this theory is correct, then depressed people on antidepressants that block REM sleep should suffer memory impairment – they don't and, if anything, report memory improvement. As psychologist Liam Hudson has also pointed out that, if Crick's and Mitchison's theory were right, people who frequently recall dreams should be more "addled in their wits" than non-recallers, a finding unsupported by research.[21]

Yet another problem with the theory is that technical advances in the recording of what actually happens during dreaming have now shown that the overwhelming majority of dreams are, in fact, quite routine, everyday experiences.[22] It is the tiny percentage of dreams that we recall that seem bizarre: dreams recorded in the sleep laboratory, when sleepers are woken as soon as they go into REM sleep, are mostly not bizarre at all. As a result of this discovery, Crick revised his theory to suggest that it might still, at least, explain those few dreams that do have a bizarre component to them. In other words, his theory has been so drastically modified that very little of it remains at all.

Finally, since Crick and Mitchison formulated this theory, not a shred of evidence has arisen to show that the human brain makes parasitical connections. That is something known only to occur with computer networks. The new research presented in this book disproves the 'we dream to forget' theory.

It is not surprising, however, that with the dawn of the information technology age in the 1960s, the new metaphor of the computer was seized upon to explain many processes, including dreaming[23,24] and one line of thinking became very fruitful indeed. Because, during REM sleep, the brain is disconnected from sensory input from the outside world by the inhibition of major muscles scientifically termed the anti-gravity muscles (we are all temporarily paralysed during REM sleep), it could be compared to an off-line computer. Perhaps the myriad of 'programs' contained by the brain could be being updated during the off-line time of REM sleep, and dreaming was somehow related to this. In other words, REM sleep might be about programming the brain. This proposal had the advantage of seeing the REM state as an active one with specific purposes. The computer metaphor prompted scientists to consider REM sleep in the fetus and newborn as a time when the 'software' of the brain is programmed, an idea crucially picked up and developed by the French scientist Michel Jouvet.

It was Jouvet who made the discovery of the inhibition of anti-gravity muscles (our major muscles) during REM sleep. He suggested that REM sleep, which he calls paradoxical sleep, might have the role of programming the central nervous system to maintain or organise instinctive behaviour.[25] He argued that the programming of instinctive behaviour on a continuous basis, rather than a once and for all basis during early development, would enable a more efficient expression of instinctive behaviour. Since the original programming must interact with the animal's experience in the real world, then REM sleep might allow either the original programming to be reasserted (nature over environment) or the effects of the experience to modify the programming (environment over nature).

When we look at the biology of dreaming later we will explore Jouvet's research in greater depth and see how his work put in place some of the essential building blocks for understanding the function of the REM state. However, as we shall see, it does not offer an explanation as to why dreams take the form they do.

Some researchers have recognised that emotion has a central role in dreaming. In the 1970s, sleep researcher Rosalind Cartwright proposed that dreams enable us to problem solve creatively in an unrestrictive setting, without being inhibited by circumstances or our emotions. Still active in this field, she holds that dreaming is a means of incorporating memories and regulating negative emotion, thus keeping us emotionally healthy.[26] We make the case, however, in Chapter 7, that problem solving is not a direct function of dreaming.

Sleep researcher Ernest Hartmann has argued that dreams are

guided by the emotions of the dreamer and are a form of psychotherapy, enabling the dreamer to make connections, in a safe place, between different experiences, thoughts and emotions. When the emotional state is clear-cut, the dream is simple but when emotions are mixed, it becomes more complicated. He suggests that traumatic or difficult emotions are gradually woven in with other less extreme experiences the dreamer has had in the past, enabling the emotional disturbance to be reduced and the dreamer to cope better with similar trauma or stress in the future.[27] However, this doesn't account for the fact that not all dreams are about traumatic or difficult emotions and that, while 80 per cent of dreams may involve negative elements, 53 per cent of dreams also involve positive elements.[28]

Antti Revonsuo, a Finnish cognitive neuroscientist also focused on trauma and proposed that dreaming evolved as a means of rehearsing threat perception and threat avoidance in a simulated threatening situation (i.e. practising our survival techniques). He and colleague Katja Valli analysed nearly 600 dreams from dream diaries kept for four weeks by 52 participants, categorising possible threats (escapes and pursuits, accidents and misfortunes, failures, catastrophes, disease and aggression) and the strength and frequency of them. They found that the main threats came in the form of accidents, misfortunes and aggression, of which the dreamers were mainly the victims. Threat situations in dreams were stronger (eg involving stabbings, shootings or being pursued by animals) and more frequent than in real life but were broadly realistic and mainly threatened the dreamer or people close to the dreamer.[29] Interesting though the theory is, again it doesn't take account of the fact that over half of dreams have positive elements.

In recent years, another theory has tried to climb the slippery pole of scientific acceptance: dreaming as a means of consolidating memories.[30] The evidence presented seemed to show that REM sleep was connected in some way with the learning of routine procedures. The theory still has enthusiastic adherents but Jouvet and others elegantly demolished it.[31] If it were true, depressed people, who dream proportionately more and more intently than non-depressed people, would have much better memories than everyone else. They don't. (We explore the dreams consolidating learning idea more fully in Chapter 7.)

It has even been suggested that dreams are the result of our brains trying to make sense of external stimuli registered during sleep. For example, the sound of a radio or phone may be incorporated into the content of a dream.[32] But this, of course, leaves a great deal of dream content unaccounted for.

By the end of the 1990s, most cognitive neuropsychologists had given up on the idea of there being any biological function for dreaming, settling instead upon the notion, along with Hobson, Crick and Mitchison and others, that dreaming is merely the result of low-level neurological processes going on during REM sleep, a biological epiphenomenon with no meaning and not selected for by evolution. Even G. William Domhoff, a leading sleep researcher who studied under Calvin Hall and who has recognised the role of emotion and metaphor in dream content, has finally concluded "reluctantly" along with the majority of cognitive neuroscientists that dreams have no important function.[33]

His outline for a new neurocognitive theory of dreaming, "sees dreams as psychologically meaningful in that they are coherent, relate to other psychological variables, and are continuous with waking conceptions and concerns, [but] it does not claim any purpose or function for dreams. Based on current evidence, it is most likely that dreams are the accidental by-product of two great evolutionary adaptations, sleep and consciousness. However, their frequent dramatisation of emotional preoccupations and their parallels with the figurative dimensions of waking thought may explain why many societies have invented cultural uses for dreams, usually in conjunction with religious ceremonies and medicinal practices."[34] He then triumphantly rams his point home: there can't possibly be a meaningful function for dreams, he insists, when most of the time we completely forget them. But he was incorrect in these assumptions, as we shall show.

Over half a century since the start of modern sleep research, despite dozens of theories, only a few of which we have outlined here, ignorance about sleep and dreaming is something of an embarrassment to scientists. In mid-2003, in a *New Scientist* report on a conference on sleep research in Chicago, a pertinent comment was made about dreaming: "Try to think of another fundamental biological phenomenon to which we can't assign a role. You'll draw a blank." Craig Heller, a sleep scientist at Stanford University, was quoted as saying, "It's the biggest unanswered question in neuroscience."[35]

But Heller was wrong. The question *has* been answered, but by a psychologist, not a neuroscientist. Scientists get so wrapped up in their own particular approach to a problem they rarely step back far enough to see what other people in different fields have done. (Joe first published his findings in 1993.[36])

The dream theories so far described all fall short of meeting the criteria for a holistic theory that combines the developmental (why dreaming evolved), the phylogenetic (dreaming occurs across different species) and the psychological (the richness of the feeling of meaning our own dreams have) aspects of dreaming, or why we almost always forget them. The various reductionist biological theories of dreaming put forward over the last few decades see dreaming either as essentially a meaningless epiphenomenon, an insignificant by-product of a biological process, or as somehow connected to learning or programming. There is no consensus. Even those that recognise the central role of emotion have not put all the pieces together. All the various lines of research have created a scientific logjam. Indeed, when reading reports of scientific conferences on this subject, we are reminded of the parable immortalised by Rumi in his *Mathnavi* over 700 years ago and projected again, for its contemporary relevance, in the West, in the 1960s and 1970s by Idries Shah.[37] In this now familiar tale, a team of men from a city where all the inhabitants were blind were sent off to examine an elephant. Each became convinced that they understood what an elephant was like, depending on which bit they managed to touch. One felt a leg and described the elephant as a kind of moving tree. Another passed his hands over an ear and declared it to be like a living carpet. A third grabbed its tail and said it was a rope. A fourth explored the trunk and was convinced an elephant was a hose or snake ... and so on. When they reported back to the city, it was clear that each had felt only one part out of many. Each had perceived it wrongly. And each went on to attract bands of supporters convinced that one or other description was the true one.

Any new theory of dreaming, if it is to conform to the highest scientific tradition, should mesh with the major biological findings of recent decades and also reconcile a much wider-ranging set of findings and variables than existing theories. It should generate novel predictions that are capable of validation. In other words, it must describe 'the whole elephant'.

3

AN EXPERIMENTAL ADVENTURE

"My Lady Seymour dreamt, that she found a nest, with nine finches in it. And so many children she had by the Earl of Winchelsea, whose name was Finch."

JOHN AUBREY, (1696) 'MISCELLANIES UPON VARIOUS SUBJECTS'

We are now going to explain the key experiment which broke the scientific logjam. It is, of course, for you to decide whether you think the evidence supporting Joe Griffin's theory of the origin, meaning and function of dreams meets the scientific criteria described at the end of the last chapter, and whether or not it reconciles all the available information collected about dreaming so far. But you don't need to rely on statistical probabilities or gut feelings to do that: you can replicate the experiment yourself. No sophisticated technical equipment is needed; you can do the science by working on the content of your own dreams. In the twenty-odd years since the theory was first published, we have been unable to disprove it and thousands of people have checked with their own experience of dreaming and found it holds true.

There are well established precedents other than Freud and Jung for using one's own dreams in dream research. For example, the method Joe used to collect representative samples of dreams was used by Ebbinghaus in his research on memory as long ago as the late 1800s.[1] He studied the rate of forgetting nonsense syllables rehearsed prior to going to sleep by waking himself during the night at regular intervals and testing his recall. His methodical approach, and the fact that many of his research findings have stood the test of time, demonstrated clearly that scientific method could be applied successfully to one's own subjective experience. Indeed, studies based on recall of dreams is staple fare in much modern dream research. Sleep researcher Bill Domhoff lists four sources of dream reports used in analysis: individuals woken during dreaming for sleep laboratory research; individuals keeping dream diaries as part of psychoanalytical psychotherapy (though such patients are few and unrepresentative of the general population, so this source is used only in case studies, not systematic studies); dream journals kept for personal, artistic or intellectual reasons – valuable in establishing the consistency of what people tend to dream about, although there may be gaps or omissions; and classroom collections, wherein students provide their most recent recalled dream or keep dream journals for a few weeks.[2]

In fact, even hardened cognitive neuroscientists have come round to the view that self-report is a valid, if not essential, part of a scientific approach to dream research – one which has been neglected. As Erin Wamsley and Robert Stickgold report, "For the most part, cognitive neuroscience has abandoned the behaviorist notion that conscious, subjective experience is not a suitable object of empirical investigation. Research in the last two decades has moved beyond the philosophical question of mind-brain relationship and begun in earnest to study the neural correlates, for example, of motivation, emotion, attention, mental imagery, and episodic memory. Very often, mapping the brain basis of these subjective concepts relies on taking participants' verbal reports of experience at face value. Yet surprisingly, neuroscience has been slow to formalise the study of spontaneous subjective experience during 'offline' states, when responses to sensory stimuli no longer drive the system. While research on the 'default' mode of brain function has brought attention to the importance of spontaneous brain activity occurring during periods of rest and sleep, surprisingly, virtually none of this work has examined participants' own reports of what is going through their mind at rest. Data on spontaneous cognition during sleep has been even more lacking. Neurophysiological studies seeking to shed light on the neural basis of dreaming have often relied merely on describing the physiology of REM, or else have dichotomised conscious experience as either 'present' or 'absent', without exploring the actual content of this mentation."[3]

It is in this new climate of greater scientific acceptance that we re-present the findings from Joe's own dream recall over a period of years. (Naturally, of course, research findings based on one's own subjective experiences have to be checked against other people's, to validate their universality.) Joe's original research project began when he woke up one morning and then, still drowsy, drifted back to sleep and found himself dreaming about a castle:

Dream 1

> I start to climb the castle wall. As I get nearer to the top I notice that stones are coming loose and falling down. I feel myself to be in great danger of serious injury.

He woke up still thinking about the dream and realised that, just before he had drifted back to sleep, he had remembered an incident from childhood when he had been playing in the road with a ball, which bounced over a boundary wall made of stones. He ran to climb over the wall to get his ball back but, as he pulled himself up onto the wall, a loose stone came away in his hand and he fell backwards. Unfortunately, the stone followed him, making a large bloody gash in his forehead that required medical attention. (He still has the scar.)

The dream can easily be seen as a pictorial representation of part of his earlier thoughts – very much as Hall's research suggests. There were, however, some significant changes made in the dream images. The boundary wall, which in reality was just a few feet high, was changed in the dream to a castle wall. The single stone that had come away in his hand was changed in the dream to the collapsing of an entire castle wall. Perhaps these changes were nothing more than artistic licence – Calvin Hall, as we described earlier, thought dreams were like a work of art, through which the dreamer expressed personal concerns. But the dream did not seem to Joe to be a reflection of a specific ongoing problem; it appeared to be a translation of his waking thought pattern into a different set of images. His curiosity was aroused. There and then he resolved to collect more of his dreams and compare them with waking concerns of the previous day, to see if this pattern held good across a series of dreams.

To begin with, he recorded dreams whenever he woke up and found, as so many had before him, that it is essential to make a record of the dream story immediately on awakening, no matter how memorable the dream may appear to be at the time, otherwise, within a short space of time, it is usually forgotten.

If the effort is made to wake up and consciously recall the dream, then the dream can be processed through the waking brain and become a conscious memory. To be on the safe side, however, it is usually better to write the dream down or record it immediately. It took Joe some time to acquire the ability to do this consistently, but, eventually, he became so proficient that he would frequently wake up immediately after a dream sequence and be able to record it there and then.

It proved, however, much more difficult to recall and reflect on his thoughts and experiences of the previous day, something he needed to do, of course, to see if the dream was a reflection of yesterday's waking concerns. Since the dream is the more recent experience, rich in sensory impressions and emotional content, at first it can seem difficult to find any significant correspondence with some half-forgotten waking experience of the day before.

He soon found that the best way to find these correspondences was to rewrite clearly the scribbled dream accounts that had, so often, been hastily written during the night. By carefully writing out or typing up the scribbled account of a dream, he was able to fix it in his memory and he could bring it back to mind a number of times during the course of the day. Almost invariably, a memory of an experience from the previous day would spring to mind and it was this fact that convinced him of an overwhelmingly structural and symbolic correspondence with the events of the dream.

Over the next nine months, he continued to collect both his own and other people's dreams and worked hard at identifying the corresponding waking experiences of the previous day. This procedure clearly indicated that dreams were not simply a continuation of ordinary waking thoughts expressed pictorially. They all appeared to be concerned in some way with *emotionally arousing* experiences or thoughts of the previous waking period. Moreover, these concerns were always expressed in symbolic or metaphorical imagery.

The following dream, told to Joe by a patient who had come to him for psychotherapy, perfectly illustrates the process.

The patient had recently started a new job, which involved a training period with other new recruits. He had also been experiencing a degree of anxiety in his social encounters in the period before taking up his new position. One of the things that caused him anxiety was a sudden, almost uncontrollable, desire to laugh at inappropriate moments when in company. His inclination to laugh usually occurred when someone spoke intensely or emphatically. To relieve this desire to laugh he had learnt to make a semi-jocular remark and then laugh at his own joke. However, in his new job, one or two people had not responded well to this behaviour. When he told Joe about this problem, Joe ventured the opinion that perhaps his desire to laugh was due less to his perception of humour in the situation than to an effort to relieve the anxiety generated in himself by seeing the tension he was creating in the other person. A couple of days later the patient reported this dream:

Dream 2

I am in church and I want to go up to read the gospel but people keep getting in my way. Suddenly Terry Wogan is standing alongside the altar. The church has a wall dividing the altar from the main body of the church where the audience is seated. Now I am on the other side of this wall and I am urinating. Terry Wogan can see what I am doing (but no one else can) and is laughing at me. The people in the church assume I have cracked a joke and all start laughing.

The correspondence between the subject's waking experience and the dream is self-evident. Terry Wogan, the radio and television personality, represented his public image as he imagined it. (He thought people saw him as witty like Terry Wogan, whom he had recently seen in person and with whom he shared his Irish nationality.) He assumed they would think, when he laughed, that he had cracked a joke when really he was laughing at his own embarrassment. There is also the connection with the common vulgar expression 'pissing myself', to denote a state of tension and anxiety, and 'pissing myself laughing' to denote a state of uncontrollable laughter.

The church setting is also particularly appropriate because the patient saw himself as religious, with a responsibility to promote 'the gospel'. His problem with relating to people made it difficult for him to fulfil that responsibility. This is symbolically expressed in the opening sequence of the dream, when he tries to go up to the altar to read the gospel but finds people keep getting in his way. The barrier in the dream between him and the people, who can see Terry Wogan laughing but not him urinating, can be viewed as an analogy for the dichotomy of himself as other people see him in company ('laughing') and as he really is ('pissing himself').

The dream can therefore be seen as a metaphorical expression of his waking anxiety from the perspective that Joe had put to him during the previous therapy session. Thus, this dream would appear to confirm Hall's theory that dreams express the dreamer's self-conceptions in an artistic form: it converts the dreamer's concepts into perceptions enabling the communication of the dreamer's ideas, very much as artists communicate their ideas through works of art. But Joe wasn't satisfied. However aesthetically pleasing dreaming might be, surely, he reasoned, it must have evolved to serve some adaptive function for the organism, i.e. us.

He felt that the most surprising finding from his research up to that point was that the dreams always gave metaphorical or symbolical expression to waking concerns. This applied not just to concepts but to people as well. For example, a husband who was seen as behaving in a dominating manner was replaced in one dream by a forceful schoolmaster known to the dreamer.

At this point in his exploratory research, having decoded several dozen of his own and other people's dreams, Joe decided it was time to adopt a more systematic approach to dream collection. This was because he could not yet claim that the dreams he had collected and decoded were representative of dreaming as a whole. It could, for instance, be argued that the dreams that spontaneously cross the threshold into waking consciousness are in some way more memorable or more coherent than the average, unremembered dream.

He knew from extensive review of the experimental dream research of recent decades that dreaming is strongly associated with REM sleep. REM periods tend to be shorter at the beginning of the night and lengthen as the night progresses. Armed with this information, he decided to set his alarm clock for two hours earlier than normal and immediately record any dreams he could recall at that time. Often a dream would be easily recalled but equally often only a vague memory of dreaming would come to mind. When that happened, he discovered, to his surprise, that the act of writing down the few details of the dream that he could still remember triggered a clear memory of further dream material.

Whilst doing this early waking and recording, he also continued to record any dreams he could remember when he woke at his normal time in the morning. He found that it was important to record *all* dreams, irrespective of how irrelevant or even nonsensical they might appear at the time of recall. Later, those apparently meaningless image sequences made perfect sense when he identified the waking experience to which they related. On some mornings, he recorded up to five dreams, on others only two, in which case several themes might be recorded within a dream and the dream sequence would, as a consequence, be unusually long. He kept up this method of dream collection for three weeks.

At the end of that time, he found that the subject matter of the recorded dreams were, as expected, related to his waking concerns. His previous finding, that dreams are not simply a visual expression of personal concerns but a metaphorical visual translation of them, was also supported.

In addition, he found that not only do all dreams use metaphor but the entire dream sequence is a metaphorical expression of a waking concern. This means that everybody and everything in a dream sequence is an analogous substitute for some person, thing or event in waking life. In other words, the plot, or theme, set out while awake, is preserved in the dream but the locations, props and entire cast are replaced. Dreamers are aware of themselves in dreams – an awareness is different from a perception – but where the dreamer has been objectifying their own identity, or part of it, then that identity is also represented in the dream but by someone else. We saw an example of this in the second dream where part of the dreamer's persona was represented by Terry Wogan.

That dreams use metaphor has been noted by many theorists but that *all* elements of *all* dreams appear to be metaphorical was a new finding. The metaphor is not used as a dramatic device to highlight certain principles or concepts, as might be seen in the creation of a work of art, but rather as the translation of a waking concern into an analogous sensory scenario (the dream). The concerns themselves can be seemingly quite trivial. The next dream of Joe's illustrates this:

Dream 3

Scene I

I got my hair cut in a new style, with spiky bits sticking up in the air. A man passes me by as I walk down the road. He thrusts his hand out, like a referee at a football match, and calls, "That hairstyle doesn't suit you!" I feel crestfallen and immediately flatten my hair.

Scene II

I have put on a new Harris tweed suit. It looks very good, except that it has a kind of skirt wrapped around the trousers. I feel a bit embarrassed about this feature. I detach the skirt and look in the mirror, thinking to myself that it looks okay now.

On the previous day Joe had bought two sweatshirts in a London street market where there were no facilities to try them on. Thinking about his purchase on the way home, he reflected that one of the sweatshirts might look too young on him because of two white bands across the body which made it look rather like a football shirt. He decided that it definitely would not suit him and he would have to get rid of it.

These thoughts are expressed in the dream but translated into a metaphorical sensory scenario. In the dream, the unsuitable 'too young' style of sweatshirt is replaced by an 'unsuitable' new style of haircut. (He had recently seen a young man get this new style while waiting his turn to have his hair cut at the barber's.) This image expresses his expectation that the sweatshirt would be more suited to a younger person. The person thrusting his hand out like a referee and telling him that the hairstyle was unsuitable expressed the reservations he himself had had on the way home from the market. The behaviour reminiscent of a referee at a football match is a visual reference to Joe's waking thought that the sweatshirt looked like a football shirt. By flattening his hair he got rid of the hairstyle, just as in waking life he had resolved to get rid of the sweatshirt.

The second scene in the dream relates to the purchase of the second sweatshirt. He had hesitated to buy it because the pastel colour was a shade more usually worn by women. On further reflection, he rejected this sexist attitude and decided that, if he liked it, he would buy it anyway. On the way home, he thought that, unlike the other sweatshirt, this one would suit him. Later that evening, by chance, he saw a TV programme about the island of Harris and the manufacture of Harris tweed. The programme concluded with a display of Harris tweed suits, the style of which he thought unorthodox, although he liked the fabric. We can clearly see that the analogy used in the dream came from the TV programme. The Harris tweed suit stands for the second sweatshirt. The skirt wrapped around the trousers is an analogy for Joe's sexist views concerning the colour. His removal of the skirt is analogous to his discarding his concern that the colour was too feminine. His expectation that the sweatshirt would look all right is made manifest in the dream when he looked in the mirror and saw that the suit looked well on him, once the skirt was discarded. There is also a pun in the analogy of a suit for the sweatshirt because this is the sweatshirt that he anticipated would 'suit' him.

Interestingly, Freud maintained that part of the manifest (obvious) content of dreams came from the waking experiences of the previous day, which in the case of this dream can be seen to be true. But what Joe's research clearly shows is that the latent (hidden) content of a dream also comes from the experience of the previous day.

Up to this point, Joe's findings indicated that dreams represent our emotionally arousing waking concerns, expressed in metaphors. If this hypothesis was correct, he reasoned, in principle it ought to be possible for people to predict the themes of their own dreams from a consideration of their own waking concerns. In all our reading of the research, we have found no instance of any scientist attempting this experiment before. Joe's decision to do so was to prove the turning point in dream research.

In practice, of course, there are a number of foreseeable difficulties that might arise from such an experiment. For example, would it be possible to maintain the continuous self-monitoring that identifying likely waking concerns would require? Would this process of self-monitoring and prediction affect the dream process? And how could the need to collect a representative night's dreams, to check their content, be resolved? Notwithstanding these difficulties, Joe resolved to persist with the experiment.

After reflecting on the concerns that had occupied his attention during the day, he wrote down predicted themes prior to going to sleep. To get as complete a collection of each night's dreams as possible, he used an alarm clock to wake himself every two hours, and then recorded whatever dreams he could remember. The first time he tried this, he had, by morning, recorded three dreams.

The first dream theme related to a domestic incident of the previous day, which was one of the predicted sources of dream material.

It was an accurate symbolic representation of his perception and emotional reaction to the incident. The next two dream sequences portrayed different aspects of a predicted theme, which related to his reflections concerning the analogical theory of dreams. He had been rereading his notes on his previous year's research, which included a summary of existing dream theories. Whilst doing this, he again noticed how Freud had mentioned that the previous day's experiences were reflected in the manifest content of the dream. This is what Freud referred to as the "day's residue". Joe realised how, in his own collection of dreams, there was usually an item or two in the manifest content of the dream that was related to the previous day's experiences. He was reminded that Freud had not observed that the latent content was also a reflection of the previous day's experiences.

Joe thought that Jung's concept of the 'shadow' might have come from Jung observing the self as an object metaphorically expressed in dreams, as in the case of the Terry Wogan character, described earlier. He also realised that other dream researchers besides himself were investigating dreaming from the perspective of finding the adaptive significance of dreams. The 'sentinel hypothesis', for instance, saw sleep as putting an animal at risk from predators.[4] It was suggested that the periodic activation of the brain by the REM state, followed by a brief awakening, might leave animals better prepared to deal with danger. But the problem with this idea, Joe reflected, was that, even if such an adaptation had taken place, it could scarcely account for the complexity and metaphorical nature of human dreaming. Montague Ullman put forward similar thoughts.[5] He saw dreaming as possibly preparing humans for the kind of reality they are likely to encounter on awakening. But this hypothesis was incompatible with the evidence about dreaming that Joe was gathering.

So, one of Joe's major waking preoccupations that day was a consideration of the work of other theorists and his search for points of similarity that existed between their work and his. The professors to whom he would submit his findings (in the form of a PhD thesis in psychology) were psychoanalytically oriented, so he remembered wondering intently if it would be necessary, when he eventually reported his findings, to detail these points of correspondence. That evening, as he reviewed the day's activities to make his list of dream predictions, it seemed likely to him that his preoccupation with studying other dream theories during the day might well become a theme that featured in his dreams that night. As expected, one dream that night did indeed reflect that theme.

This was the dream:

Dream 4

Scene I

We are searching for buried treasure under a collapsed pile of bricks in a field. I'm wondering if we will divide the treasure between us or if it is a case of 'finders keepers'.

Scene II

Then it seems we are back in time, a time shortly after a Christ-like figure has lived. Now we are digging a well. We have a bottle of water with us. Someone finishes the bottle off. I am aware that everything will be all right because the well will be full in twelve hours.

The first scene of the dream obviously relates to Joe's reading of other people's theories and wondering whether, when he wrote up his work, he should point out the parallels with certain aspects of his own ideas on dreams. The symbol of the buried treasure is appropriate for the search for the meaning of dreams, given that he placed a high value on such research.

The Christ-like figure in the second scene refers to Freud, whose photograph had always brought biblical associations to Joe's mind. The pile of bricks in the first scene relates to the present state of Freud's dream theory, as Joe saw it – collapsed in ruins.

The well is a symbol for creativity and is used as such in Chinese literature (as had recently come to Joe's attention). The specific creativity involved in this instance is the discovery of the meaning of dreams. This is an appropriate symbol, not only because one has to dig under the ground to find water but because one also has to dig, as it were, under the obvious content of the dream to find the hidden content.

The bottle of water refers to the parallels between other theorists' work and his own – a small amount compared with a full well of water and representing small discoveries about the dream process. In the dream, he doesn't mind who drinks the bottle of water. That is to say, he doesn't mind who gets the credit for these discoveries. The well being full in twelve hours means that, in twelve hours, he will have his night's collection of dreams, which he expected to be full of creative insights.

The final dream in the sequence relates to the experiment itself:

Dream 5

We are looking for buried eggs. There is a hen nearby. Someone finds a single egg buried near the hen. This egg was very close to the surface. I say, "It's an old egg – probably been there for days – but there's still a whole pile of eggs buried somewhere."

The hen represents the REM state or dream generator. The egg that was found only lightly buried near the surface relates to the manifest (obvious) content of the dream. It is found near the hen, and the fact that it is lightly buried means that it is easily identified with the dreamer's waking experience. This relates to those aspects of the dream that Freud had observed relate to the dreamer's waking experience of the previous day. The egg appears to be 'old' because the observation about the manifest content was made by Freud many years ago. The pile of eggs that Joe is looking for refers to the dream themes he had identified and listed the evening before, and which he expected to find buried in that night's dreams. As he was aware, chickens develop from the genetic code hidden in the egg and, in a very real sense, dreams can be decoded to show that they are a translation of specific information from the past into a new sensory structure.

This dream can be seen as a clear metaphorical expression of Joe's hopes and reflections of the day before, concerning the dream experiment he was planning. The dream is not a wish fulfilment, as might be expected from Freudian theory. It doesn't show him finding the eggs; it expresses his expectation that the dream themes will be found 'buried' in that night's dreams. We can see clearly that the dream does not go beyond the waking thought in another medium, as Hall's theory might lead one to expect. Just like the other decoded dreams, it is simply a translation of the experience had whilst awake into a sensory metaphorical analogue.

Joe's results were, therefore, supportive of the hypothesis he was testing. Two of the three recorded dreams related to predicted themes. One dream related to the experiment itself. On the other hand, he had predicted five dream themes, three of which failed to appear as recorded dreams. This might be because he failed to record the relevant dreams, but it could also be because, for some reason as yet unknown, not all his predicted themes resulted in dreams.

He continued the experiment for another four nights and found he successfully predicted two or three dream themes each night. As the experiment progressed he found it easier to recall his dreams and collected a great number. It became clear, however, that, whilst he could predict some dream themes, completely unpredicted themes also featured. Although these were also metaphorical representations of waking concerns, it was by no means clear to him why they should have been chosen as dream themes in preference to his predicted themes. At this point, a further complication emerged. Careful reading of his predictions and his notes about specific dreams showed that, even when a predicted theme featured in a dream, he had not usually predicted the particular aspect of the waking concern that was featured. The predicted dream themes tended to be fairly general whilst their expression in a dream was much more specific.

So, at the conclusion of the experiment, he had mixed results. On the one hand they convincingly supported the hypothesis that dreams were metaphorical expressions of waking concerns but, on the other, the basis on which those waking concerns were chosen as the subject matter of his dreams was unclear.

Joe had begun the experiment, not unreasonably, with the assumption that the most pressing waking concerns would form the subject matter of his dreams and, indeed, had used that as the criterion on which to base his predictions about which waking concerns would generate his dreams. Some of the dreams from the experiment showed, however, that this was not the case. Not only did less important waking concerns become the subject matter of dreams but a major concern, which he had expected to form the subject matter of at least one dream, did not feature at all in an extensive night's collection! It seemed likely to him that, if he could identify the basis on which waking experiences were selected by the brain to be the subject matter of dreams, this would provide a significant clue as to why we dream.

Over the next twelve months Joe busily continued to collect and decipher his own dreams, as well as those offered to him by other people, in the hope of solving this problem.

Although the many dreams he collected and decoded continued to provide evidence that dreams are sensory analogues of waking experiences, still no clue emerged as to how the brain selected specific waking experiences to become the subject of a dream. The fact that some dream predictions, based on the perceived importance of the waking concern, successfully predicted dream themes, showed that the perceived importance of the concern might be one criterion. But it was clear that there must be some other modifying factor involved because not every exciting waking experience became a dream.

As he puzzled over this, he decided to write up his research findings to date. And it was then that he made his discovery – the breakthrough that revealed what dreams are all about. Suddenly, the significance of a predicted dream theme that failed to materialise as a dream became clear.

This is how it came about. As Joe read over and wrote up his notes, he saw that, by the third day of the experiment, he was finding the whole process of trying to predict dream themes extremely stressful. The increasing tiredness and the consuming effort of constant reflection on the previous night's dreams were getting him down; he became increasingly short-tempered and irritable. The experiment was also proving stressful for his wife, Liz, a busy nurse who needed her well-earned sleep. She was beginning to resent being disturbed by the alarm, which was going off every two hours each night, so that Joe could wake, turn on the light and record his dreams. This stress bomb finally exploded on the third night of the experiment, as they were about to go to bed. They had a row about it. When they finally did get to bed and turned out the light, their respective frustrations fully vented, Joe calmed down and started to think that this heated exchange with his wife, in which he (temporarily) saw her to have changed from a supportive ally of his research to a hostile and unsympathetic critic, must surely form the basis of a dream. So, risking further fireworks, he turned the light on and hastily added this theme to his list of dream predictions.

The next day, however, it was clear that the row was not reflected in any way in the dream experiences of the previous night. Of course, it could be argued that, perhaps, he had failed to record the dream in which this theme was expressed. However, he had recorded five dream sequences from that night and could not help contrasting the failure of this theme to appear with the number of times the theme of the experiment itself was featured during the first night's dreams. Was there some significant way in which these two waking concerns differed that might account for the reason why one was apparently repeatedly selected as dream material, whilst the other was apparently ignored?

Yes, there was. And the implications were astonishing.

During the row with his wife, Joe realised, he had discharged his feelings straight away. In contrast, the feelings aroused by the prospect of the experiment were not discharged. Because the highly aroused feelings related to an event in the future – the prospect of the experiment – and so could not be discharged in the present, he searched for the buried treasure in his dream; he searched for the buried eggs; he dug the well.

As he thought about this, a previous argument with his wife, one that did become the subject matter of a dream, came to mind:

Dream 6

> I'm wearing punk-type coloured spectacles, which I refuse to change, since I have already paid for them. I'm aware that my wife is telling her mother that I'm unwilling to change them.

This dream is based on another occasion when Joe had a strong disagreement with his wife prior to going to bed. In this row, he saw himself as the injured party. In bed later, his wife indicated, by playing 'footsie', that she was willing to forget the incident. But, still perceiving himself as the injured party, 'having paid the price' of being mistreated, he maintained his somewhat aggressive attitude, turned his back on her, and refused to make up. This is metaphorically represented in the dream as his unwillingness to change his 'punk-type spectacles'. He had reflected that his wife must see him as unwilling to make up and forget the issue, while he felt that he was the injured party and therefore entitled to his viewpoint – he had paid the price.

His wife's mother appears in the dream sequence as a stand-in for his wife's objective self, to whom her subjective self explains that he was unwilling to change his perspective, just as he had imagined her doing before he went to sleep. Clearly, in this scene, unlike in the previous row, he had not yet expressed – acted out – his feelings and views on the situation.

Joe had already established that everybody and everything in a dream is a metaphorical or analogical replacement for somebody or something from waking life. Now a question arose. Joe's wife's identity didn't change in the dream. Why? The reason he came up with was that he didn't actually see her in the dream. But he was aware of what she was doing. He knew she was close by, but she didn't actually appear. Her objective self, the self he had imagined her talking to, is analogically represented in the dream by her mother, with whom she enjoys a close relationship. This dream is, therefore, a metaphorical acting out of Joe's introspected *but unexpressed* views and emotions concerning a row with his wife.

Joe had arrived at a watershed moment. He realised that the waking experiences, including thoughts, which result in dreams are ones that involve the arousal of feelings that are not acted out or given expression during the day. This was the brain's qualifying criterion for what becomes a dream. Suddenly everything made sense.

The expectation fulfilment theory of dreaming

Joe had made the hugely significant discovery that the subject matter of dreams is not derived from our emotionally arousing concerns *per se* but from our unexpressed emotionally arousing views about those concerns – in other words, our expectations. It has led to what is now called the expectation fulfilment theory of dreaming.

Whenever we become emotionally aroused during the day – whether by anger, desire, excitement, anxiety or whatever – these impulses activate the part of the nervous system known as the autonomic nervous system to enable it to respond accordingly. We throw something to relieve our temper; we eat an appetising meal to alleviate our hunger; we make the bungee jump we've craved to do. When we act at once like this, our heart rate returns to normal. The arousal is discharged. But what if a man's desire is aroused by an erotic scene in a television drama? What if a woman on a strict diet refuses the mouthwatering lemon meringue? What if a child's long-anticipated trip to a theme park has to be cancelled? In such examples the expectation that has been set up fails to be fulfilled and the arousal it produced remains active in the brain. Like a telephone answering machine that is continually scanning for incoming signals as it awaits a message, whether a call comes in or not, so part of the brain remains occupied in scanning the environment, in readiness to act out the expectation that, in fact, is not going to be fulfilled. But the brain doesn't know that. So it stays in a state of alertness, ready to respond to any thought, feeling or event that recalls the original expectation or concern (part of a process we call pattern matching – the associating of like with like).

It makes sense to surmise, therefore, that, without the ability to discharge all the emotional arousal caused by unfulfilled expectations throughout the day, our brains would become overloaded to breaking point with 'unfinished business'.

This is what Joe has proposed is the function of dreams – they are a metaphorical acting out of undischarged emotional arousal from our unfulfilled expectations of the previous day. When Joe reviewed all the dreams he had collected, and the waking experiences on which they were based, every single one verified this new understanding. For example, in the dream that occurred after Joe had purchased two sweatshirts in a street market without trying them on, it is clear that the resultant dream sequences were metaphorical translations of his anticipated reactions about whether the sweatshirts would suit him, in terms of colour and style. These anticipated reactions did not take place because, when he did eventually try them on the next day, they both turned out to be too small, and so he gave them to his wife. Thus, the expected reactions did not take place at all during waking. They were, however, expressed in metaphorical form in the dream.

Over the next several years, Joe continued to collect his own and other people's dreams, gradually identifying the various reasons that certain types of emotionally arousing introspections are not acted out during waking. For instance, our expectations are not just concerned with the here and now. Even when we use our imaginations to think about an emotionally arousing event that occurred in the past, or that might happen in the future, the effect is just as real (we have probably all experienced the pumping of anger when we recall an old injustice or the tingle of trepidation, when we think about a test to be taken in two weeks' time). The brain experiences arousal and expects an imminent means to discharge it. This is because the autonomic nervous system cannot distinguish between past, present and future arousing events. It responds to what is on our minds now. Clearly, however, the expectation cannot be discharged in such circumstances, either because the event is long in the past or else it is still in the future.

When we spend time imagining how an anticipated event might turn out, the emotional arousal caused will necessarily remain undischarged – we can't experience the scenario we are imagining, again because it is in the future. So the imagining becomes metaphorically translated into dreams. Dreams can also result from introspections about emotionally involving books, television programmes, news items, films, computer games and what other people might be posting about them in the world of social media. Our reactions to, or identification with, the experiences of the characters remain, in effect, at second hand, and so the pattern of our arousal stays uncompleted. (Examples of dreams resulting from these types of experiences will be given in a later chapter.)

In the course of his development of the theory, Joe realised another significant advantage of the brain's ability to discharge unexpressed emotional arousal through dreams. Not only did it allow the brain to save the energy required to keep seeking completion of accumulated unfulfilled arousals, the dream mechanism also allowed instinctive reactions to remain intact. If an instinctive behaviour is inhibited, or not acted upon, for a long enough period of time, it will become conditioned out of us. For instance, a laboratory animal that is restrained may learn it can do nothing to avoid electric shocks – and thus fail to take evasive action, even when not restrained. The instinct to flee has been eroded. If all of our unacted upon arousals were deemed by the brain to be thwarted in a similar way (the autonomic nervous system, as we said, is unaware that the arousal can't be fulfilled), many important instinctive reactions might be weakened or lost.

The expectation fulfilment theory of dreaming has elements in common with both Freud's and Hall's theory of dreams, but also differs from them in several important ways. It supports Freud's idea that dreams have a hidden (latent) meaning. It diverges from Freud's theory in three distinct ways:

- The origin of the dream lies in conscious expectations and not in 'subconscious infantile impulses'.
- Dreams are not disguised or distorted wishes; they are sensory, metaphorical analogies (pattern matches, drawn from our memories) of the *unexpressed* emotionally arousing expectations from when we were last awake.

- Freud's theory of dreams is based on the idea that dreams are attempts at wish fulfilment, but a major problem with this idea is that it cannot realistically be argued that people would wish to have nightmares. According to Joe's theory, it is not our wishes that are fulfilled but our expectations; whether they are happy, sad, anxious or angry ones presents no difficulty for his theory.

The expectation fulfilment theory has in common with Hall's cognitive theory the suggestion that dreams relate to the conscious emotional concerns of the dreamer. But, unlike Hall's theory, which sees the dream as a continuation of waking thought in another medium, the new hypothesis specifically states that the dream is a replay of certain previous emotionally arousing thoughts from waking. It also differs from Hall's theory in that it specifically predicts that *all* dreams are expressed in the form of a metaphorical translation.

So, Joe's research to date had provided strong evidence for the function of dreams, which can be summarised in the following three points:

- Dreams are metaphors for emotionally arousing introspections that are still active at the onset of sleep.
- The expression of these emotionally arousing thoughts as a sensory analogue (the dream), completes the emotional circuit and thereby deactivates the emotional charge. This frees the brain to deal with the emotionally arousing concerns of the next day.
- With the completion of the previously unacted-out patterns of arousal, the instinctive templates on which they are based – anger, sadness, fear, desire, joy etc. – are preserved intact, ready for future use.

The autosymbolic effect

By accumulating quantities of individual dream accounts, Joe was able to gather a great deal of convincing evidence to support the expectation fulfilment hypothesis. But, however convincing such evidence might be, it would be even better, he thought, if we could actually see a demonstration of this process of translation into metaphor taking place. Fortunately, thanks to the psychologist and one-time follower of Sigmund Freud, Herbert Silberer, we can do just that. It is astonishing how often important information can lie hidden and unappreciated for long periods of time. Through his researches, Joe came across the forgotten work of Silberer and found that he had discovered one of the most powerful explanatory principles in psychology – the autosymbolic effect – yet it had lain buried in the clinical literature for nearly a hundred years, since it was published in 1909.[6,7]

Silberer discovered that, if he tried to master some intellectual task when he felt drowsy, a point would come when the feeling of drowsiness would temporarily overcome him. He would then wake up a few moments later and realise that he had dreamt a symbolic representation of what he had wanted to achieve. This was what he called the 'autosymbolic effect'.

The following five examples make this effect clear.

1. Silberer describes how he is trying to improve a halting passage in an essay. This results in the following dream fragment: "I see myself planing a piece of wood." Here we see the anticipated behaviour replaced with an analogical sensory representation of that behaviour – in the dream fragment he metaphorically smooths out the rough passage in his essay.

2. Silberer is reflecting on the ambiguity of the human condition by, "probing into the foggy and difficult problem of the 'mothers' in *Faust, Part II*". This results in the following dream fragment: "I stand alone on a stone jetty extending out far into a dark sea. The water of the ocean and the dark and mysteriously heavy air unite at the horizon." Silberer explains that the jetty extending out into the dark sea corresponds to probing into the problem. The unity of the air and water at the horizon symbolises, as with the mothers, "all times and places shade into one another, so that there are no boundaries, no here and there, above or below".

Again we can see that this dream fragment provides a clear metaphorical representation of his introspections or anticipation concerning the solution to the proposed problem.

3. Silberer is "trying to think of the purpose of the metaphysical studies I am about to undertake". He decides that the purpose is to "work my way through ever higher forms of consciousness; that is, levels of existence, in my quest after the basis of existence". He then dreams that "I run a knife under a cake as though to take a slice out of it". The cake in question has a number of layers, corresponding to levels of consciousness. The running of the knife through the layers of the cake is an analogy for working through the levels of consciousness. The knife has to be pushed under the cake to remove a slice, corresponding to getting to the basis of consciousness.

   Here we have another example of his anticipation being converted into a metaphor. Silberer called this type of dream symbol a 'material' symbol because it dealt with the material he was contemplating. He also described what he called 'functional' symbolism, which he thought related to the state of consciousness of the dreamer. An example he gave was when he tried to recall what he was thinking about but found that he had lost the connecting link. He dreamt of "a piece of typesetting with the last few lines gone". However, the key point that Silberer's description misses is that the dream sequence is *not* simply symbolic of his state of consciousness but rather of his introspection, or anticipation, concerning his state of consciousness. His dream can be clearly understood as a completed metaphorical representation of his conscious introspection about, or anticipation of, having lost the connecting thread of his argument.

4. Silberer is thinking about something but, whilst "pursuing a subsidiary consideration, departs from the original theme". When he attempts to return to it, he dreams the following fragment: "I am out mountain climbing. The mountains near me conceal the farther ones from which I came and to which I want to return".

This dream fragment is clearly a metaphor for the difficulties he is having in completing his anticipated mental journey.

5. Silberer says: "Before falling asleep I want to review an idea in order not to forget". He dreams that "suddenly a lackey in livery stands before me as though waiting for my orders". Silberer tells us that, in this instance, he experienced no difficulty in thinking and expected to carry out his task. This dream fragment example is therefore interesting because it introduces a higher level of complexity than previous ones. He wants to carry out a certain task and anticipates that he will have no difficulty doing it. His anticipation then includes a reflection of the subject as object, i.e. there is the self number one that is anticipating that self number two will have no difficulty carrying out the task. In the dream fragment, self one is of course himself, the self we are aware of. The livery man waiting for instruction is self two who will be able to carry out the task without difficulty. This dream fragment is again a metaphorical image of the subject as object willing to carry out the instruction.

Besides material and functional symbolism, Silberer noted a third type of autosymbolic effect, this time arising from bodily sensations. One example he gave was of a time when he had had a sore throat and fever, which forced him to swallow saliva steadily. When drifting off to sleep, each time he was about to swallow he saw a picture of a water bottle that he was supposed to drink from. Clearly each swallow had become a consciously anticipated behaviour, and the water bottle a sensory metaphor for his mouth holding the saliva.

Curiously, in this last example we are not really dealing with symbols, if we take symbols to stand for something abstract that can't be represented any other way by the senses. Clearly, a mouth with saliva is not an abstract concept. So what we must be dealing with is a sensory analogical process that can apply both to *abstract* ideas and to *physical*, sensory concepts.

Silberer was a supporter and minor colleague of Freud and tried to make his findings compatible with Freud's dream theory by arguing that our brains may not be able to support certain ideas, for intellectual as well as emotional reasons. He suggested that, whenever a thought or idea proved too difficult to be supported by a given state of consciousness, as when we are drowsy, we regress to thinking in symbols because, he assumed, this required less effort.

Ironically, although he never realised it, Silberer had already found the key that would unlock the secret of dreams – and sold it for a mere bauble: a grudging acknowledgement from Freud that he had made a minor contribution to *Freud's* work. In order to keep his findings compatible with Freud's, Silberer even suggested that the symbolisation process could be caused by Freud's mechanism of repression. This was absurd. There was no logical basis for that at all – he was just trying to make his own work an acceptable adjunct to what he thought was the important work of Freud.

This analysis of Silberer's findings, however, shows that the underlying principle in all three categories of symbolism he describes is actually the occurrence of introspections or uncompleted patterns of arousal, and that these introspections are translated into matching sensory analogues. This occurs even when the type of thinking involved includes physical sensations, such as swallowing, rather than abstract thoughts. What he was describing therefore, and we can all observe this happening in ourselves once it has been pointed out, is a switching over from logical, left-brain information processing to right-brain metaphorical pattern matching just prior to sinking into the first period of deep, slow-wave sleep.

Freud treated Silberer's contribution rather warily in the later editions of his book, *The Interpretation of Dreams*. He was, of course, acutely conscious that it was a two-edged sword. On the one hand, it gives first class evidence for the process of symbolisation taking place. But on the other, what is being symbolised is straightforward emotionally arousing conscious material and not subconscious material that is a threat to the ego, which Freud believed to be the function of dream symbolism. It was probably for this reason that Freud spent some time in his book diverting his readers into a pedantic consideration of Silberer's functional symbolism which, as we have seen, is a distinction of little relevance because the same process of introspection underlies all three categories Silberer identified.

What must have haunted Freud was the question of whether *his* theory was actually needed to explain dreams or whether the process observed by Silberer, of waking thoughts being converted into metaphors at the onset of sleep, could be used to explain what's happening with *all* dreams? He must have realised that, if the latter were the case, the entire basis for psychoanalysis would collapse. He had good reason, therefore, to bury Silberer's insight in obscure trivialising meanderings about "threshold symbolism" in later editions of his dream book. Freud concludes his discussion of Silberer's work with the dismissive suggestion that it may not, after all, be that relevant to a study of dreams and "can be more appropriately treated elsewhere."[8] However, as will be shown in the next chapter, it is now known that dreaming is not confined to the REM state but is recorded in other stages of sleep, such as the brief twilight period between wakefulness and sleep proper (known as 'hypnogogic sleep'). And so the process that Silberer discovered was very relevant indeed to dreams. (Sadly Silberer, who was more independent-minded than most of Freud's followers, paid for his freedom tragically. He committed suicide shortly after being excommunicated from the master's circle. He died gruesomely, hanging himself and leaving a flashlight shining up into his face, so his wife would see him when she came home.)

Silberer's important work confirmed two of the main aspects of Joe's expectation fulfilment theory of dreaming. Firstly, that the symbolism, or analogy, relates to the entire dream scene and everything in it, including the dreamer when he has been the object of his own thoughts. (The Freudian view sees only part of a dream, or certain images, as symbolic.) Secondly, Silberer's findings also beautifully illustrate the actual conversion of the uncompleted patterns of emotional arousal into a sensory analogue. They make it possible to observe both the formation of the incomplete pattern of arousal and its conversion into a sensory analogue taking place one after another, whereas with REM dreams these are separated in time.

Joe was fortunate that, in his own serendipitous discovery of this process, his waking memory and thoughts about falling off a wall as a boy and being struck by a stone had involved sensory images rather than abstract thoughts. This meant that it was apparent to him from the start of his research that dream images appeared to involve a translation of waking introspections into sensory metaphors, rather than just being pictorial representations of abstract thoughts, as both Hall's and Silberer's work had inclined them to suppose. However, the expectation fulfilment theory can be seen to apply equally well to abstract and other more complex dreams, as we will show in a later chapter.

Bill Domhoff, having studied under Calvin Hall, is very ready to acknowledge the significance of the metaphorical content of dreams. He is concerned, though, "that the few attempts to undertake systematic studies of metaphor in dreams suggest that most dreams do not seem to relate very obviously to primary metaphors. Most dreams seem more like dramas or plays in which the dreamer acts out various scenarios that revolve around a few basic personal themes".[9] Joe's work indicates that this is indeed so and is not a problem: the metaphors used in dreams are often extremely personal to the dreamer – for instance, Terry Wogan representing the witty public image one dreamer, described in this chapter, perceived that he himself had. Having recognised that dream content relates to waking concerns, Domhoff also pointed out, in 2008, that it is difficult to confirm this with more accuracy because "no one has compared waking and dreaming thought with the same people as yet".[10] He was wrong. This comparison is the very one that Joe had meticulously applied to his own dreams.

The question might here be asked: Why does the brain need to convert emotionally arousing introspections into a metaphor? Why does it not simply act out the introspections as they are?

Joe felt sure the answer could be found by reviewing the major findings of the research into the biology of dreaming. When he put all the pieces together, he indeed found that dreaming expressed in the form of metaphor is exactly what the biology of dreaming would lead us to expect would be the case.

In carrying out his review of the biological research, set out in the next chapter, it occurred to him that his approach was consistent with the advice given by Robert Farr, professor of psychology at the London School of Economics, when he was discussing scientific method: "Once you have the right theory ... it can be used to reinterpret what is already known ... It is not so much new evidence as new thinking that is called for ... It is foolish to ignore what we already know from experimental research."[11]

It was Joe's aim, therefore, not only to introduce new data in support of this new expectation fulfilment theory of dreams, but also to demonstrate the wide, if unrecognised, support for this idea that is present in existing experimental research. This is what the next chapter is about.

4

OUR SLEEPING BRAINS

"Sleep that knits up
the ravelled sleeve of care,
the death of each day's life,
sore labour's bath,
balm of hurt minds,
great nature's second course,
chief nourisher in life's feast."

WILLIAM SHAKESPEARE

In the last 50-plus years, sleep research has become a major scientific enterprise, yielding a wealth of new biological data. The major stimulus for this research was the breakthrough already referred to: the 1953 finding of Aserinsky and Kleitman that a regular change in brain waves occurred during sleep.[1] Electroencephalogram (EEG) readings of electrical brain patterns (made by placing electrodes on the skull) showed that sleep consisted of two discrete types, or phases, which alternated throughout the night. (This was a surprise because, up until then, it was widely believed that sleep was on a simple continuum.) One phase was clearly accompanied by rapid eye movements and for that reason it was called REM sleep.

A more detailed study by Dement and Kleitman in 1957 confirmed that REM sleep occurred about every 90 minutes and, when all these periods were added together, occupied on average one and a half to two hours of total sleep time.[2] When people were woken up from REM sleep they could vividly recall a dream on 80 per cent of occasions, whereas people woken from non-REM sleep, later to be called slow-wave sleep, could only recall a dream on around seven per cent of occasions and then not with the intensity associated with REM sleep dreaming. It was suggested that the small percentage of dreams recalled from slow-wave sleep might represent memories of dreams persisting from earlier REM phases. The researchers also noted that recordings from slow-wave sleep could be further divided into four stages according to progressive changes in the slow-wave pattern. We now know that, during sleep, we usually pass through five phases known as Stages 1, 2, 3, 4, and REM. These stages progress in a cycle from Stage 1 through to REM, which then starts over again. Adults in normal health spend about 50 per cent of total sleep time in Stages 1 and 2 (shallow sleep), about 25 per cent in Stages 3 and 4 (deep sleep) and about 25 per cent in REM sleep.

The relationship between dreaming and non-REM sleep, however, is not as clear cut as Dement and Kleitman's 1957 paper suggested. Dreaming does occur outside REM sleep. In fact, about sixty per cent of non-REM awakenings result in reports of mental activity of some sort. It was a researcher called David Foulkes who found that dreaming is not completely confined to the REM state but is recorded from other stages of sleep as well, such as hypnogogic sleep, that brief hinterland between waking and sleep.[3] (In the hypnogogic stage, strange visions, voices, sensations and even, sometimes, deep insights can occur as we drift away from normal consciousness into sleep.) He noted that, during the short hypnogogic dreams that can appear when we first begin to fall asleep (Stage 1 sleep), EEG readings taken from the brain are similar to those taken during REM sleep. More often than not, as David Foulkes showed, reports of dreaming at these times are characteristic of a dream fragment, not a dream scenario.[4] (This all clearly fits with Silberer's experience, which we described in the last chapter.) Foulkes suggested that these less than full-blown dream periods might be a kind of revving up of the dream production engine and could throw light on the dreaming process proper.

(The idea that the REM state shows a maximum activity of the dream production system but that it can also have a lesser involvement in other sleep states is also compatible with the evidence that some of the processes of the REM state can be activated at other times, such as in daydreaming, hypnosis and psychotic states,[5] which we will explore later.)

Some research on dreaming cats, carried out by Professor Michel Jouvet and his colleagues, identified further important facts about REM sleep.[6] They noted that the state was also accompanied by an inhibition of the major muscles known as anti-gravity muscles – creating, in effect, a state of paralysis, termed 'tonic immobility' because the muscles are immobilised. (This discovery led to the internationally agreed system for recording sleep phases, comprising the recording by electromyograph (EMG) of signals coming from the muscles, together with the recording of eye movements by electro-oculograph (EOG) and brain waves by EEG.) As research intensified, it soon became apparent that the REM state was characteristic not only of humans and cats but also of nearly all viviparous mammals – those that produce live young (rather than eggs). It was even found in birds, though lasting only for brief periods of five to fifteen seconds at a time.

Then a fascinating pattern of electrical signals, called PGO spikes, was discovered. Triggered off in the brainstem, these play a key role in both the generation of the REM state and in dreams themselves. The signals arise in, and progress through, three areas of the brain. They start in the pons (the lower brainstem) and travel up via a part of the midbrain called the geniculate body to the occipital cortex in the higher brain. (Thus the name PGO spikes – ponto-geniculate occipital spikes – from pons, geniculate and occipital.)

An important distinction was made by Professor Mourizzi when he noted that the REM state could be divided into tonic and phasic components.[7] The tonic component is the underlying passive state where muscles are immobilised. This lasts throughout REM sleep. The phasic component is periodically superimposed upon this passive state and consists of bursts of activity when the PGO spikes occur – the eyes dart about, there is fine muscle twitching, changes to heart rate and breathing patterns.[8]

The phasic components are not strictly confined to the REM state. PGO spikes can be observed moving through the geniculate body prior to REM.[9] In 1967, Jouvet established that tonic and phasic components are based upon different anatomical mechanisms, showing that, under certain conditions, tonic and phasic components can be separated.[10] William Dement concluded that an important principle was suggested by these results, namely that at least two distinct neurological systems must be responsible for the REM state: a system that generates the active element, particularly the PGO spikes, and a system that produces the passive phenomena which last throughout REM sleep.[11] *In other words, the REM state is separate from the dream: it is the theatre the dream is acted out in.* This important distinction has also been made by leading sleep researcher Bill Domhoff: "REM sleep and dreaming are not the same thing, so whatever functions REM sleep may have cannot be taken as functions for dreaming and dreams."[12]

These findings importantly suggest that a number of processes come together during REM sleep which may also occur discretely at other phases of sleep. Thus the similarity in the brain waves that occur at sleep onset (known as Stage 1 sleep), and in REM sleep, and the fact that dreams have been recorded in both, might mean a similar form of data processing goes on in the brain during both stages. As Foulkes suggested, sleep-onset dreaming may involve partial engagement of the dream production system, whereas in REM sleep, it is fully engaged.

Researchers next started to wonder, was REM sleep vital for well being? Dement carried out the first systematic studies of REM deprivation.[13] In his sleep laboratory, he prevented REM sleep in volunteer participants by having them woken up at the onset of a REM phase, and found that, the next night, when they were not woken up, they spent markedly longer than usual in REM sleep. Further studies showed that not only was there an increase in REM sleep time but also an increase in the frequency of phasic events (the eye-darting and twitching, etc).[14] When Dement tried this on cats, he found that, sometimes, on being woken at the onset of a REM period, cats' REM sleep could be effectively derailed while still allowing a discharge of a large number of PGO spikes. After two days of this procedure, the cats experienced just a small rebound, or no rebound at all, in REM sleep. This indicated that it is particularly the phasic component of REM sleep that the brain has to compensate for, after REM deprivation, rather than the tonic component (the passive immobility of the REM state).

Dement also found that prolonged REM deprivation in cats brought about an increase in their general level of arousal, especially primitive emotions such as sexual desire and rage.[15] He had expected that the REM deprivation would lead to hallucinations, and that EEGs would show a considerable firing of PGO spikes. However, nothing happened initially. Then, a few days later, he gave the REM-deprived cats a drug called parachlorophenylalanine (PCPA), which inhibits the synthesis in the brain of the 'feel-good' neurotransmitter serotonin. After administration of the drug, EEGs of the cats' brains taken when they were awake showed PGO spikes firing wildly. The cats also exhibited the hallucinatory behaviour that Dement had originally expected and they underwent profound personality changes, resulting in hypersexuality, rage and overeating. As time passed, the spike discharge became evenly dispersed throughout waking and sleeping and the animals grew very lethargic.

These findings suggested to Dement that there were two systems by which we could express our instinctive appetites – for food, warmth, sex, etc., – and that we had only a finite amount of energy with which we could do so (our energy could become depleted). The first system operated when we were awake and was concerned with instinctive behaviours, such as eating, drinking, survival and sexual urges. The second operated when we were asleep, when the mechanism for discharging instinctive impulses was by means of the PGO spikes. (PGO spikes are not observed on the EEGs of animals when they are drinking, eating, mating, etc., so clearly the two systems are not operational at the same time.) He concluded that the primary role of REM sleep was to provide a 'safety valve' outlet for the discharge of instinctive impulses – the letting off of steam through the act of dreaming.

He was not entirely happy with this notion, however, because he wrote elsewhere, "It seems naive to suggest that the REMs exist in the adult organism to prevent the nervous system from becoming over-excitable". The major evidence that Dement accumulated to suggest two systems for discharging instinctive drives still stands, but the expectation fulfilment theory of dreaming shows that the function of the REM drive discharge system is far more vital and sophisticated than the safety valve version he suggested.

Dement's 'two systems' idea inspired Gerald Vogel's thinking, after he found that people suffering from depression showed improvement when deprived of REM sleep.[16] For a sustained improvement, REM sleep deprivation has to last for about three weeks. Vogel suggested that depressed people might discharge too much drive (or motivation) through REM sleep and that preventing REM sleep increased the motivation available to them when awake. Although REM sleep deprivation led to some increased arousal in non-depressed individuals, the effects were not as dramatic, he suggested, because non-depressed people were already near 'the ceiling' for excitability. To support this idea, he referred to a well-established finding that antidepressant drugs, which suppress REM sleep, have little effect on non-depressed people, yet can raise the motivation of depressed people. Vogel concluded that one of the functions of REM sleep was to modulate instinctive behaviour, so as to permit greater flexibility in its expression in higher organisms: in other words, to damp down instincts.

Whilst it is hard not to agree with Dement that this idea of damping down instincts is rather crude, we plan to show that Vogel's idea had some merit. We will have a lot more to say too, later in this chapter, about what the effects of REM deprivation tell us.

Dement also co-authored a very different theory of the function of the REM state, the so-called 'ontogenetic hypothesis', which was put forward to explain one of the most surprising discoveries about REM sleep.[17] Research had shown that REM sleep occurs most frequently in the young and decreases as we get older. During the last trimester of pregnancy, the fetus spends up to 80 per cent of sleep time in REM sleep. This declines to 67 per cent at birth, then declines further to approximately 25 per cent later in childhood and stays around this level until old age, when it declines still further. The amount of REM sleep at birth is directly related to the maturity of the animal when born. Those species born with their brains and physical abilities well developed experience little REM sleep. In contrast, species that are born very immature experience high levels of REM sleep. A species such as the guinea pig, which is well developed at birth and within minutes can run around and nibble grass, is in REM sleep for only about 15 per cent of its sleep time, whereas the rat, which is born blind and immobile, spends over 95 per cent of its sleep time in REM sleep. As the rat matures it has less and less REM sleep and, within a month, REM has declined to 30 per cent of its total sleep time. Dement and his colleagues concluded, therefore, that the primary role of REM sleep is in the very young and that it may serve to provide stimulation to the developing brain in the stimulus-poor intrauterine environment. But that answer simply begs the question: what is it that REM sleep achieves for adults? There can be little doubt that any comprehensive theory of REM sleep must be able to explain both its preponderance during gestation and early childhood, and REM sleep in adulthood.

In Chapter 2, we referred to Michel Jouvet's idea that the REM state evolved to program mammals (while still in the womb) with instinctive behaviour, and that the REM state persists in adulthood to allow that instinctive behaviour to be continually modified in some way. Jouvet had shown that REM sleep is controlled by a very primitive part of the brain and that, when the most recently developed 'thinking' part of the brain, the neocortex, is removed, slow-wave sleep stops but REM sleep still occurs. When he removed a small area of cats' midbrains, the cats seemed to act out their dreams: during REM sleep, they did things such as chasing or attacking an invisible object, displaying fright, or making grooming, mating or drinking motions.[18,19]

Consistent with Jouvet's theory that REM sleep in the womb is a programming period is the observation that newborn babies display during REM sleep what appear to be sophisticated emotions, such as perplexity, disdain, scepticism and mild amusement, which are not observed during waking.[20] Young babies smile in REM sleep weeks before social smiling is observed when they are awake.[21] It was suggested by J. Allan Hobson that, because babies know how to breathe and swallow as soon as they are born, these behaviours are somehow learned in REM sleep in the womb.[22] He notes that observation of fetal lambs has shown breathing movements of the chest wall in REM sleep, even though, of course, there is no air in the womb to breathe. It is possible too, therefore, that other behaviours are programmed or rehearsed in REM sleep, the use of which will only be identified later in social life. Fetuses are now commonly seen on scans apparently rehearsing a whole range of emotional expressions, including smiling, disgust and surprise. However, Jouvet's theory becomes less plausible when we consider REM sleep and the older child and adult. No analysis of dreams from REM sleep has shown a consistent pattern of interaction between waking behaviour and what might be considered rehearsal of instinctive drives or behaviour. Still, taking Dement's and Jouvet's research findings together, a nice integration becomes possible between the role and function of REM sleep in the fetus and the newborn.

The process of pattern matching

What possible implications can be drawn from all this so far? Well, instinctive behaviours are widely regarded as inherited patterns which allow a prepared response to stimuli that an animal, once born, might expect to encounter in its environment.[23] Moreover, these patterns can have only partially specified parameters in order to allow for the range of variation that individual members of a species might encounter within their particular habitat. For example, there can be no predetermined pattern for exactly what a mother's face will look like, what her voice will sound like and, in humans, what language she will speak. The more unspecified the parameters of genetically anticipated stimuli (and responses) are, the greater the range of flexibility in the animal's behaviour and the environmental learning component of their instinctive behaviour (for instance, which language to speak). So, instinctive behaviours have to be installed in 'metaphorical form', which, in effect, convey to the baby, "When you get out into the world, look for something *approximately* like this". They are internal patterns for which we seek completion in the environment.

This metaphorical pattern-matching process is carried out by all creatures. The diversity of shape, size, composition and location of the nests built by birds of the same species shows how wide a variation there can be in the execution of what appears to be a highly controlled instinctive behaviour.[24] Consider how many mammals use their unique vocal patterns so that parents and young can recognise each other. The genetic pattern cannot possibly specify the voice pattern of a particular bird. The pattern has to be sufficiently indeterminate that any voice from the whole range of voices that could possibly be encountered is capable of being selected and recognised as an analogue of that pattern. In other words, analogues from the world of sensory experience (the 'outside' world) have to be identified to complete the internal pattern.

As Jouvet has noted, there can be little doubt, from the study of monozygotic (identical) twins reared together and apart, that the expression of intelligence and personality in humans is to some extent influenced by genetic factors.[25] It is probably fair to say that, for the human species, the parameters of genetically inherited behaviours are the least precisely defined. This gives us the widest latitude in the identification of environmental analogues and permits us greater flexibility in the expression of our behaviour. Our brain is the world's supreme metaphorical pattern-matching organ.

Let us consider human languages again. We know that there is a genetic substratum to language acquisition – Lev Semenovich Vygotsky's so-called 'language acquisition device'[26] or Noam Chomsky's 'deep structure'.[27] The native language is acquired as a social analogue which completes the genetically programmed language acquisition pattern. Jerome Bruner tells us that it was "Vygotsky's genius to recognise the importance of language acquisition as an analogue".[28] We believe he was right.

Suppose a child failed to develop the basic instinctive programs that underlie human behaviour. We would expect this child to show profound developmental deficits, possibly including an absence of language, an inability to relate to people and an inability to learn how to express emotions appropriately. We would also expect to see idiosyncratic and inflexible behaviour patterns. The syndrome that these symptoms typically describe is, of course, childhood autism. Not only do autistic children fail to develop normal human interactive behaviour, they do not attend to sounds or visual stimuli in the way normal children do. Autistic children are literally in a world of their own, without access to the instinctive templates that would enable them to connect appropriately to people or places. We have previously mentioned Jouvet's theory that instinctive knowledge is programmed during REM sleep. Interestingly, a number of studies by Edward Ornitz and his colleagues have shown that, in younger autistic children, differentiation in the pattern of their brain waves is delayed, compared with normal children of the same age.[29] It is as if a program has not finished running out in them.

Asperger's syndrome is sometimes regarded as a milder form of autism. The child grows up with normal language and mental development but the templates for instinctively reading other people's emotional responses and continually prioritising their own responses to changing situations appear not to have been 'laid down' in them and they show severe and sustained impairment in empathy, social skills and the ability automatically to read context and react appropriately. Asperger children clearly lack the instinctive basis for interpersonal interactions. Without the instinctive templates to guide the development of these skills, the child can only be taught external rules to guide them. Unfortunately, external rules are a poor substitute for the direct perception of the subtleties involved in social interactions and how the child should behave in different contexts. Consequently, people with Asperger's syndrome continue to have major problems with forming and managing relationships throughout their lives.

Because the patterns of different human cultures are so diverse and varied, it follows that human beings must have a very flexible innate mechanism for instinctively connecting to any one of them. In other words, we employ highly subtle, sophisticated and analogical thinking abilities to enable us to make sense of whatever patterns we are confronted with. The diversity of language is again a fine example – there are said to be up to 8,000 different languages in use today and, if the genetic basis of language were rigid, we would not have had the capacity to develop so many. It is the genetic basis of language, the incredibly subtle and flexible pattern passed on to us in our genes, that allows children to learn any one (or even several) of those thousands of different languages easily and automatically in the first few years of life.

The model of REM sleep put forward on the basis of the experimental biological evidence suggests that REM sleep in the fetus and newborn is what programs instinctive behaviour – genetically programmed anticipated experiences (expectations) amassed over millions of years of evolution. Since the anticipation of sensory experience cannot actually be that specific future experience (as we have seen, our genes cannot predict exactly which language we will need to speak or what our mother will look like) it must be an analogue of it. In other words, incomplete patterns are completed by the identification of analogous sensory experiences in the real world. But, as is recognised, this still leaves the problem of the role of REM sleep in the adult, as there is no evidence that instinctive behaviours are further modified during adult REM sleep. Yet there *is* an explanation that would fit what we know about the role of REM sleep.

Since the dreams of REM sleep have a sensory content, it follows that, if they too are based on anticipated drive patterns of experience, these patterns must have had a sensory component assimilated prior to expression in REM sleep, as instinctive patterns themselves have no sensory content. (For instance, anger is an instinct but the sensory component of the pattern is the anger experienced but not expressed *in a specific situation*, such as our boss dumping another job on us just before home time.) This means that dreams are the analogical expression of anticipated experiences or unfulfilled expectations from when we were awake that have aroused the autonomic nervous system. Because these 'arousals' (unfulfilled expectations) are not deactivated by the anticipated experiences actually happening that day, we carry them into our sleep where they are deactivated by the dreaming process. An unfulfilled expectation from waking life, unlike a genetic expectation, must have a sensory description or content. Thus its release during REM sleep can lead to its completion and deactivation when it is pattern matched to an analogous sensory experience drawn from memory (the dream). This, of course, cannot happen for the originally programmed instinct patterns. Since they have no sensory content they cannot be matched from memory; they must be matched in the real world.

This explains the sensory content of dreams and fits perfectly with the expectation fulfilment theory of dreams. When patterns of arousal are not discharged by completion, they are carried into our sleep where they are deactivated by the dreaming process. There is even further evidence from biology that supports why this is likely to be so.

The orientation response

We have described the busy discharge of PGO spikes during the phasic component of REM sleep. In the 1980s, Adrian Morrison and his colleagues showed how these PGO spikes are in fact part of an alerting, or orientation, response which, in the waking state, accompanies the perception of novel stimuli – leading us to turn towards a loud noise, for instance.[30,31]

Movement is crucial to the evolution of brains. Living things that don't move, such as trees, don't have brains. But an organism that is capable of movement needs a brain to predict the best moves it should make to survive. We cannot stress too much the importance of the fact that our brains expend a massive amount of energy on trying to anticipate the future. Mostly this is happening unconsciously. At all times the brain has a frame of reference – a model of what it expects to happen next – that it is orienting to. When the incoming data conform to that model, we just accept it. So, after dark, we are quite comfortable in seeing the familiar shadows of the trees at the bottom of our garden and barely register them. It is when there is a discrepancy that we suddenly become 'aware'– when we suddenly notice for example, among the tree shadows, a smaller, moving shadow in the shape of a man. It is the orientation response that alerts us to the new, unexpected shadow. The PGO spikes fire off from the brainstem whenever a discrepancy is registered between signals from the environment and the anticipated model. Consequently, the model of anticipated reality we hold in our brains is being constantly updated.

This response is also associated with processes characteristic of the REM state: we freeze; our higher brain goes into overdrive to make sense of what is happening; and related physiological reactions occur. It has even been suggested that, in effect, the orientation response is a mini REM state in itself, similar even in the elevated brain temperature, the fixation of attention and the brain waves that are generated (hippocampal theta rhythms).[32] But what, in the absence of any external stimuli, could be the function of the intense production of these orientation responses during sleep? We suggest that, in triggering many of the phenomena of the REM state itself, they serve to alert the cortex to the imminent arrival of aroused unfulfilled expectations that need to be completed.

It is the orientation response that signals to the midbrain and neocortex, at the onset of a REM sleep period, that something warrants attention. Because sensory information from the sense organs is blocked from reaching the brain during REM sleep,[33] the signal cannot be matched up with information coming in from the outside world. But the unfulfilled expectation patterns need to be completed to be de-aroused, so if the brain can't pattern match from the environment to complete them, the only other option is to make a pattern match from the sensory content of stored memories. The brain pulls out from its memory banks metaphorical equivalents – which create the dream – to complete and thus switch off the unexpressed expectations. (The right hemisphere of the brain, which is dominant during dreaming, is recognised as working through metaphor.)

Perhaps, for example, a lawyer feels badly treated by her boss. She thinks angrily at some point during the day, “I want to get back at my bully of a boss for treating me unfairly”, and imagines how she might do it. The unfulfilled expectation that requires discharge during REM sleep has a clear sensory description – the imagined scenario with her boss. This cannot itself be used to complete the expectation and be discharged during REM sleep, however, since it is the very pattern that is seeking its completion via a pattern match from memory. As noted earlier, the pattern match must be found in an *analogous* sensory scenario if it is to complete the unfulfilled expectation. So, in this scenario, she might see herself telling a bossy doctor in no uncertain terms why his behaviour is so unacceptable.

As we have seen, the orientation response prepares the organism to respond to what may be significant new stimuli. Any pattern match is a perception, and perception is a constructive process. Hence, we sometimes misperceive people and things – as when we think we recognise someone, for example, and then realise we were mistaken, or when we see objects and shapes that turn out to be different from what we first thought they were. Perception always has an emotional content. Our hearts can miss a beat when we first see a body lying motionless in the road but, on closer inspection, the ‘body’ can turn out to be a bag of rubbish. Perception is always our *best informed guess* at what we think we are seeing, hearing or touching in any given situation. Similarly, during sleep, when the PGO spikes start firing furiously as part of an internal orientation response pattern, in the absence of outside information the brain can only base its ‘best guess’ on significant information that it is actively anticipating – the unfulfilled emotional arousals. So these are released during REM sleep and analogically processed as ‘real’ perceptions which match up to, and complete, the arousal patterns. These are our dreams.

It is our *introspections* about unexpressed emotional arousal that give rise to dreams, not the arousal itself. For instance, it has been found that viewing erotic[34] or violent[35] films immediately before going to sleep does not usually result in sexual or violent dreams content.

This is not surprising, in light of the expectation fulfilment theory: the arousal is being expressed through the watching of it being acted out on screen.

A review of the *biological* data, therefore, is highly supportive of the conclusion that Joe's *psychological* research led him to: that dreaming is deactivating highly aroused emotional thinking and that it has to use pattern matching or metaphor to complete the circuit, because that is how the brain, and therefore the REM process, works. Joe's theory also comfortably links the demonstrated programming functions of REM sleep seen in fetuses and the very young to the continued experience of REM sleep in adults.

Why we dream in metaphor – and forget our dreams

There is another key explanation for why we dream in metaphor, which also explains why we forget our dreams. We do so to prevent our memory stores from becoming either corrupt or incomplete. For instance, let's imagine that the sales manager at the firm where Katie works thinks it is fine to give her a pat on the bottom when he passes. Katie finds this behaviour offensive but she is fearful, rightly or wrongly, of losing her job if she makes a fuss, so she says nothing. Inside, though, she is steaming with anger. So, at night, in line with the expectation fulfilment theory of dreaming, after such an occasion she will need to complete the expectation aroused, both to discharge the still 'live' emotional expectation that is taking up brain space and also to preserve the integrity of her emotional instincts. But there is a problem. If in her dream Katie acts as she would like to have acted, swiping his hand away and giving him a good push that propels him into the filing cabinet, she will be creating a memory that is partially false. It might be argued that we are perfectly well able to distinguish dreams from reality – we do so whenever we happen to remember our dreams. However that is because we are dreaming in metaphor, so the remembered scenario, whatever it is, never actually happened. And, even then, it is only *afterwards*, if the dream is remembered, that it can be rationalised, because during dreaming lines of connection to the rational part of the brain are closed and so everything feels very real while we are in the process of dreaming it. Imagine how hard it would be, then, to distinguish a dream from a memory of an event if we dreamed out exactly what happened, embellishing it only in terms of acting out our emotional arousal in some way.

If, on the other hand, Katie does dream out what really happened, along with acting out her arousal, and then forgets her dream, as most of us do, she will have gaps in her memory of what *actually* happened, since the dream involves both real (the bottom-patting incident) and fantasy (fighting back) experiences. As we use our memory of experiences to help us predict how to react in similar circumstances in the future, a memory system with significant memories missing would be next to useless for this purpose.

These two undesirable consequences explain why it makes sense for the brain to expend the extra energy required to dream in metaphor: if we dream the real scenario and how we would like to have acted, we have set up a partially false memory; if, on the other hand, we forget that dream, we have introduced memory gaps that could have significant adverse effects. Using an analogous experience as a means of completing the arousal provides a perfect solution. It enables the arousal to be discharged and the metaphorical dream material can be safely forgotten, but the original record of what happened (the bottom patting) is able to be remembered. So Katie may dream that someone else comes on to her inappropriately and she stands up for herself. The dream can be forgotten but the original memory is safely stored, reminding Katie to be wary whenever the sales manager is around. What has been discharged is the arousal associated with the instinctive urge but, importantly, the instinctive urge itself in the context it was experienced is remembered.

All this also explains why it is actually important that we forget our dreams. When we are awake, the hippocampus, the conscious memory store, holds our memories of recent events and quickly deconstructs those memories and sends them to various parts of the cortex – the parts concerned with vision, hearing, touch, etc – for storage. It does that to facilitate efficient pattern matching. But, as discussed above, if the dream is allowed to be stored as a real memory, it will corrupt the memory store and greatly diminish our ability reliably to predict the outcome of similar experiences in the future. PET scans and other types of research have shown that, in dreaming, the pre-cortex is not active. This effectively prevents the hippocampus from sending the metaphorical dream information to the cortex for long-term storage – which in itself strongly indicates that dreams are not intended to be remembered.[36]

But sometimes we do recall our dreams. Might this not undo all our good dream work? The answer is no, because the arousal is switched off once the expectation is acted out. And, once we are awake, the cortex is switched back on, enabling us to compare dream content to what is really happening around us and, thus, to distinguish between dream and reality.

This also neatly explains why, as we are often asked, people who suffer from post-traumatic stress continue to experience emotional arousal, even after dreaming about the stressful event in some form. Shouldn't the dreaming deactivate the arousal? The answer is that, as explained above, the memory of an event must remain intact. So, although the arousal experienced on any particular day is deactivated in dreams that night, next day the amygdala (the brain's 'security guard') is again on alert for any circumstance that could be matched to the traumatic event and signal danger. As we know, pattern matching is relatively crude. So, if the traumatic event was associated with dimmed lighting or petrol or the sound of a kettle boiling, re-experience of just that element could be sufficient to reactivate the trauma memory and associated emotions – unexpressed arousals which will need discharging again that night.

People sometimes claim that certain dreams which they remember are definitely not metaphorical – they dream about an instance exactly as it happened. In some non-REM stages of sleep, such as lighter Stage 2 sleep, a certain amount of thinking (termed 'mentation' by researchers) and fantasy still occur. It isn't dreaming as such and, if woken from sleep at such a stage, the sleeper may recall what is, in effect, a brief replay of an event that they were thinking about.

In other cases, a dream recalled on waking which is apparently almost an exact replica of a lived event may still, in fact, be metaphorical. For instance, a young woman told Joe that she had driven her widowed mother to a social group but, on arrival, her mother refused to get out of the car, saying that she was anxious about going. The daughter felt she had wasted her time, as she could have been at home getting on with an essay she needed to deliver. She dreamed that night that she and her mother were in a car. She kept trying to persuade her mother to get out but her mother refused, saying there was an obstacle outside preventing her from opening the door. Eventually the daughter got out and tried to yank the door open. The young woman wondered why her mother appeared so clearly in the dream, acting almost as she had acted earlier in the evening, if, as the expectation fulfilment theory holds, real 'characters' in dreams should be changed in some way. Joe asked whether her mother might be representing some aspect of herself. For instance, was she feeling blocked? The young woman then realised that, in fact, she had been worrying about not knowing how to go on with her essay. Her mother's inability to go into the club had in the dream represented her own inability to get on with the essay – not because she had wasted time driving her mother but because she was stuck about how to proceed. So what appeared to be an almost exact memory was metaphorical after all.

Another question that some people ask is why, if dreams are designed to deactivate arousal, do we sometimes wake up with a feeling of dread or anxiety? This is because, if the level of anxiety that is being discharged metaphorically is extremely high, the neocortex may become activated ("what is going on here?") and this wakes us up. The dream was doing its job but it was interrupted. If we fall back to sleep, the deactivation will continue. Sometimes, however, people start introspecting about why they are feeling anxious, or why they were dreaming such a strange and frightening scenario (not realising that it was metaphorical), which keeps them awake – and which becomes the subject of another dream the next night.

Why we evolved to dream

We can next show that, from the viewpoint of evolution, if the expectation fulfilment theory of dreaming is correct, REM sleep confers significant advantages.

Homoiothermia (warm-bloodedness) gave more freedom of behaviour to higher vertebrates (animals with backbones) because the ability of mammals and birds to keep a constant internal temperature conferred great advantages on them in terms of mobility. As they evolved, this mobility was accompanied by a "complexification of the brain".[37] Michel Jouvet suggested that REM sleep, being warm-blooded and the flexibility of instinctive behaviour were all linked – he thought that REM sleep may have evolved to permit more freedom in the expression of instinctive behaviour, in the way that we have described.

The new ability of mammals and birds to keep their internal temperature constant and to express instinctive behaviours more freely would have come at a great price – more than a fivefold increase in basic energy expenditure over cold-blooded creatures.[38] Such a massive increase in metabolism obviously had to be compensated for by a corresponding increase in energy supply. This could hardly be achieved by simply extending the time spent looking for food. What was required was a matching increase in productivity: a more productive return from the energy expended in seeking food and the energy gained by acquiring it. This could partly be achieved by conserving energy whenever possible – sleeping, for example, when prey or other sources of food were not available. (This can be seen as one of the functions of 'slow-wave' sleep.) But, although reducing energy expenditure by cutting out nonproductive time does conserve energy, it doesn't actually provide any. And, as we have seen, a massive increase in energy gain is required to compensate for the demands of being warm-blooded. Clearly there was a need to develop the ability to employ this new high-powered energy system in more productive ways.

What was required was the ability to increase survival chances through prediction, planning and the motivation to pursue purposeful, goal-directed behaviours. This, of course, is the function ascribed to the greatly expanded neocortex in mammals. Paul MacLean summed this up well when he wrote: "A remarkable feature of the neocortex is that it evolves primarily in relation to systems receiving and processing information from the external world. ... It was as though the neocortex was designed to serve as a more objective intelligence in coping with the external environment."[39]

This would include the ability to inhibit particular instinctive drives if circumstances or goals should warrant it. Once an instinctive pattern (e.g. the desire to eat or mate) is activated, the normal outcome is that the programmed behaviour is carried out and that deactivates the drive. But the neocortex has the power to inhibit an activated arousal pattern if it is deemed inappropriate in the circumstances. No animals would pursue a sexual opportunity if a predator was heard rustling in the bushes, for instance. For humans, inhibiting an activated arousal pattern might mean desiring a fried breakfast but resisting the temptation for health reasons, or having to come up with a different solution when childcare plans are thwarted. The resources of the neocortex can then be directed towards inhibiting the arousal pattern and focusing attention towards another goal. Clearly, to avoid overloading the neocortex in this way (which would result in a weakening of its ability to influence instinctive behaviours), it would be advantageous to have a means of deactivating the activated, but unacted upon, arousal patterns. The expectation fulfilment theory of dreaming neatly demonstrates how REM sleep fulfils this function every night through dreams, releasing the neocortex to cope more effectively with the emotionally arousing events of the following day.

As mentioned earlier, but worth repeating in this context of evolutionary development, a further benefit of acting out the unexpressed instinctive impulse is that we maintain its integrity. We continually inhibit the desire to flee, for instance, because the threats nowadays are more usually not a risk to life or limb but a feared bawling out by the boss or the prospect of taking an exam. If these arousing scenarios were not acted out metaphorically in our dreams, we might lose the natural instinct to flee, failing to accept that danger is real when life really *is* at risk. In other words, if this didn't happen, vital survival instincts would be conditioned out of us.

Thus we can see the beautiful economy of nature. The same process that programs instinctive behaviour is also used to preserve its integrity and to deactivate 'left over' activated, but not acted upon, patterns of stimulation from our waking state.

REM sleep deprivation

If this new theory is correct it leads, of course, to a prediction of the consequences of REM sleep deprivation (some of which we mentioned earlier, when looking at the work of Dement). The theory would predict that, if an animal were deprived of REM sleep, its autonomic nervous system would become more aroused. This would result in a more uninhibited expression of instinctive drives, with increasing inability to control or express instinctive behaviour patterns (i.e. react) in appropriate ways.

The effect would be similar in human beings, although we might expect that social constraints would help people control the expression of those desires. But we all know that when we become very tired, for example, we experience increased irritability and find it harder to concentrate or be polite. We would expect people deprived of REM sleep to feel that they were at the mercy of events. The overloading of the neocortex would impair their ability to analyse and decide for themselves matters of personal importance, and they would be more easily influenced. Also, they would be increasingly unable to cope with stress. (Indeed, we can even think of stress as the accumulation of uncompleted arousal patterns held in the brain, which causes the feeling of being overwhelmed and out of control that people under stress so often describe.)

Many of these REM-deprivation effects can be observed in people who have suffered torture at the hands of regimes that come down hard on those with dissenting opinions. Such torture typically involves not letting people sleep. The effects are also evident in the behaviour of members of cults and certain religious orders whose leaders use sleep deprivation to 'brainwash' or indoctrinate people into their beliefs.

It has long been known that lack of sleep can kill. We also know that REM sleep is essential throughout life, although just how essential has only been clarified over the last few decades through the many experiments on REM deprivation carried out on animals and humans. One of the great veterans of sleep research was Allan Rechtschaffen who, with enormous ingenuity, devised experiments that enabled scientists to study the effects of 'net' sleep deprivation on test rats without other variables getting in the way. His control rats slept normally but in every other way were treated the same as those deprived of sleep. He found that there was no doubt that sleep deprivation alone was responsible for the death of the test animals.[40]

Rechtschaffen and his colleagues searched and searched for explanations. At first they suspected a drop in body temperature might be the cause, because all the test rats showed a decline in body temperature. But, when the experimental rats were kept warm with heaters, they still died. Breakdown in bodily tissues caused by accelerated metabolism or systemic infections was also ruled out in a series of elaborate experiments.[41]

Even though Rechtschaffen's studies failed to uncover the direct cause of death in his sleep-deprived rats, they did provide us with new information. One consistent observation was that the test rats ate increased amounts of food while, at the same time, losing weight. These changes suggested that sleep-deprived animals have an increased metabolic rate, as though they have an increased need for energy. In fact, near death, the sleep-deprived animals showed an energy expenditure two to three times above normal. This, the researchers surmised, might be caused by excessive heat loss or by a dramatic change in the set point of the brain thermostat.

Rechtschaffen thought hard and went on to devise more ingenious experiments which showed that, indeed, the set point of the brain mechanism that keeps internal heat at a constant level was increased by sleep deprivation. Rats who had been deprived of sleep for two weeks preferred to remain in a 'heat corridor' where the ambient temperature was 50 °C (122 °F). The control rats found that unbearably hot and fled as fast as their legs could carry them to the part of the corridor where the ambient temperature was 30 °C (86 °F). Clearly, if the test rats preferred to be in a much hotter environment, their internal thermostats had been altered. This sleep deprivation in some way disrupted the activity of the brain cells responsible for temperature regulation.

In further experiments, Rechtschaffen found that rats that were prevented from having REM sleep were unable to keep their body temperature stable. It became clear that REM sleep deprivation did not cause a change in the brain thermostat *per se*, but rather caused disruption in heat conservation. The link between the evolution of warm-bloodedness and the REM state in the brain could not be more clear.

Interestingly, when sleep-deprived animals were near death and then allowed to sleep, all of these changes could be reversed. Most remarkable was that the animals showed large amounts of REM sleep rebound. In other words, they had to catch up on what they had missed. On the first day that they were allowed to sleep without interruption, overall length of REM sleep was five to ten times greater than normal. Rechtschaffen's conclusion was that "the need for paradoxical [REM] sleep may exceed the need for other sleep stages".

Supersleep

Other eminent researchers, building on more recent work, go much further. "REM, it seems, is some sort of supersleep," said Hobson.[42] He gives three reasons to support this. The first is that, "although it normally occupies only about 20 per cent of the total time we sleep each night, it takes only six weeks of deprivation of REM sleep alone to kill rats, compared with four weeks for complete sleep deprivation. Based on its relative duration of only 20 per cent of sleep time, we would predict that five times as long a deprivation period would be required if both states were equally life-enhancing." Calculated on this basis, one minute of REM sleep is worth five minutes of non-REM sleep.

His second reason to support the idea of REM supersleep is one that will please catnappers around the world. Short naps are surprisingly beneficial "if they occur at times in the day when REM sleep probability is high. Daytime naps are different from night sleep in that we may fall directly into a REM period and stay there for the duration of the nap. Since the time of peak REM probability is greatest in the late morning, the tendency of naps to be composed of REM sleep is highest then and falls thereafter till the onset of night sleep (about 12 hours later)." The implication is that a little bit of sleep, at the right time of day, may be more useful than more sleep later on in the day.

The third reason is that "following the deprivation of even small amounts of REM sleep, there is a prompt and complete repayment. The subject who has been denied REM sleep launches into extended REM periods as soon as he is allowed to sleep normally. In recent drug studies, when REM sleep was prevented the payback seemed to be made with interest. More REM sleep was paid back than was lost."

He then goes on to propose "a link between brain-mind states and genetics" which makes sense, given the evidence that our instincts are laid down from our genes in the REM state.

Perhaps the most consistent finding from sleep laboratories has been the fact that both humans and animals deprived of REM sleep show a rebound when allowed to sleep normally after the deprivation. The pressure to have REM sleep was forcefully observed during the deprivation experiments. On the first night, researchers would have to wake up subjects at the onset of REM sleep on average seven times a night, but by the fifth night 30 awakenings might be necessary. The REM rebound phenomenon therefore seems to indicate a strong biological pressure for REM sleep – a fundamental need.

Overall though, the results were a disappointment to experimenters because they had expected to see hallucinations and gross personality disturbances with subjects deprived of REM in this way. However, the results were much in line with what we would expect from the hypothesis set out in this book. For example, REM deprivation resulted in higher autonomic arousal as indicated by the following facts:

- An increase in heart rate from 160 beats a minute to a mean of 200 beats a minute after 30 days of REM deprivation, arising from a lesion in an area of the brain that has the effect of entirely suppressing REM sleep[43]
- A lowering of seizure threshold for convulsions in rats following REM deprivation for six days[44]
- A lowering of the auditory recovery cycle in cats suffering REM deprivation[45]
- Dement reported that primitive behaviour was greatly enhanced in cats after REM deprivation using a mechanical method.[46] The cats ate nearly twice as fast as normal and some showed disturbed sexual behaviour – such as compulsive mounting of anaesthetised male cats
- Psychometric tests of human subjects showed heightened neediness and emotionality, together with a significant increase in the expression of neurotic concerns.[47]

These findings clearly indicate that REM deprivation results in an increase in autonomic arousal and heightened instinctive drives, which is what we would predict if the expectation fulfilment theory of dreams is correct.

The effects of REM deprivation on autonomic arousal in humans are much less pronounced than in animals. This may be partly because less stressful and less efficient methods are used to wake up humans compared with the mechanical methods usually used with animals.[48] Hypnotic drugs such as tranquillisers inhibit REM sleep to varying extents, but again without any gross disturbances in the behaviour of normal subjects. However, as we know, dreaming does occur to some extent outside of the REM state. It may be that REM-suppressing drugs merely displace dreaming into another sleep stage. The purpose of taking these drugs is to reduce arousal so we would expect there to be less need for REM sleep since fewer unexpressed arousals would have taken place.

Antidepressant drugs inhibit REM sleep and, as Gerald Vogel has shown, REM deprivation is helpful in the treatment of depression.[49] He also found that subjects who failed to show an improvement in symptoms after REM deprivation were also less likely to respond to antidepressant medication. A possible explanation for these findings is that REM deprivation lowers the threshold for triggering instinctive drives when people are awake, thus enabling those suffering from depression to motivate themselves sufficiently to rise out of their apathy on waking in the morning. Such an explanation would be consistent with the expectation fulfilment theory of dreaming. The theory also explains why antidepressant drugs can have a therapeutic effect: they inhibit REM sleep.

Depressed people spend proportionately much longer dreaming in the REM state than non-depressed people. Since, as we have seen, REM sleep lowers our autonomic arousal level, the excessive REM sleep of depressed people could be expected to lower their arousal level much more than would be normal in a healthy person. This is the reason, of course, that depressed people wake up feeling exhausted – their arousal level has dropped drastically due to an excess of REM sleep.

The question that has puzzled psychiatrists for decades is why depressed people have excessive REM sleep. But, in the light of Joe's theory, the answer is obvious: dreaming is caused by emotionally arousing introspection that is not acted upon. And what do depressed people spend enormous amounts of their time doing? Worrying! Worrying puts an immense strain upon the REM system, leading to excessive REM dream sleep, which in turn leads to brain exhaustion. Also, the prolonged firing of the orientation response during the excessive dreaming exhausts the brain's ability to orientate itself when the person wakes up. If you recall, Dement discovered that there were two systems of discharging instinctive impulses, either via the orientation response or through instinct-driven behaviour. He found that, when the reservoir of attention energy was exhausted by constant triggering of the orientation response, an animal became exhausted and unable to take an interest in life. This, we are saying, is why depressed people become so apathetic and unable to find life interesting. The excessive firing of the orientation response, due to excessive dreaming, exhausts their ability to engage in motivated behaviour – which is what gives the sense of meaning to what we do in our lives. This, of course, has clear implications for the treatment of depression, which we will look at in a later chapter.

Most other theories that seek to account for the function of REM sleep in adults find REM deprivation studies a major problem. The theory we are presenting, however, not only explains the effects so far discovered but can also predict ways that those effects can be even more fully demonstrated: increasing the number of uncompleted patterns of arousal that load the brain as a result of lack of REM sleep should, if the theory is right, cause a person's ability to cope to deteriorate rapidly, compared with that of a person who has a proper amount of REM sleep. This is clearly so.

Interestingly, Professor Peretz Lavie, head of the Sleep Laboratory at the Technion-Israel Institute of Technology in Haifa, even speculated on whether or not we need REM sleep at all, after his experiences with a patient whom, he discovered, had had little or no REM sleep for years.[50] This patient had been injured in the Arab-Israeli war and was found to have a shrapnel lesion in the very spot in the brainstem that Jouvet had discovered was responsible for triggering REM sleep (the pons). Professor Francis Crick, the Nobel prize winner whose 'dream to forget' theory we described in Chapter 2, was taken aback by this finding. He urged Professor Lavie to do further extensive tests to discover if there might not be some subtle malfunction of the patient's memory. But, in spite of extensive observations, Professor Lavie could find no malfunction in the patient's memory or thinking. Since the war, the patient had developed a successful law practice and was also particularly adept at doing crossword puzzles, activities which would be impossible for a person with amnesia. This is not an anomalous finding from the perspective of the expectation fulfilment theory. In fact it is predictable, as we shall explain.

The onset of REM sleep is controlled by the acetylcholine neurons in the brainstem. These cells also trigger the orientation response which focuses our attention on any sudden change perceived in the environment and in turn triggers the physical changes that gear the body up for 'fight or flight' in the event of danger. It is, as explained, the activation of the orientation response accompanying certain introspections that, if unresolved that day, gives rise to dreams. (Remember the firing of the PGO spikes at the start of REM sleep.) So, if this mechanism is deactivated, not only will there be no dreams, there will be no need for them. Professors Lavie and Crick were looking for cognitive or memory impairment, but their results might have been more revealing if they had checked whether this patient was capable of responding with arousal to novel stimuli. The deactivation of the fight or flight mechanism would make such a response unlikely. The absence of this process would impair performance on occasions, such as when driving, when it is crucial to react instantly. We would also expect this patient to be an emotionally cool person – perhaps the kind of person who would find complex crossword puzzles a compelling activity.

Until fairly recently it was thought that dolphins, whales, the primitive egg-laying Australian mammal known as the duck-billed platypus and the spiny anteater (a primitive, egg-laying marsupial), did not experience REM sleep. This was a tremendous paradox. One suggested explanation for this seeming lack in dolphins and whales was that the muscle paralysis that accompanies REM sleep would cause them to drown. The mystery was: if they were not going into REM sleep, how were they surviving without it? One suggested answer was that, since they have a much bigger neocortex than would be expected in creatures of their complexity, they used the extra brain capacity to compensate in some way. This would make sense if, as we are saying, one of the benefits of REM sleep is that it releases resources in the neocortex that would otherwise have had to be expended in continually scanning the environment for uncompleted patterns to fulfil its expectations. But, then, how would an animal not going into REM sleep give vent to frustrated instinctive impulses? Wouldn't it destroy its instinctive repertoire if it had no way of acting out uncompleted impulses to complete the patterns?

This remained a mystery until it was discovered that dolphins and whales have their own 'trick' to enable them to give expression to their impulses.[51] The phenomenon has been filmed and what they do is to go into the REM state for extremely short periods. During that time they roll over; their muscles stop working and, in a state of paralysis, they start to sink. This would provide enough time for the discharge of unexpressed instinctive impulses. They then return to the surface, take another breath of air, and sink back down again for another short period of REM dreaming. By having very short periods of REM sleep, these creatures have found a way round the problem of drowning.

The case of the duck-billed platypus has proved even more revealing. For a long time it was thought that this animal did not go into the REM state at all. But that was because sleep laboratories are warmer places than the duck-billed platypus is used to. The REM state is highly sensitive to ambient temperature. When the ambient temperature was lowered to one that a duck-billed platypus finds comfortable, it went into the REM state just as other mammals do – but for incredibly long periods.[52] It had more REM sleep than any other mammal so far observed. Not only that, but the type of REM sleep it experienced was characteristic of that seen in the fetus.[53] In other words, what it is likely that we are seeing in the duck-billed platypus is an earlier stage in the evolution of REM sleep, before unacted upon arousals could be discharged in dreams, leaving the instinct intact. The duck-billed platypus, it would appear, must reprogram an entire instinctive behaviour each time it represses a particular instinct. Consequently, its REM sleep lasts much longer. However, its arousal circuits remain switched on in its brain (since it doesn't dream and can't therefore act out its instincts to preserve them) until the reprogramming is completed – thus it needs a comparatively large neocortex compared to other animals.[54] This constant reprogramming is probably what all primitive mammals had to do before they evolved the tool of dreaming.

We have to recognise that something different started happening once dreams began to accompany REM sleep in mammals. The difference is that, as well as having access to instinctive programming processes, the REM state now also allows an awareness of the presence of sensory content from the memory of real experiences, which enables it to use these memories to make analagous sensory pattern matches. If the REM state initially evolved to programme in genetically anticipated patterns, these patterns could not possibly have had sensory content from outside encoded in them. Fetuses in the womb are programmed with instinctive knowledge – what we now call the human givens (because nature has given them to us through our genes). This innate knowledge includes physical behaviours, from breathing, swallowing and grasping, through to focusing attention and building rapport (which babies start doing with their mothers within moments of birth). This programming cannot have any psychological content, partly because the newborn baby has had no outside experiences yet, and the brain is insufficiently developed to process any, and partly because the genetic programmes only partially specify the patterns the baby will try to match to.

The sensory element of dreams develops gradually. Clearly, children's dreams could not be expected to have the complexity of adults' dreams because dreams are derived from waking thought processes – introspections – and are translated into metaphorical imagery based upon memories. Adult memories are more complex than the memories children have to draw on. Research on children's dreams done by David Foulkes shows that the type of dreams they have up until the age of six are very simple. They cannot even properly be called narrative dreams because, invariably, they consist of very short imagery sequences. Moreover, the imagery often involves animals, – very young children don't have the mental sophistication to see similarities between human beings in terms of qualities, and so may tend to replace human beings with an animal caricature that encapsulates the characteristic that they see in a human being. An aggressive barking dog may stand in for an angry person shouting, for instance. But perhaps more interesting still is that, up to the age of five, children do not have an articulated and well-defined self-concept. The complexity of our internal narratives always depends upon having a sense of who we are, and that requires a certain level of intellectual maturation. It is only when we have a sense of who we are that we can reflect on how that sense of self has been impeded or impinged upon by another person or an event. As children grow older and establish fuller self-consciousness, we find that their dreams begin to have more of a thematic story to them and increasingly develop the complexity that we tend to associate with adult dreaming.

In his own considerations for a new neurocognitive theory of dreaming, leading sleep researcher Bill Domhoff made a statement which would clearly support the above: "The fact that specific neural defects can lead to the loss or impairment of dreaming, when considered in conjunction with the fact that dreaming develops gradually in children, suggests that adult-like dreaming depends on the maturation of the neural network for dreaming. For example, the complete loss of dreaming in adults due to injuries to either inferior parietal lobe, when placed alongside the finding that increased dream reporting in young children correlates with visuospatial skills, suggests that the ability to dream in children depends in part upon the development of the neural network for spatial construction centered in the parietal lobes."[55] The parietal lobes are primarily concerned with our sense of ourselves as separate beings.

How other recent research findings support the expectation fulfilment theory of dreaming

Since the expectation fulfilment theory of dreaming was first developed, no findings from dream research have ever disconfirmed it and most, in fact, add weight to it. For instance, researchers have only recently shown that, after a night's sleep, people are less emotionally aroused by emotionally affecting stimuli encountered the previous day. Thirty-four participants were twice asked to rate the emotional intensity of 150 pictures, some of which were quite alarming. All saw the pictures for the second time 12 hours later but for half, that was after a night's sleep. The other half carried out their viewings in the morning and evening, with no sleep in between. The intensity of the ratings decreased after a night's sleep but remained the same or increased when participants stayed awake. The researchers report, "These findings describe an overnight de-potentiation of neural (amygdala) and behavioral (subjective) responsivity to previously encountered affective stimuli. Moreover, the success of this depotentiation was predicted by REM sleep gamma EEG activity."[56]

A similar experiment showed a similar result after a 90 minute nap. Thirty-six students had to rate faces on a screen for intensity of the emotion showed – a mix of fearful, sad, angry and happy expressions. Half were then given the opportunity for a 90-minute nap and, afterwards, all participants were asked to rate the expressions again. Those who did not have the nap showed a heightened sensitivity to the fearful and angry expressions, whereas those who napped were less affected by these but more sensitive to the happy faces. Also, the nappers reported more decrease in negative mood, whereas those who didn't nap felt worse than before. EEG recordings taken while the nappers slept showed that those who experienced REM sleep were more likely to have reduced sensitivity to negative emotions and increased sensitivity to positive ones.[57] The expectation fulfilment theory of dreaming would clearly predict these findings.

In some cases, the expectation fulfilment theory suggests a different, perhaps more logical or realistic, explanation for some recent dream research findings. Selterman and colleagues gave questionnaires to 61 undergraduates to assess their feelings about their relationships with their partners (the couples had to have been together at least six months). The participants then kept dream diaries for two weeks and a daily report of how much they interacted with their partner, felt warm towards them, conflicted with them, etc. The dreams were coded by the researchers, who then looked to see if dream content relating to the partner predicted behaviour towards them the next day. The researchers found a correspondence – for instance, dreams about infidelity were followed by less closeness the next day, but only in those who felt less securely attached to their partners. They conclude that dreams can prompt behaviour within relationships.[58]

This doesn't really make a lot of sense until one considers an explanation for the findings in line with the expectation fulfilment theory. This would hold that individuals who dreamed about infidelity would have been introspecting about it at some point the previous day – introspections varying, perhaps, from the speculative "I love him/her so much – wouldn't it be awful if he/she was ever unfaithful to me!" for those securely attached, to the "I wonder if he/she is being unfaithful" anxiety of the insecurely attached. The former would clearly be no less likely to feel warmth towards their partner the next day, whereas the latter would be acting on fears they already had.

Revonsuo's assertion that the function of dreams is to help us to rehearse how to practise survival techniques in threat situations (see page 17) can also be better explained by our theory. Through analysing 592 dreams from 52 subjects, Revonsuo found that dreams contain more frequent and more severe threats than waking life does; that dream threats are realistic; and that they primarily threaten the dreaming self, who tends to respond defensively.[59] As we show in the dream examples given in Chapters 3 and 5, the brain may use any easy-to-grab analogous scenario for a metaphorical representation of an emotionally-arousing experience, often picking an image that literally expresses what we may have ruminated about in figurative languge – "I could have clobbered her!" "I want to kill him!" Thus it might pick an event from a violent scene viewed on television that evening to express a relatively benign real-life situation in which annoyance or frustration was felt.

Some dream research has quantified what sort of dream content occurs most often, whether women and men dream differently, whether dreams are consistent over time and so on.[60] It is now known that the content of dreams over time is remarkably consistent. This would reflect the fact that our waking concerns stay largely the same, in broad terms, and that the brain is economical in using the same metaphorical representations again and again to reflect them.

It has also been established that men dream twice as often about men, often strangers, as they do about women, whereas women dream fairly evenly about both men and women. Women experience less physical aggression in dreams than men but more scenarios in which they experience perceived rejection. Women's dreams are evenly divided between friendly and aggressive whereas men's dreams are more likely to involve aggression. All this would make sense, in line with the theory. Because of our evolutionary past, men are more likely to perceive threat from other men and this could more easily form the content of unexpressed emotional arousal, whereas women are more attuned to the quality of relationships with both sexes.

Interestingly, even a study of the dreams of people who are paraplegic can be seen to support our theory. Researchers found that people who are paraplegic can walk in their dreams, even if they have never walked in real life. They studied ten people who had lost the use of their limbs up to sixty-four years previously, mainly in military service, and five who had congenital paraplegia. All recorded their dreams for six weeks, along with fifteen able-bodied participants of similar ages. Only one paraplegic participant did not record a dream in which he was moving and, overall, the paraplegics dreamed of walking just as often as the able-bodied participants. Length of time spent paraplegic had no bearing on whether people experienced leg movements in dreams. Just over half of paraplegic participants recalled dreams in which they were in a wheelchair but all openly admitted ruminating from time to time about wishing that they could walk.[61] It is, therefore, not surprising to us that they would often dream out that desire – the metaphorical form being the fact that they *could* walk.

We will turn finally, in this chapter, to what modern sleep researchers themselves observe about the overall content of dreams, and relate that to the dream theory we have proposed. Many researchers have commented on the correspondence between what happens in daily life and what appears in dreams and the fact that the connection is not straightforward. For instance, in one study, 29 people kept a log of daytime activities, events, and concerns for 14 days; they also wrote down any recalled dreams, and scored the dreams for incorporation of any waking experiences. While 65 per cent of a total of 299 sleep mentation reports were judged to reflect aspects of recent waking life experiences, the episodic replay of waking events was found in no more than one to two per cent of the dream reports.[62]

In another paper, Erin Wamsley and Robert Stickgold put this observation eloquently: "Despite the strong influence of waking experience on subsequent sleep mentation, dreams rarely consist of an exact 'replay' of a life event. Instead, sleep mentation incorporates isolated elements of a waking episode, intermingled with fragments of other recent memories, as well as remote and semantic memory material, thus creating novel and sometimes bizarre scenarios which do not faithfully represent any particular waking event."[63] This fits exquisitely with the expectation fulfilment theory of dreaming – the mind pulls in whatever metaphorical images may suit the purpose, sometimes using seemingly overly strong ones, sometimes trivial ones, and even on occasion puns or plays on words to express an unexpressed emotional arousal.

To sum up, the new expectation fulfilment theory of REM sleep is applicable not only to humans, young and old, but to other species as well. It explains the predominance of REM sleep in the fetus and newborn. It can account for the effects of REM sleep deprivation and predict how those effects can be enhanced. It predicts metaphorical thinking to be a major feature of human thinking – which the evidence clearly confirms – and accounts for why we dream in metaphor and forget our dreams. It also makes specific predictions about the content and form of dreams, and is testable at a psychological level. It has not been disconfirmed by any current findings from sleep research. For the first time, we have a theory which is both consistent with the major biological facts of dreaming yet which gives us an explanation for the occurrence of symbolism in dreams. In the next chapter, by looking at more of the dreams that Joe has collected over the years, we will show that the theory holds good even when the content of dreams is complex – and we later explain how, unlike the baffling constructs of Freudian and Jungian dream analysis, remembered dreams can often be put to straightforward, practical use in therapy.

5

THE PSYCHOLOGY OF DREAMING

"All night long and every night,
When my mama puts out the light,
I see the people marching by,
As plain as day, before my eye."

ROBERT LOUIS STEVENSON

As we have seen, Joe's psychological findings, based on the psychological and biological evidence, suggest that dreams arise from emotionally arousing expectations that are not acted out when the dreamer is awake. The introspections that give rise to unfulfilled expectations are what we refer to as 'uncompleted patterns of arousal'. His expectation fulfilment theory states that these uncompleted patterns of instinct arousal are translated into sensory analogues and metaphorically acted out in dreams. We can see this happening in its simplest form in the following account of a boy's first 'wet dream' which he had when he was about 13 years old:

Dream 7

I am happily cycling along a country lane on my own with no one around when I come to a 'T' junction. A beautiful girl cyclist is by the roadside and she has had a puncture. Her front wheel is off. I stop and she asks me if I would pump up her inner tube. I am shy but oblige her very intensely. I find myself pumping up the tube faster and faster. I can't stop myself. I had a strange, growing feeling of panic and woke up with a hot, wet patch in my pyjamas.

The day before, the boy, who went to a boys-only school and was not used to the company of girls, had cycled for some distance behind a girl on her way to her school. He felt attracted to her, which was a novel experience because, up until that point, he had had no interest in the opposite sex. He found himself longing to talk to her, but she went her way and he went his without a word being spoken. This is a clear example of how an uncompleted pattern of instinctive arousal is metaphorically acted out in a dream.

It took many years of research, as we have said, before Joe was able to work out the precise rules by which the images in our awake minds are converted into dream images. While carrying out the key experiment reported in Chapter 3, he collected hundreds of dreams, both his own and those of relatives, friends and volunteers. After a time, he became so proficient at this that he would wake up spontaneously four or five times a night to recall dreams. To ensure a representative sample, he systematically collected dreams for a period of a week or longer. He then compared the dreams to a detailed examination of his experiences during the corresponding waking hours prior to sleeping. By looking at other people's dreams and waking experiences in the same way, he ensured the general applicability of the evidence for his hypothesis.

One thing he found was that a dream rarely reveals its corresponding waking experience on first examination. There are two reasons for this. Firstly, it is almost impossible for our logical mind to separate itself from the rich, sensory immediacy of the interweaving dream content *and* consider at the same time every element and person in the dream as a replacement for something else. It is, therefore, necessary for the logical mind to examine the dream structurally and to ask questions about who or what each character or event in it could be representing. In other words, what, from the previous day's experiences, prompted a particular emotional behaviour sequence, or dream story line?

If, after doing this, the connection between dream imagery and a corresponding waking experience didn't suggest itself, and more often than not it didn't, Joe found it best to leave the problem alone for a while so that his metaphorical thinking processes could start to work on it. (You can do this yourself with your own remembered dreams. By consciously thinking about the dream, and what it might mean, sooner or later the experience from the previous day that caused it should pop into your head and, on examination, it will be clear that the dream is in fact a metaphorical translation of it. It also becomes clear that the dream is not simply a sensory analogue of an event that occurred, but concerns our emotionally arousing thoughts, i.e. our expectations, about what *might* happen.)

Another reason that it is so difficult at first to connect a dream to its appropriate waking scenario is, of course, that the dream has turned off our emotional awareness of that experience – it has done the job it was designed to do. The dream, by deactivating the emotional charge from what caused the dream, has sent the waking memory of the cause to the back of the queue, as it were, and that's why we have to make an especial effort to bring the relevant scenario back into waking consciousness.

We will analyse some straightforward dreams, to help clarify the process and show just how varied the metaphorical representations can be, and how they often even include puns. Some of the dreams are Joe's and some are dreams that have been sent to us by people who read the first edition of this book and have applied the theory to their own dreams. The following dream is one of Joe's.

Dream 8

I am travelling in a car with my brother. I said that I had made an offer to buy a house in the area and that I had the key in my pocket. My brother was noncommittal about the house as we walked through it. To my surprise, there was a huge room at the back of the house. The end wall was completely made of glass and a swimming pool was set in the floor. My opinion of the house's value immediately increased. We went out into

> the garden and looked at the back. The rear view of the house looked enormous compared to the front. In the dream I never actually saw my brother; I was just aware of his presence.

The previous day Joe had told his brother about a house he had made an offer on. His brother had expressed reservations about the proposed purchase because he thought the price was rather high. Joe argued that the area where the house was located was becoming increasingly popular and that a house there could be expected to increase in value in the near future. Although Joe impressed himself with the argument, his brother remained unimpressed. But Joe was convinced that the property might be worth even more than he was offering.

His brother can appear as himself in the dream because Joe was aware only of his presence and did not actually see or hear him. The dream makes analogically manifest what Joe anticipated would happen with regard to the house. It does this by showing the property, which he had made an offer on, transformed to represent the way he had anticipated it would be affected by the changing market. The house increased in size by means of an extra large room, analogous to the anticipated increase in value of the house. The swimming pool is a metaphorical way of showing that it had gone 'up market'. The rear view of the house was much bigger than the front – with hindsight one could see how much the property, and hence the property value, had increased. The effect of seeing the extra large room at the rear of the house was to make Joe increase his valuation of it, just as, in the waking situation, the effect of his expectation of what the market forces would do to the house's value made him reflect that the house was probably worth more than he had offered.

We can clearly see, therefore, that this dream, in an analogous form, simulates feelings which Joe had anticipated whilst he was awake but which could not be discharged because the anticipated events lay in the future.

Dream 9

> I was at a school reunion with old friends. A man I didn't remember from school was talking to me and being over-familiar, touching me inappropriately. I turned on him and yelled at him to leave me alone.

This is the dreamer's explanation: "Earlier that day, the door bell had rung and, when I opened the door, a man whom I didn't recognise was standing there. However, he greeted me like an old friend and I was momentarily confused, searching my brain as to who he could be, while at the same time responding in a friendly manner. Then, to my extreme annoyance, he proceeded to try and sell me double-glazing. My instinct was to be rude to him but instead I just said I wasn't interested and bid him goodbye. Inside I was fuming! I felt somehow tricked into being friendly with him when I didn't even know him.

"After my dream, I could see exactly where the scenario of a strange man behaving inappropriately came from, and that I was acting out what I would like to have done in reality, but I didn't know why I'd dreamt about a school reunion. Then I remembered that the previous evening my husband had told me he was going to a reunion lunch the next day, with people he had used to work with."

Dream 10

> Many years ago I kept having re-current dreams about the Norman Invasion – I was being attacked, running away from the arrows, etc. I couldn't understand why it kept recurring, as it didn't link with anything I was studying or interested in. Then the penny dropped and the dream stopped. I was receiving persistent invites for a date, which I did not want to accept, from a man called Norman!

This dream, which was sent to us, is a nice example of the inventiveness of the brain in generating relevant images.

Dream 11

Scene I

I am walking with someone whom I'm aware must be my wife. We are walking off the main road, through lovely countryside. Suddenly the ground gets marshy. I warn my wife that we must be careful picking our steps and try to get back to the main road without losing our footing.

Scene II

I go to an experimental theatre. I am aware that I am accompanied by my wife. We arrive early for the play. On the way out we find that members of the staff have pulled back the floors by means of mechanical levers. We have to try to cross the open space by balancing ourselves on the metal bars which supported the floor. I tell one of the young actors to put the floor back and that he should have some manners, as I assumed he had some talent.

This is another dream about Joe's worries about buying a house. The first dream scene represents Joe's initial worrying anticipation of the consequences of buying a house in a particular suburb. Whilst the idea was attractive – like walking through the countryside – it was still a long way from the really popular areas – 'off the main road'. If they didn't 'pick our steps carefully', they might buy in an area where it could later prove difficult to sell and find themselves on very dodgy ground – 'marshy ground'. This would make it difficult to move back to a popular area if it proved necessary – 'try to get back on the main road'.

The second scene deals with other concerns that he had had about looking for a house. He thought they could 'experiment' with looking for a house, although they were starting 'early' – because they couldn't yet afford one. The floor being pulled back analogically represents the floor being taken from under them, which was how he had felt when he actually looked at the price of prospective houses. Joe and his wife would have to do a very fine financial balancing act (represented by the physical balancing act in the dream), if they were to proceed further now that the floor had been taken from under them (metaphorically speaking), by the huge cost of houses. On further reflection, Joe thought to himself that the estate agents were bound to have a few houses in his price range. There was therefore no need to feel embarrassed about talking to the young man from the agents. In fact, he could afford to be quite assertive. This was expressed metaphorically in the dream, when he told the young actor (estate agents do tend to put on a bit of an act!) to put the floor back, as he assumed he had some talent – that is, a range of houses in Joe's price range.

You can see that this dream metaphorically makes manifest what Joe had expected to happen when he and his wife went looking for houses. In the dream his wife could appear as herself because her presence was intuited rather than directly perceived. This was possible because she was not playing a direct role in the dream and, consequently, there was no need for her to be perceived. (Similarly, we can be ourselves in our dreams, because we are not directly observing ourselves – just intuiting.)

Dream 12

> I dreamt that I was walking through a shopping arcade when a large, thickset man in rugby kit loomed into view from the street and was framed in the bright light at the end of the arcade. He dropped his shorts and defecated on the tiled step that led up from the arcade onto the street. Immediately two Keystone Cops came from the same direction and, taking him by his arms, dragged him off, with his shorts around his ankles.

Here is the dreamer's explanation: "The day before, I had drawn up behind stationary traffic at a busy junction in town. I noticed the car in front had a pretentious registration plate and I wondered what kind of person would sport it. I could see the driver's silhouette against the brightness of his windscreen. He had a large neck, which made it look as if the sides of his head descended straight to his shoulders. I thought of him as a 'bullet head' and that his profile was consistent with the registration plate. At that moment, a half-eaten pasty or pie came arcing from his car window and landed with a splat on the road. Then his arm emerged from his car window and bowled a scrunched-up greasy paper bag over the roof of his car. I sat there in the queue, fuming about his behaviour and his blighting the environment for everyone. I wished I could have remonstrated with him but couldn't leave the car. The traffic started moving and he went a different way and I didn't have to think about him any more.

"But clearly I had become highly emotionally aroused and thus the dream I had that night. The man now 'sports' a rugby kit and his physique (thick neck) is that of a rugby player. He blights the environment in the crudest way. The cops represent my own desire to bring him to justice and take him down a peg and perhaps my thoughts about him being a bullet-head also influence the imagery of cops getting involved. I recognised the arcade where the incident takes place. It is gloomy inside but, looking towards the end, one can see a bright rectangle of light. This appears to represent my recall of looking through his car to the bright windscreen."

Dream 13

I'm on a car ferry travelling from Ireland to England. I'm aware that I am a member of a group of undesirable aliens whom the secret service or army would like to arrest and persecute. I huddle into a position in a corner beside my sister. Suddenly, I notice two official-looking gentlemen, one in some sort of army uniform jumper

> and the other in plain clothes, standing near us, although they don't appear to see us. I'm about to leave when a member of my group signals to me to stay where I am. The signal, however, is ambiguous and I still move off. My sister stays behind as I head in the direction of where some of our group are positioned at the head of the boat. I am jumped on by the two officials referred to earlier who grab me about the shoulders and say they have already arrested the people I was heading towards.

The dream relates to experiences encountered the previous day when Joe and his family went to Windsor Safari Park. He was afraid that the chimpanzees would attack and damage his car by leaping onto the bonnet (they would then be more than shoulder high). All the cars were in convoy driving through the compound. Joe had recently travelled to Ireland and his car, like all the other cars, had been driven on to the car ferry in convoy fashion and garaged in a compound. This was the source of the boat analogy used in the dream. From the point of view of the chimpanzees, he felt that his family were intruders – 'undesirable aliens'. The car in front stopped. It wasn't clear to Joe whether they should try and bypass it or stay behind (hence the ambiguous signals in the dream). He suddenly noticed chimpanzees on his left. One of them had a thick mane around his neck (which corresponds to the army jumper worn by one of the officials in the dream). Note also the pun with 'jumper' as he was afraid the animal would jump on the bonnet. Joe urged his wife (his sister in the dream), who was driving, to move forward but she seemed unaware of the danger.

In the dream Joe did actually walk forward, which is analogous to his waking anticipation of driving forward that he hadn't been able to complete because he wasn't the driver. One chimpanzee did jump on the car a couple of places ahead of them and when Joe's car eventually began to move, two chimpanzees near it suddenly became aware of their presence and appeared, to Joe, about to attack his side of the car. In the dream, the anticipated attack does actually take place – when the two officials grab him about the shoulders. The attack on the car ahead corresponds to the sequence in the dream where the officials say they have got his friends stationed ahead.

Dream 14

I'm sharing a house with three brothers who are members of the famous pop group, the Bee Gees. One of the three brothers looks much younger than the other two. I like them but I feel a little uneasy, something of an outsider. I'm looking out from the window of the house at two of them playing a game of hurling. I pick up a hurley but I quickly drop it in case they see me, as I don't feel myself good enough to play hurling with them.

This dream shows how a television programme can provide the obvious content of a dream whilst a second television programme, more closely identified with by the dreamer, can provide the hidden content. In this case, the obvious content was inspired by a television programme Joe had seen about the Bee Gees pop group, who were returning to England to buy a house to live in. The hidden content was inspired by another television programme in which there was a scene with which Joe strongly empathised. The programme was an episode in a drama series which glamorously portrayed the world of diamond merchants and dealers. In the series, a family of two brothers and a nephew controlled the family business and, in the episode he had seen, a share in the family business had been offered to a key employee. Joe found himself imagining that, if he were the employee, he would be flattered by the offer but he would always feel a bit of an outsider and perhaps a little embarrassed to push his own point of view.

The Bee Gees pop group metaphorically represents the three men involved in the glamorous and lucrative business of diamond trading. The house that he shares with them represents the family business. The game of hurling is an analogy for running a family diamond business. (Hurling is a national sport in Ireland, where Joe grew up.

He was never good at it and did not enjoy playing it competitively.) In the dream, the game of hurling that he doesn't participate in expresses the feelings he had anticipated he would have if he were the man in the television programme being offered a share in his employer's family business. It expresses the feeling that he would not be able to participate fully in the 'game' of running the family business, because he was an outsider.

There is also the connection between the fact that only two brothers were playing the game of hurling and the fact that, in the television programme, one brother was a silent partner in the business. The young brother in the dream corresponds to the nephew in the television programme. This dream, therefore, illustrates how feelings, which are anticipated or introspected upon simply through empathising with a character in a television programme, are expressed in metaphorical form in our dreams.

Dream 15

> I dreamt that I was watching a TV screen, which occupied my entire field of vision. On screen was an opinionated sports commentator with hair so over-groomed it looked like plastic. He was wearing an ugly, multicoloured sports jacket, although the colours of the jacket were muted, not garish like the ones a certain celebrity sports commentator wears. The sports commentator in my dream began to vent his opinions. I couldn't understand a word he said: it was gibberish but had the tone and rhythm of someone clearly in love with the sound of his own voice. As he droned on, the muted colours of his jacket suddenly occupied the entire studio set.

The previous evening the dreamer had been worrying about his behaviour at work. Having been anxious and reticent when he was first promoted to a managerial position a year or so before, he'd noticed that he had now become quite the opposite. He had also observed, in some other colleagues, that confidence and decisiveness can, unchecked, turn into arrogance and egotism and cause any number of problems in the workplace. On the evening of his dream he was worrying that this was happening to him, too. "I was starting to feel that I could say and do anything I wanted at work and never have to answer for it. What I needed to do, I thought, was book a session with my fitness trainer. He had a way of so putting me in my place that for days or even weeks afterward, I'd feel far less cocksure and more like my old self.

"In the dream, the sports commentator, modelled on one that I consider pretentious, represents the arrogant me, losing my real identity (hair like plastic). He needs muting, just as I felt I did, and this is expressed through the colours of his jacket. I assume my brain chose someone connected with sport as I planned to contact my fitness trainer to help me."

Dream 16

> There was a Christmas present all beautifully wrapped up on the top of my wardrobe, waiting for Christmas. There was also a beautiful doll. Daddy got the doll down for me and I nursed it in my arms.

The above dream was told to Joe by his eldest daughter, Mona-May, when she was six years old. When he asked her if the doll in the dream was a new one, she said she'd never held it before but Mummy had let her see it many times. And as she remembered the dream she held her arms as if gently holding the doll or a baby and had a beatific smile on her face. She said she could remember exactly how the doll felt to her as she held it in her arms.

The previous day her mother had taken her shopping. They had gone to look at prams for the baby her mother was expecting in seven weeks' time. The children's toy department was on the same floor. Mona-May asked if she could have a toy. Her mother had said no because it was not Christmas yet.

The dream is clearly a metaphorical manifestation of the anticipated events, triggered by this experience: the anticipation of receiving her Christmas present, which she knew to be stored on top of her parents' wardrobe ready for Christmas (*her* wardrobe in the dream) and her other anticipation triggered by shopping for the baby. Her mother had been telling her often that she was having the new baby for Mona-May, and encouraged her to feel the baby move when it kicked. In the dream, she analogically represented her mother's involvement of her with the baby by having her father (Joe) get the doll down from the top of the wardrobe for her. Her awareness in the dream that her mother had let her see the doll many times represented her mother's letting her "feel the baby many times before". The fact that her mother is not mentioned means that she was not perceived directly in the dream; Mona-May was simply aware that it was her mother who had previously allowed her to see the doll (feel the baby). The baby was due before Christmas and can also be anticipated in its actuality (the doll in the dream) unlike presents, which must be wrapped up and remain an unknown quantity until Christmas day.

The next dream was collected from a patient.

Dream 17

> I was writing a letter to my husband on striped paper. I realised that it is all wrong to send it on striped paper. It should be more romantic; it should be on flowery paper.

The dreamer of the above went on to explain that the pattern of the striped paper corresponded exactly to the lining of her baby buggy. It had been on her mind that her husband had complained a couple of nights previously that she now always wore her unattractive winceyette pyjamas to bed. She wore these pyjamas because they made it easier for her to breast-feed her baby.

Her introspections concerning her husband's complaints led her to realise that, by wearing those pyjamas, she was sending the message to him that she was more interested in the baby than in romantic experiences. This is analogously expressed in the dream by writing a letter to her husband on striped paper that matches the baby's buggy lining. She realises in the dream that this is "all wrong" and that she should be writing on "romantic flowery paper".

The dreamer also revealed that the letter she was writing was in the form of a collage rather than writing *per se*. At the start of the letter she used a picture of an eye to stand for 'I'. This is a metaphorical way of showing that the message she is giving out to her husband is a nonverbal one – to the 'eye'. This dream, then, is clearly a metaphorical representation of the dreamer's emotionally arousing worries, or expectations, of how she should respond to her husband's criticism.

Dream 18

> I woke up from a nightmare. In the dream I was relaxing, watching television, when I suddenly felt guilty and panicky about where my four-year-old daughter was. I rushed to our downstairs toilet to see my daughter totally submerged in it, very clearly dead. I then became aware that there was also a small boy kneeling next to it, staring in at her. Although I knew it was my daughter, the little girl I saw drowned in the exaggeratedly large toilet bowl didn't look at all like her. I stared at her face, and the full magnitude of the finality and horror of her death, and my responsibility for it, hit me with a vengeance. That was when I woke.

The dreamer explains: "I was extremely relieved to wake up and realise that it was only a dream, as the emotion and distress had been so intense. Then, knowing about the expectation fulfilment theory of dreaming, I thought about the dream for a few moments and realised that it related to three quite brief emotionally arousing thoughts that I had had the previous day.

"The first was in the evening when I thought I should go and check that my daughter was all right, as I normally do, but didn't because I was feeling very tired (her bedroom is at the top of our three-storey house and I was at the bottom in our living room). The significance of the toilet in the dream at first eluded me but then I recalled that the previous day, when my daughter had had a little friend over for lunch, the friend had gone to our downstairs toilet to wash her hands and I had been torn between checking on her and serving up the lunch, which all the cooker alarms were signalling was ready, as we were in a hurry to go out. I didn't go and, of course, she was fine, but the emotional arousal must have stayed in my system.

"I couldn't make any sense of why there had been a small boy kneeling by the toilet until I remembered that, the previous evening, I had been watching a drama on television in which a young boy had led the police to an injured man, who later died. As I watched, I had felt frustrated that the police hadn't realised the significance of the boy leading them to the victim (it turned out the boy's own father was the killer). So the dream had discharged those three separate, brief emotional arousals. Also significant to the imagery of the dream, I later realised, was the fact that I had recently finished reading a book about the true case of the brides who were murdered in the bath – at least one of whom had been found totally submerged, just as I 'saw' my daughter. If I hadn't known about the expectation fulfilment theory of dreaming, which enabled me to relate the dream back to minor concerns of the previous day, that nightmare would have unsettled me for quite a long time."

Dream 19

I am in my flat with a friend. She comments that the fish in the fish tank look as if they are dying. The water in the fish tank looks horrible. One of my fish is still alive and jumps out, flaps itself along the floor and out of my living room. Outside the living room is not the corridor that should be there but the outside of the house. It didn't seem odd at the time, in the dream. The fish continued to flap across the ground away from the house and I was sad that it would die. As I followed, trying to catch the fish to get it back in the fish tank, a fat cat

> suddenly pounced on the fish and ripped its head off. When I got to the dead fish, it had turned orange and was hollow inside. This upset me. I wanted to cry.

This dream was told by a friend to someone who used the expectation fulfilment theory of dreaming to make sense of it for her. The friend had found out at short notice that over half the staff in her team were going to be made redundant. This had upset her as she got on with those that were leaving and had concerns over whether the company was viable enough to keep going (fish dying, fish flapping out of the building, dirty fish tank). She felt that it was the employer's fault that the staff were being made redundant (fat cat killing the fish) and there would be too few staff left (fish's head bitten off). She also felt that work was going to seem empty and, as she didn't really get on well with the staff member left working with her (who happened to have ginger hair), she had wished he was one of the staff going instead (hollow fish, dead fish turning orange).

Dream 20

> I was going down some stones steps into a stylish, trendy, cellar restaurant. It was dimly lit. Around the sides of the room I saw aquarium tanks. In one tank a large, iridescent blue fish swam. I walked closer and then saw that the tank had no glass, yet somehow the water was holding itself up. I felt panicky for the fish's safety. I thought that either the water might just fall out or the fish, not knowing the glass wasn't there, might swim out into the air and perish.

The dreamer said, "On reflecting back on the dream, I was puzzled at first as to why I should be so worried about the fish. Over the years I have had similar dreams about fish being 'out of water'. And then it struck me. The fish was me! When I thought back to the previous day I had been considering the new future career I had been training for and was feeling daunted. I had spent the previous fifteen years as a happy 'stay-at-home' mum and was worried about how I would adapt to a new unfamiliar environment and role. I felt exposed and unprotected. Once I had this realisation I did not dream about 'fish out of water' ever again."

Dream 21

> I'm taking a tube journey. My two eldest sons get out at the Park stop. I go on to Mansion House stop. I feel awful. I must get back to the Park stop.

The previous day the dreamer had visited a new playschool to assess whether to register her baby's name for a place there in the future. The new playschool was rather regimented and alien to her artistic temperament (she's an artist by profession). Later that day, a friend praised the school's discipline methods saying the children were not allowed to use polish until they had first mastered how to fold a duster properly. This really made her even more convinced that the school was unsuitable for her son and caused her to reflect that she must go and register him at the playschool near the park, which her second son currently attended, and which her eldest son had also attended before starting proper school, which was also beside the park.

The dream metaphorically simulates her actions and introspections concerning these events. In the dream she is taking a tube journey whereas in real life she walked. Mansion House was the name of a famous brand of polish and so, analogically, represents the new playschool with its particular attitude towards the use of polish. Mansion House also sounds very like Manor House, an area of London which has a tube station of that name and which happened to be the place where her uncle had died. Again, this neatly expresses her attitude towards the new playschool, which she sees as likely to kill the child's creative impulses.

Her negative feelings towards the new playschool and her desire to go back to register her son in the park playschool, which her other sons attended, is analogically represented in the dream by her unpleasant feelings at discovering she is on her way to Mansion House, and that she must get back to the Park stop where her sons have already alighted.

The subject matter of our dreams is as complex and varied as our introspective lives. If we fantasise about being wealthy, we will dream about being rich. If we fantasise about having sex with someone we are attracted to, we will have sexual dreams. If we fantasise about things that might go wrong in our lives – worries and imagined catastrophes – we will have dreams full of anxiety and dread. But the dream content will always be metaphorically translated, so the person you are attracted to in your dreams will be a stand-in for the person you are attracted to in real life (a piece of knowledge which itself might prevent much anxiety!).

We will now look at a number of structurally more complex dreams that Joe collected and show how the metaphorical sensory translation process always operates by the same rules, however complex the waking introspections might be.

Dream 22

> My sister's husband died. My sister was concerned that the paperwork relating to two properties which he had wanted to leave her had not been properly completed. She wanted me to correct the paperwork but I refused, saying that it would be wrong and would be immediately spotted.

In the dream Joe was actually aware of his sister's frustration at the possibility of being disinherited, yet he felt that there was nothing he could do about it. Joe is quite close to his sister and has always admired her ability to write well. The previous day he had been thinking about two scientific theories he was working on and reflecting that, given the state of his notes, no one would be able to understand the theories if he were to die. Joe further reflected that, if he were to rush things and write up the theories now, he would probably get them wrong. There is in the dream, therefore, Joe's 'me' that is imagined to be dead – we'll call this *self one*. There is the 'me' that is imagining that self dead and who is feeling frustration at the thought of the work being incomplete, and who then experiences a desire to complete the work quickly in order to get rid of the feeling of frustration – let's call this 'me' *self two*. Finally there is the 'me' who, reflecting on this desire of self two, experiences a desire *not* to carry out this behaviour because it would result in the work being wrongly completed and would be shown to be incorrect by fellow researchers – *self three*.

The dream acts out this imagined situation with each of the three levels of self reflection appropriately personified. There is self one who is imagined to be dead, personified by Joe's brother-in-law who had recently suffered from a serious heart condition. There is self two, personified by his sister who, being the wife of his brother-in-law, is the closest person to him. His sister is also appropriate for this self as she takes a keen interest in his research. She and Joe have a great rapport and it is easy for him to identify with her feelings. This leaves the way clear for the emotions experienced by self three to be directly experienced by Joe in his dream.

By appropriate metaphors, this dream beautifully represented the contradictory emotions and levels of self-reflection that had resulted from Joe's anticipation of his own death.

Dream 23

I am watching a couple, my friends Sam and Janice, committing suicide. Those around them seem powerless to help. They are breathing in carbon monoxide, sitting in their chairs. They seem wrapped up in their own experience. I know I have to, and want to, say something meaningful to them. I think about saying that, if there is a next life, I will see you there, but I am not happy with the phrase. I put my arms around Sam, I say to him, "I love you", then I put my arms around Janice and say, "I love you". Janice reacts and says, "Why am I doing this then?" I carry her quickly away from the poisonous gas.

> I notice Sam has become more alert and I shout to someone to get him too. They are both rescued just in time.

In this dream, Sam and Janice stand for two people Joe was seeing for psychotherapy whom we will call, for reasons of confidentiality, Seamus and Jean. Joe had been thinking a lot about them the previous day. Their attempted suicide metaphorically represents the way their emotional problems were killing their happiness (and one of them had actually attempted suicide before). Two days previously, Joe had attended an advanced workshop on psychotherapy in which the trainer talked about the importance of not just being a master of techniques, but of doing therapy "with a heart". The night before Joe had been reviewing both Seamus's and Jean's case notes and was aware of feeling that his next session with the couple would be critical for both of them, and of hoping he could usefully apply the new therapeutic approach he had learned.

Putting his arms around them in the dream and saying,"I love you" is, of course, an analogical way of expressing Joe's anticipation of doing therapy with them – the therapy "with a heart" that the trainer in the workshop had talked about. Joe's initial thought of saying, "If there is a next life, I will see you there" is rejected by him in the dream as this approach appears to be not only heartless but ineffective. Therapy "with a heart" analogically represented by the phrase "I love you" does prove effective in both cases. The words "I love you" actually came from a wedding anniversary card that Joe had bought his wife a couple of days previously. It showed a street of shops and clubs with signs everywhere saying "I love you". This phrase appears in the dream by virtue of its appropriateness and recent prominence.

Both Seamus and Sam, who is metaphorically standing in for him, are of Irish extraction, work with their hands and are of a similar age. Janice represents Jean in the dream. Both women are of English middle class background and have the same qualities of femininity about them. Janice responds first to Joe's intervention in the dream, just as in real life Jean has shown more rapid progress. Sam and

Janice both respond to Joe's interventions and their lives are saved, analogous to real life where he anticipated his therapeutic intervention would improve the quality of Seamus's and Jean's lives.

In the dream Joe called to someone (whom he didn't see) to rescue Sam. Joe had anticipated that, in the psychotherapeutic intervention he had planned to do, Seamus might want to deal with an incident that had occurred when he was young, which involved someone's death and about which he felt guilty. As part of the therapy Joe planned to have him imagine the dead person giving his views about what had happened in a way that would absolve Seamus of his guilt – rescue him. The reason why Joe didn't see the person that he called to help him in the dream is because he is long since dead and the client is going to imagine his presence. This dream, therefore, represents a metaphorical enactment of Joe's anticipated experiences from the previous day concerning the couple's future therapy.

Dream 24

> We are going to a party. My family is there. I am walking along the road with my cousin and all our aunts and uncles. We call into a shop for sweets. My cousin gets served but the girl behind the counter doesn't seem to understand my instructions. She keeps getting the wrong bar of chocolate and seems very rude. We go into another shop and I get an old-fashioned bag of Maltesers and we eat these small balls of honeycomb covered in milk chocolate. We then see other aunts and my mother walking up the road. All of them look as though they have been put through a chocolate machine; they all appear as different types of chocolate. I notice that my mother appears as my favourite chocolate. She is some distance behind my aunts. I am annoyed that they are not waiting for her. My family are talking about a skirt that had been given to them by granny. It is decided to give it to me. I try it on and it fits me perfectly.

This dream was told to Joe by a nurse and is based on the following waking experiences:

1. A member of the dreamer's family had invited her to a party the previous day. The anticipated party provides the setting for the dream.
2. A senior nurse, on her ward round the previous day she had been accompanied by an inexperienced junior nurse who seemed unable to carry out correctly the instructions she gave her and had been rather insolent. This is represented in the dream by her difficulty in getting served by the rude shop assistant.
3. The old-fashioned bag of chocolates relates to her weakness for chocolate (she had actually bought some on the way home from work the previous evening). The 'old fashioned' relates to her view that this weakness is handed down through the generations in her family.
4. The image of her aunts and mother as bars of chocolate relates to a conversation she had had a couple of days earlier with her boyfriend, concerning her diet and weight. He had said that, unless she was careful, she would continue to put on weight, as all her family were overweight – hence her perception of her aunts and mother as bars of chocolate. These ideas were restimulated (i.e. introspected about) by her guilty feelings at buying chocolate on her way home.
5. Another dream theme is the annoyance she feels when she sees her mother falling behind her aunts and her aunts not waiting for her. This reflects her concern for her mother, who had recently had heart trouble. She felt annoyed when she learned that her aunts were rushing to their doctors to have their hearts checked without waiting to see how her mother got on. Thinking about weight had led her to recall her annoyance at her aunts' recent behaviour.
6. The final theme is that of the skirt given by her grandmother which fits her perfectly. Her aunts and her mother inherit their figure from her grandmother. The 'perfectly fitting' skirt is an

analogy for inheriting the family 'figure', caused by liking sweet things, which she thinks she has inherited.

What is really interesting about this dream is that, at first sight, it seems to be an exception to the rule. All our examples of dreams so far have illustrated the rule that everything perceived in a dream is a metaphorical representation of something else connected with a waking event. (This rule is not, of course, contradicted by those dreams where the dreamer is aware of a person's presence without actually perceiving them in a dream.) The difference with this dream is that the dreamer's mother and her aunts actually appear as themselves, but the dreamer's introspection of them as being overweight as a result of their liking for sweet things has – bizarrely – metaphorically transformed their bodies into different types of chocolate bars.

This makes it clear that what is going on in the dream is not a symbolic replacement in order to disguise identity, à la Freud, but rather a metaphorical manifestation of the introspected waking perception. Usually this involves replacing a real person with someone else who stands in a metaphorically similar relationship to the dreamer, but in this case it was the bodies of the people that were introspected about when awake that were used to express the analogy, whilst leaving the aunt's and mother's perceived identities intact. This gives us more evidence that dreams express themselves in analogies rather than symbolic disguise.

The next two short dreams again show how a person's body can be used to express an analogical relationship with a waking perception whilst letting the person's identity remain the same.

Dream 25

I am pushing a bundle of old branches down to the cellar. The head of the upstairs tenant keeps appearing and disappearing at the centre of the heap of old wood.

The person who told Joe this dream had been lying in bed the previous evening listening to the noises being made by the upstairs tenant. He tried to dismiss this person from his mind with the thought of what a useless load of rubbish he was. This is expressed analogically in the dream when he pushes the tenant, in the shape of a bundle of old wood, down to the cellar (which is where they put 'old rubbish' in their household). Here, again, the tenant's identity stays the same, but his body represents, in metaphorical form, the emotionally arousing introspection concerning the dreamer's view of the tenant – a useless load of rubbish. The dreamer's attempt to dismiss the tenant from his mind is represented by his pushing him down into the cellar.

Here is another example of this process from one of Joe's own collection of dreams.

Dream 26

> I saw a relative lying on a bed. His body was emaciated beyond recognition; only his face was familiar. I told myself that there was no need to worry because he could now start to eat properly again and regain his weight loss.

The previous evening a relative had telephoned Joe and told him that he was going on a starvation diet for forty days. From his knowledge of this person's personality, Joe knew that any attempt to dissuade him would only make him more determined in his action. Joe had then thought to himself that his relative should be able to survive a month without food after which he could then build his strength back up again. The metaphor identified during REM sleep does not require a new identity for the dieting man. Instead his present body is changed into a form that is metaphorically representative of the anticipated image of him being reduced to skin and bones – like a famine victim. This dream expresses, in the simplest and most obvious way possible, the essence of the introspection that caused it.

All human thinking is suffused with metaphor and entails varying degrees of abstraction, and the dream story, which has to be expressed as sensory perceptions, expresses each aspect of the introspection as a metaphor or symbol. Thus the person seen as a load of rubbish becomes, in the dream, a load of old sticks; the aunts, whose excess weight is seen as being caused by eating too many sweet things are turned into different bars of chocolate, and the man contemplating going on an extreme diet becomes the sort of image one sees on television documentaries about people starving in the third world.

A woman recently told us of another dream that illustrates this. It featured a person she had only known a short while. This person was himself in the dream but appeared much younger, the way he had looked long before she first met him. In the dream he had long hair and was wearing clothes that were in fashion 30 years ago. She had recently seen him looking that way in a photograph. The REM process had replaced the man she actually knew with a man she had only seen but never met, albeit the same man.

In most instances in dreams, however, what is anticipated or introspected is not a change in a person's identity, or how we imagine them physically; rather, the person is part of an anticipated pattern of stimulation and the REM search for a suitable metaphor results in the replacement of *all* the people and objects in the anticipated or imagined expected scene with an analogous cast of characters, objects and behaviours.

Dream 27

> Mummy, I was upset last night, I had a bad dream. I dreamt I was in the car and it burst into flames.

This dream is included because the analogy with the waking experience is so immediately obvious. The dream was told by a 12-year-old girl with Down's syndrome to her mother, who is a friend of Joe's. The previous day her daughter had gone on an outing with other children on a hired bus. At some point on the journey they had to abandon the bus when smoke started coming out of the engine. The dream is clearly a metaphorical recreation of the original experience which the young girl must have replayed in her imagination. The bus is replaced by her parents' car. The smoke is replaced by flames. The dream might perhaps have been caused by worry that the relief bus, which took them home, might also be found to have smoke coming from the engine.

The next dream of Joe's is interesting because it shows how even a complex psychological theory can be translated into a metaphor by the REM state.

Dream 28

I'm walking down the street. I see a man throwing stones. I tell him off. He then directs his attack at me. I run and start yelling for a policeman. The man runs after me. Now there is a policeman on the scene. The man who threw stones starts to talk loudly to the policeman, using emotive language and blaming me. I reflect I had better speak up quickly or this guy will convince the policeman he was right. I start to shout loudly as well. I'm aware that the policeman can't listen to both of us at the same time, but at least I'm preventing the other guy from winning over the policeman to his viewpoint. The policeman says he will arrest both of us if we don't sort it out between us. I talk to the other guy and explain what the policeman said because it was evident that he hadn't understood the words. He is then prepared to be friendly.

I go into the car park to get my bicycle, as I live some distance outside the town. I find that my bicycle isn't there and I must have left it at home. I can't remember how I got into town. I must have got a lift from someone else, without thinking how I was going to get home. I realise that, without my bicycle, I have no means of getting home. I walk out of the car park and, as I do so, I repeat to myself the sentence that I had used to explain to the other fellow what the policeman had meant. The fellow is walking behind me and he also repeats what I said. I feel embarrassed and ignore him.

The previous evening, before having this dream, Joe had been reading a book on the lateralisation of the brain by Thomas Blakeslee,[1] which describes studies showing that the left and right cerebral hemispheres process information differently.

He read of a patient who had undergone the 'split-brain' operation (which involves severing the corpus callosum, the dense bundle of connecting nerves that joins the two hemispheres together and through which the two sides of the brain communicate), in order to relieve severe epilepsy. This man had been observed to use his right hand to signal his wife to come and help him, even as his left hand pushed her aggressively away. The right hemisphere controls the left side of the body and the left hemisphere controls the right side. The man's experience was used to demonstrate that strong emotions are more associated with the right hemisphere.

Joe also read of another patient who had had his right hemisphere removed completely and who, as a consequence, was unable to find his way back from the bathroom. This and other examples given in the book confirmed that spatial intelligence and sense of direction are primarily right hemisphere activities. The right hemisphere also appeared to be more active in activities involving motor skills, such as getting dressed. After certain tests designed to stimulate the right hemisphere, subjects were observed going into a dreamy state where they spoke little, sometimes not even responding to their own names, but carried out the tests more efficiently. It seemed as though the subjects had gone into a trance state. Left hemisphere consciousness (our normal state), on the other hand, is much more concerned with speaking and comprehending language, a skill only meagrely possessed by the right hemisphere. The two hemispheres compete for dominance at any one time. As the left hemisphere has a slight genetic advantage for language development (except in a small percentage of left-handers), it becomes primarily the language brain whilst the right hemisphere becomes more able at processing spatial data. Usually, the hemisphere that is best qualified for any particular task currently in hand takes control. (At the time Blakeslee's book was published, to talk of 'right and left hemisphere consciousness' was, in the view of many scientists, to take speculation beyond that justified by the experimental evidence. More recent research, however, has confirmed that such major differences in the functioning of the right and left hemispheres are real.[2] But Joe's dream is not concerned with an objective view of the evidence; rather it concerns his subjective reactions to the views presented in Blakeslee's book.)

Finally, that evening, Joe read about stuttering. Experimental evidence was cited which showed that some stutterers don't have a well-defined left hemisphere dominance for language. In the book, Blakeslee quotes a study of four patients who had stuttered since childhood. Each of the four had a damaged speech area on one side of the brain. The damage was of recent origin and unrelated to the stuttering. A Wada test (a research procedure which helps determine which cerebral hemisphere is 'dominant' for speech and whether memory is functional on one or both sides of the brain) showed that the speech of these stutterers was controlled by *both* hemispheres; but after the damaged area was surgically removed, the patients ceased stuttering and regained normal speech. The patients' stuttering had evidently been caused by both hemispheres having developed a capacity to control speech. A postoperative Wada test showed that speech had become controlled by one hemisphere only. Joe reflected that the repeated false starts which a stutterer makes when he tries to speak could easily be caused by both speech areas trying to control speech at once.

The dream metaphorically acts out Joe's introspections concerning these aspects of brain lateralisation, as the following points make clear:

1. The man throwing stones as he walked down the street represents the aggressive potential of the right hemisphere, as demonstrated in the example of the 'split-brain' man, whose left hand tries to attack his wife, even as his right hand seeks her help. Joe, representing the left hemisphere, reprimanded the man (representing the right hemisphere), which is what he had imagined the previous evening would actually happen in such a situation.

2. In the next dream scene, Joe calls a policeman who represents control of the brain. When the policeman arrives the stone-throwing man talks loudly in emotive language to try to get the policeman to accept his version of events. The man's emotive language represents the right hemisphere's better ability to understand the emotive connotations of language. Joe (the left hemisphere consciousness) realises that he will have to compete with this guy if he is to prevent the policeman from accepting his viewpoint. This scene metaphorically represents the competition between the two hemispheres to win control. The policeman says that, if they can't sort it out between themselves, he will arrest both of them (arrested development).
3. Joe (left hemisphere) has to explain to the man (right hemisphere) the meaning of what the policeman has said, thus analogically demonstrating the left hemisphere's better language comprehension and expression. After his explanation, the man is prepared to be friends, metaphorically demonstrating that the hemisphere best qualified to take charge usually does.
4. In the next scene, Joe goes into the car park to get his bicycle, only to find that it's not there and he has no idea how he arrived there or how he is going to get back. Joe assumes someone else (right hemisphere) must have given him a lift. This scene metaphorically represents the left hemisphere's dependence on the right hemisphere's superior spatial ability and sense of direction. (In explaining the unconscious mind to students, Joe often uses the example of riding a bicycle as an acquired skill that has become an unconscious motor programme, something we do without thinking about it. In the same way, Blakeslee suggests we depend on the right hemisphere to take us to and from familiar places without having to think about it.) In the example given in Blakeslee's book, the person who had had their right hemisphere removed could not find his way back from the bathroom. At first it seems rather surprising to look for a bicycle in a (motor) car park, until we realise that the dream is using the car park as an analogical

image to represent the right hemisphere's greater involvement in our unconscious motor programmes that the brain has acquired, such as cycling and getting dressed. Note also that we look for a 'space' to park our motors in a car park, and these programmes are concerned with spatial intelligence.

5. The final scene represents the last point from Joe's reading of the previous night, which he had intensely introspected about: the possible influence of brain lateralisation on the development of stuttering. When a person stutters they repeat the same syllable or word over and over again. This is represented analogically in the dream when Joe (left hemisphere) repeats the same sentence he had already said. This sentence is repeated again by the stone-throwing man following him – Joe's 'right hemisphere'. This scene, then, is a metaphorical representation of stutterers having language ability controlled by both sides of the brain and the fact that dual control causes interference leading to the repetition of the same words or syllables. The fact that Joe (left hemisphere) says the sentence twice, and the right hemisphere, represented by the man following him, says the sentence only once analogically demonstrates the greater involvement of the left hemisphere in language production. In the dream, Joe feels embarrassed by the repetition of the sentence and ignores it. This is what the stutterer usually does; he presses on with what he is trying to say, despite his embarrassment caused by the repetition.

When Joe first remembered this dream in the early morning, he thought it an incomprehensible jumble of images but, from previous experience, he knew that this was a typical and misleading reaction derived from his left hemisphere's logical thinking. The ability to discover metaphors is known to be a right hemisphere activity, so he forced himself to record the dream before he forgot it. When he started to think about the possible meaning of the dream a little while later, and also reflected on what he had been doing the previous day, he quickly saw the analogy with his reading about the left and right hemispheres in Blakeslee's book. Joe didn't see all the metaphors straight away but, once his analogical thinking process was stimulated by thinking about the dream's possible meaning, all he had to do was wait. A couple of hours later the meaning of the car park – a parking place for motor programs – flashed into his mind. A little later the meaning of the repeated sentence – its metaphorical relationship to stuttering – also flashed into his mind. This process is just like the one we all experience when our left hemisphere struggles to remember or understand something, gets nowhere and gives up the struggle in frustration. Then, some twenty minutes or so later, the memory or answer pops into our mind, as if out of the blue – because the right hemisphere has been given the chance to go on a metaphorical search in the meantime.

Decoding the various metaphors in a dream requires the ability to break down the dream into individual scenes and then consider what the possible meaning of those scenes could be, in the light of our previous day's activities. This process will stimulate an ongoing metaphorical search that usually leads to the discovery of where the meaning lies. Then we have to compare the individual components of the dream to the components of the introspective waking experience we have identified, to see how good the fit is. Sometimes the fit is simply not good enough and components are left unmatched. The search for metaphorical connections then has to continue until a satisfactory match between all of the components of the two patterns is found. Only then can we be sure that we have identified the analogous waking introspective experience on which a dream is based. These processes are similar to those involved in creative discoveries and problem solving, as we will see when we look at creativity in a later chapter.

Since this last dream was concerned with the relationship between the right and the left hemispheres of the brain, this is an appropriate place to consider a relevant study by Klaus Hoppe.[3] He reported on research that had been carried out with 12 commissurotimised patients (patients whose corpus callosum had been severed) and another patient (Mrs G) whose right hemisphere had had to be entirely removed because of recurrent glioma (a tumour of glial cells in the central nervous system). Mrs G recounted a dream in which a doctor and a psychiatrist drove her to a restaurant and treated her to a lobster and martinis, *exactly as had been the case in waking life.* Joe's theory leads us to suggest that Mrs G must have thought about the experience in her waking imagination and, consequently, the experience manifested in a dream but, without a right hemisphere, it could not be translated into metaphors. This finding fits neatly with the evidence, already available around that time and much added to since, that the right hemisphere is biased in favour of processing analogical and metaphorical thinking, whilst the left is biased in favour of digital language and logical analysis.[4,5,6]

Hoppe's study of the 12 commissurotimised patients' dreams showed that these also appeared to be conscious daydreams without symbolisation. Again, the finding suggests that waking introspections gave rise to dreams but that, as a result of the right hemisphere's being severed from the left, they retained their original format and were not, therefore, converted into metaphorical sensory experiences. Normal dreaming, however, demonstrates that our right hemisphere's endless quest for metaphor continues even in sleep.

Dream 29

I am trekking through America with David Niven and a younger man. Presently I am in a toilet with a door which is half made from glass. School children can look in. I see some blood on my clothes and I realise my period has started. I go into a shop to purchase sanitary towels. The shop assistant is not very helpful. He tries to sell me things I don't need and seems reluctant to sell me what I want. By the time I get what I want, I am getting very worried as it is getting very late and is dark outside.

The subject who recounted this dream told Joe she thought it was related to a television play she had seen the night before, in which a school teacher appeared to rush out of the classroom because her period had started. The television programme provided part of the metaphor for the pattern expressed in the dream but, more importantly, it had reactivated for her the memory of traumatic events that had occurred in previous weeks. These became the subject of a dream. The dream metaphor can be understood as follows:

David Niven represents her husband in the dream. (Her husband was at that time reading a biography of David Niven.) Although, unlike her husband, David Niven was an old man at this time, this can be seen as a pun for her 'old man' (a common English nickname for a husband). The younger man stands in for her young family doctor, who had instigated a series of investigations to find out the cause of their infertility – hence the trek through America, land of pioneers and explorers of unknown territory.

A few weeks previously, at the hospital where she worked as a staff nurse, she had suddenly developed a severe pain in her pelvis and had had to stop work. (Note the analogy with the television programme where the young teacher rushes out of the classroom because her period had started.) She was admitted to a ward with a door that had shutters on the outside, which could be pulled back allowing the nurses to look in. These nurses were mainly student nurses. This door is analogically expressed in the dream by the half glass door which the school children could look through.

The unhelpful shop assistant relates to the medical registrar who continued to explore a diagnosis of ectopic pregnancy, despite her conviction that this could not be the case. A subsequent operation showed that she had endometriosis, involving the rupturing of blood-filled cysts near her reproductive organs: hence the analogy of her period starting. In the dream she starts to get worried when she realises it is getting late and she is still waiting for the correct article to absorb the blood. In the real life situation, she was discharged from hospital and an operation was scheduled for the following week. Continued pain, whilst waiting for the operation, made her fear that the operation might come too late, explaining her worry in the dream that it is getting late and dark outside.

We can see, therefore, that the dream expresses in metaphorical form her reactivated worrying anticipations about the events leading up to her operation. The emotionally arousing memory of those traumatic events in the recent past was reactivated by an event in the present – the TV play.

Dreams and psychotherapy

As we know, we forget or are never consciously aware of most of our dreams, and the expectation fulfilment theory is a potent explanation for why this should be so. However, some dreams stay with us, forcefully and vividly, and the expectation fulfilment theory can be of practical help to explain these. Unravelling the significance of a dream, in terms of what dream content may reveal about the dreamer's waking concerns, can be a particularly valuable tool for therapists.

The dreams that patients bring to therapists may be a powerful metaphorical statement about how the patients see themselves, their problems or their relationship with the therapist. (Ivan once heard a psychoanalyst with the unusual surname of 'Karr', telling a story against himself about how many of his clients reported dreams of cars not starting, going slowly, breaking down, crashing or taking wrong turnings – clearly many of these dreams were metaphorical expressions of their anxieties about his ineffectiveness as a therapist.) However, as well as revealing, metaphorically, a patient's unconscious feelings about a therapist and the progress being made (or not) in therapy, the dreams can also contain clues as to how to proceed with therapy. Three dreams told to Joe during a psychotherapy workshop illustrate this point. Participants had been asked if they had any dreams that they would like help in understanding. The first dream offered was as follows:

The monster fish

I'm walking along a beach accompanied by a man I know, although I didn't see his face. There are 21st century buildings along the beach. Although somewhat fearful, I accompany the man into the sea for a swim. Our movements stir up a lot of muddy water, which

> arouses a monstrous fish, and it chases us. The fish follows us into a 21st century building, where, to the relief of both of us, the man stabs it to death with a knife.

The woman who had had the dream knew it was significant but felt alienated from the meaning offered by her therapist, who had 'explained' that the monster represented her emotional self, which didn't want to make decisions, and the man represented the decisive part of her, which the dream showed was now taking charge. The woman was convinced that she would want to understand the emotional side of herself – not kill it. She also mentioned that her therapist belonged to a school of psychotherapy that saw itself as taking the 'insights' of Freud and Jung a major step further.

Although it is not possible to be entirely certain what the dream means, it seems likely that it is a metaphorical reflection of the dreamer's introspection concerning her therapy. The 21st century buildings reflect the belief implanted in her by her therapist that her therapy is a more advanced type than other current forms of psychotherapy. The man accompanying her probably stands in for her therapist. The swim in the sea – stirring up muddy water – refers to her therapy and the investigation of 'not pleasant' experiences in her past which she said took place during the sessions with her therapist. The monstrous fish is a metaphor or symbol for what might be uncovered during this investigation of her murky past – stirring up the dirty water. The fact that the man kills the monstrous fish in the 21st century building reflects her confident belief that this futuristic psychotherapy would be able to get rid of any emotional monsters that might be released.

On hearing this explanation, the woman who had had the dream felt that intuitively it made sense, and was much relieved. Had the therapist been able to interpret her dream correctly, the patient would have felt reassured and her positive expectation of the therapy would have been reinforced. The wrong interpretation, however, had succeeded only in alienating her and lessening her faith in her therapy.

The second dream offered was one that the dreamer had had on a number of occasions for many years. The dream was as follows:

> **The stalker**
>
> There is an old castle with a central courtyard. I am three storeys high on an external stone landing that runs around the outside of the building. I am running away from a man who is following me. Part of the pathway ahead of me has collapsed. There are stones lying around. I am trying to make my way past the broken part of the landing by walking close to the building.

If we examine the above dream from the point of view of an analogy or metaphor for the way this woman views something that is happening in her life, then the dream obviously relates to a recurring anxiety that she has. In it, she is under stress from two sources: her unknown pursuer and the collapse of the pathway ahead of her. The fact that this dream has repeated itself for a number of years indicates either that a particular situation keeps recurring or that the dreamer has a characteristic way of perceiving challenging situations.

In either case, the dream gives a picture of how this dreamer sees herself reacting in certain situations – a picture that straightforward questioning within a therapy session would probably not reveal. The dream is not only an accurate metaphor of a given situation in the dreamer's life; it also presents the therapist with a powerful metaphor that can be used therapeutically. For instance, through guided imagery, the therapist might encourage the woman to see a stairway leading up or down, representing the idea that most problematic circumstances aren't either/or situations: there can be other options. The constructive use of an apparently frightening dream image is also demonstrated in the next example.

This was also a repetitive dream, one that used to be enjoyable for the dreamer, but had recently changed and taken an unpleasant turn. The initial form of the dream was as follows:

The dream pony

> I find the pony which I used to have when I was young and on which I won many riding events. I again mount the pony, wondering if it has retained its racing ability. To my joy and surprise, it has still got this ability.

The dreamer recalled having had this dream on a number of occasions at intervals of up to one year. Some months ago he had again dreamed about his pony, but the dream had changed to the following:

The dying pony

> I find my pony in a neighbour's field. The pony is dying. There is nothing I can do to save it. I feel a great sense of loss.

The dreamer, when a small boy, was given this pony by his father. It was by far the best of a series of ponies he had throughout his childhood. He was very successful in winning competitions when riding it and very sad when his father decided to sell the pony because he had got too big for it.

As the pony had been associated with achievement and personal success, it seemed likely that the first dream metaphorically reflected periods of his life when he had surprised himself by rising to some challenge. When questioned, he supported this explanation. He then described how he was having to undergo changes in his career, and that he felt insecure since he was now only employed part-time and doubted that he would ever succeed in obtaining full-time work in his new career. The change in the dream can be clearly seen as a metaphorical representation of his introspected self-doubt. Again, these dreams reveal the dreamer's predicament with a strength and vividness that a verbal description could not so easily convey.

The powerful personal metaphor of the pony could be used in many ways to help him find the personal resources needed to make the best of the possibilities within his present situation. It was important for Joe to point out that the pony in the dream is not yet dead and that, should the dreamer find the personal resources to rise to his present challenge, he might well find himself rediscovering his pony, healthy and strong, in a future dream. Joe used guided imagery to encourage this man to imagine himself bringing the pony the medicine it needed to get healthy again. When he had restored it to health in his imagination, Joe asked him to see himself riding it around the fields again, galloping and jumping fences. The man did all this, thoroughly enjoying the experience. Joe subsequently learned that, following this experience, the man had moved abroad and successfully established himself in a new career – in a different 'field' altogether.

Clearly, in the absence of accurate information, a disturbing dream may have the effect of exacerbating someone's problems – either because an uninformed therapist misinterprets it or because the dream images arouse anxiety in the client. Children may be afraid to sleep, or even to be left in a room on their own, because of a fear generated by a nightmare. Such a nightmare may have been prompted by the child's waking concerns about a particular life circumstance that needs to be addressed but, equally, it may simply be a metaphorical translation of a frightening scenario viewed on television. In the latter case, the nightmare is likely to be more alarming even than the feelings about the incident which gave rise to it. When something frightening is on television, children still have a degree of control. Perhaps they can choose not to watch it or they may have an adult to cling to while it is on. When it comes to dreams, however, there is no such sense of control. We know that the nightmare comes when we are on our own, in the dark. Even more terrifying, it comes from within our own minds. Little wonder, then, that this invasion of their private psychic space can lead children to be frightened to go to sleep, for fear of dreaming the nightmare again.

A young man, who had been seeing a psychoanalyst for a number of years for the treatment of a hand-washing compulsion recently came to see Joe, as he was not making any progress. He told Joe that one day, some years earlier, before his problems began, he had gone for a swim in the local swimming pool. In the water he found the floating body of a dead man. After this incident he was haunted by two nightmares:

Horses' heads

It is dark. I am surrounded by the heads of horses. There is no escape. I feel terrified.

The hourglass

I am watching the sand falling in an hourglass. I can hear horses breathing all around me. I feel terrified.

Why should he be surrounded by horses' heads and why should this image terrify him? The experience of seeing the dead body in the swimming pool was obviously deeply disturbing for the boy. He would naturally have introspected about it a lot. These emotionally arousing introspections would have given rise to traumatic dreams or nightmares about the incident. The first nightmare may well represent a fear of having more of these terrible dreams about the dead body. The horses' heads may actually symbolise the nightmares themselves. His brain could have picked up on 'mare', a female horse, so we could say that a mare's head is an apt symbol for a 'nightmare'. The fact that he only sees the heads draws our attention to the reality that these mares are 'head-mares', nightmares from his own head, rather than events in the real world. That he is surrounded by them shows that he feels there is no escape from them – every day is rounded by sleep in which the nightmares can return.

The second nightmare develops as a result of a further fear, that of dreaming about the horses' heads. The hourglass signals that time is passing. The hour of sleep and the nightmare is approaching. This is indicated by the sound of the horses' breathing. In other words, the hour of sleep approaches and the nightmare can already be sensed, as if breathing down his neck. Looked at in this way, this dream clearly seems to represent his waking fear of sleep time approaching and the recurrence of the terrible nightmare of the horses' heads. As the horses' heads are the subject of the original introspection, they are not perceived directly this time, only sensed as a sinister presence by their breathing.

It is immensely reassuring for people to realise why their nightmares take the form they do, and so it was with this young man. His hand-washing compulsion also seemed to have arisen in reaction to the same traumatic event. The washing of his hands was the washing away of any contamination from the dead man.

It is natural that repetitive dreams such as these may produce anxiety. We can see that, if a person reflects on the feared nightmare, and if those reflections arouse further fear, then the metaphorical structure of the nightmare changes to incorporate that fact. In the above example, the original nightmare clearly changed to a nightmare reflecting the fear of having a nightmare.

But many repetitive dreams maintain their format, no matter how many times they are dreamed. In these instances, all that is happening is that the dream is a manifestation of recurring emotionally arousing introspections about a repeated worry a person has, as is the case when someone is being bullied on a regular basis. Nature is very economical with its metaphors.

The following couple of examples are of repetitive nightmares Joe remembers having in his own childhood and as he grew up:

The kidnap nightmare

> I am walking down a road in the village where I was born. Suddenly a gypsy caravan appears and a gypsy leaps from the caravan and chases me. He catches me and takes me away with him. I am terrified.

This dream was originally inspired by an incident that occurred one day when Joe was about 12 years old. He saw some gypsies passing the gate to his family's property and he cheekily taunted them by shouting "Tinkers! Tinkers!" One of the gypsies, obviously upset by this, started to run angrily towards him. Joe fled through the fields, because his parents were not in the house to protect him and he was terrified that he would be caught and carried off. The dream is a clear replay of his introspected fear of being kidnapped. The location and appearance of the caravan and the gypsy are changed, as we would expect. In the dream, a gypsy does take him captive, thus completing the pattern. For a number of years, whenever he saw gypsies, his brain would pattern match to that experience and he experienced the frisson of the fear again. Hence the recurrence of the nightmare.

The money nightmare

> Money, in the form of coins, is pouring from the sky. I am filling a bucket with the coins as fast as I can but the ground keeps cracking open beneath my feet and I have to keep jumping onto safer ground to avoid falling into the holes.

This nightmare is an accurate metaphorical representation of a childhood concern of Joe's. He was raised as a member of a large, strict, Catholic family in rural Ireland in the 1950s, when money was scarce. When times seemed hard he sometimes daydreamed, and even prayed, that he might come into a fortune. However, he would then feel guilty about this fantasy because it was incompatible with the religious beliefs he was being taught. He recalls always having this dream the night after whenever he had prayed that he would discover the legendary 'pot of gold' at the end of the rainbow – the money from the sky. This immediately aroused guilt in him, and the fear that such selfish prayers might cause him to be sent to hell – hence the sinister cracks in the ground into which he was in danger of falling.

Therapists can do much to help their patients resolve fear associated with anxiety dreams like these. The first step is to look at the dream as a metaphor for how patients feel about some anxiety-provoking event in their lives. Usually the dreams people bring to therapy are recalled because of their dramatic and emotional intensity. (Emotion acted out in dreams generally feels more intense than the emotion experienced when merely introspecting about the issues that are the subject of dreams.) Often the parallels between the dream and current events in their lives are quite obvious. In such instances, resolving the underlying issues will also, of course, remove the anxiety that generates the anxiety dreams.

Sometimes working on the nightmare itself is advisable. One approach is to have people imagine replaying the dream on a screen while being helped by the therapist to stay calm and relaxed. People often find this easier if they speed the 'film' up in their mind, as if on fast-forward, so that it appears to last only moments. This helps individuals dissociate from the imagery, which in turn reduces the feelings of anxiety. People can also be asked to imagine stepping into the film at the point when the nightmare is over and imagine again everything that happened but quickly in reverse, as if on rewind, going through to a safe point before the nightmare started. The process, forwards and backwards should be repeated a few more times, to further deactivate the emotional power of the images. We commonly use this same method to detraumatise people suffering from post traumatic stress disorder or severe phobias, a process described in detail in *Human Givens: the new approach to emotional health and clear thinking.*[7] If carefully done, it usually results in a dramatic reduction in fearful feelings.

Another approach is to have the dreamer of the nightmare interact in a positive way with the feared situation. A person can be asked to imagine, for example, bringing into the scene whatever resources are needed to enable the feared situation to be handled more effectively. This is a particularly useful approach when children's nightmares have been inspired by some traumatic television viewing (rather than an underlying fear that needs to be addressed). They can regain a sense of control if, for instance, they can imagine themselves sprinkling magic powder onto the feared creature of their dreams and disintegrating it, or summoning a chariot to take them away from a terrifying situation. Once they do not fear the nightmare, they need no longer introspect about it or fear its recurrence, thus removing the likelihood of its happening again: no fear, no pattern to be completed in dream form.

Because REM sleep is accompanied by a paralysis of major muscles, we can sometimes be conscious, if starting to awaken from REM sleep, of the inability to move or speak properly. We may be dreaming of needing to get somewhere quickly or of being chased, but we can't get our legs to move. We may need to call out to avert a disaster or to get someone's attention, but find we can say nothing or only croak. This experience of dream paralysis, as it is known, can lead to a fear of going to sleep. When people understand that this paralysis is a natural phenomenon – necessary to prevent us from thrashing around during sleep – and that it ends spontaneously within instants of waking up, they may be greatly reassured.

The content of dreams, then, can be explored to much advantage, when they are recalled. But, as demonstrated, erroneous interpretations in line with the ideologies of the major psychodynamic schools of therapy, can do much harm indeed. In the next chapter, we look at the seminal dreams of Sigmund Freud and Carl Jung – the very dreams that led them to develop the explanations of dreams that have so misled psychology and psychotherapy. We show that, far from enabling a groundbreaking understanding of the function of dreams, the meanings of these two dreams conform in every respect to that predicted by the expectation fulfilment theory.

6

TWO HOUSES OF CARDS COLLAPSE:

The seminal dreams of Freud and Jung

"There are in fact two things, science and opinion; the former begets knowledge, the latter ignorance."

HIPPOCRATES

The dream known as 'The dream of Irma's injection' is the key dream sequence in Freud's book *The Interpretation of Dreams*.[1] Freud had this dream on the night of 23rd–24th July 1895. He regarded it, and his interpretation of it, as so significant that he called it his 'specimen dream' and devoted some fourteen pages to its analysis. He even wrote to his close friend Wilhelm Fliess on 12th June 1900, "Do you suppose that some day a marble tablet will be placed on the house, inscribed with these words: 'In this house, on July 24th 1895, the secret of dreams was revealed to Dr Sigmund Freud'?"[2]

Freud's whole system of psychoanalysis, which for a hundred years dominated people's thinking about psychotherapy, is based upon his dream theory. Not only that, much cultural thinking, fiction and poetry in the Western world has been deeply influenced by psychoanalytical ideas. So, if Freud's interpretation of this dream is not correct, the whole of psychoanalysis disintegrates and so do many of the Western cultural studies of the past hundred years. As we shall see, Freud's interpretation *was* hopelessly wrong.

It has been possible to unravel Freud's dream because, fortunately, the relevant historical evidence about the traumatic events in his life during the months preceding it, and the reactivation of concerns about these events by the remarks of a visiting friend on the evening before, are available to us. This evidence provides the key to understanding his dream in the light of Joe's findings about the purpose of dreams. And, as we shall see, this explanation is far removed from the one arrived at by Freud himself. His dream was, in fact, a precise metaphorical re-enactment of specific historical events in his life that were still troubling him greatly. The dream was described by him as follows:

The dream of Irma's injection

A large hall – numerous guests, whom we were receiving – among them was Irma. I at once took her on one side, as though to answer her letter and to reproach her for not having accepted my solution yet. I said to her: If you still get pains it's really your own fault! She replied: if only you knew what pains I've got in my throat and stomach – it's choking me – I was alarmed and looked at her. She looked pale and puffy. I thought to myself that after all I must be missing some organic troubles. I took her to the window and looked down her throat, and she showed signs of recalcitrance like women with artificial dentures. I thought to myself that there was really no need for her to do that – she then opened her mouth properly and on the right I found a big white patch: at another place I saw extensive whitish grey scabs upon remarkable curly structures which were evidently modelled on the turbinal bones of the nose – I at once called Dr M and he repeated the examination and confirmed it. Dr M looked quite different from usual, he was very pale, he walked with a limp and his chin was clean shaven ... My friend Otto was now standing beside her as well, and my friend Leopold was percussing her through her bodice saying: She has a dull area low down on the left. He also indicated that a portion of the skin on the left shoulder was infiltrated (I noticed this as he did), in spite of her dress ... M said "there's no doubt about it, it's an infection, but no matter, dysentery will supervene and the toxin will be eliminated" ... We were

> directly aware, too, of the origin of the infection. Not long before, when she was feeling unwell, my friend Otto had given her an injection of a preparation of propyl propyls, ... propionic acid ... trimethylamin (and I saw before me the formula for this printed in heavy type) ... Injections of that sort ought not to be made so thoughtlessly ... and probably the syringe had not been clean.

From Freud's discussion of the background to the dream, which on first inspection appears to be about one of his patients, Irma, we know that, on the previous day, he had received a visit from an old friend who was also the family paediatrician, Dr Oskar Rie. Earlier in his career Rie had been Freud's assistant and collaborated with him on a scientific paper. In the dream of Irma's injection Freud calls him Otto. That evening Rie had come directly from Irma's home where he had been staying with her and her family. Freud asked him how Irma was and he replied, "she's better but not quite well". Freud was annoyed by his reply as he fancied that he detected a reproof in it to the effect that he (Freud) had promised the patient too much. He gave no indication to Rie of his feelings but that night he worked late, writing out her case history to give to Dr M (subsequently identified as Dr Josef Breuer, a senior colleague and a collaborator with Freud on a book about hysteria).

In *The Interpretation of Dreams* Freud proceeds to give lengthy associations for each element in the dream and, finally, concludes that the main instigating force for the dream was a wish to exonerate himself from any blame for the lack of complete success in the treatment of Irma's condition. This is achieved by (a) blaming Irma herself for not accepting his solution, (b) pointing out that, because the pains were organic in nature, they were not treatable by psychological means, and (c) implying that Otto had caused the pains by giving her an injection with a dirty needle. These reasons are not, however, as Freud himself noted, mutually applicable. The dream also gave him his revenge on Otto, by making Otto responsible for

Irma's condition.

Now that we are aware that all the elements in a dream stand for something else, with the exception of when someone's presence is felt but not perceived, we can conclude that Freud's explanation for the dream, based as it is on the manifest characters, is wrong. Furthermore, since the publication in 1966 of a paper by Max Schur[3] in which previously unpublished letters from Freud to Wilhelm Fliess were included, we have had available the means to identify with some certainty the true meaning of Freud's specimen dream.

We learn from these letters that, in March 1895, Freud had treated a young, single woman of 27, Emma Eckstein, for hysterical nose bleeds. He had called in his friend Fliess, a nose and throat specialist, to examine her to see if there was a somatic basis to her illness. Fliess had not only operated on Freud himself but was also, at this time, Freud's major confidant and had expressed complete confidence in Freud's theories. Fliess travelled from Berlin to Vienna to examine Emma and operated on her nose on the 4th March. (Fliess had propounded a bizarre theory that the turbinal bones in the nose and the female sexual organs were intimately connected and that somatic symptoms, allegedly arising from masturbation, could be cured through nasal surgery.) Freud subsequently wrote to Fliess telling him that the swelling and bleeding hadn't let up and that a foetid odour had set in. He went on to say that he had called in another surgeon, G [Dr Gersuny], who inserted a tube to help the drainage.

Four days later he wrote again to Fliess telling him that profuse bleeding had started again and, as Dr G was unavailable, he had called in surgeon R [Dr Rosanes] to examine Emma. While cleaning the area surrounding the opening, Rosanes began to pull at a thread and suddenly at least half a metre of gauze came away from the cavity. This was followed by profuse bleeding. It turned out that Fliess had left a piece of iodoform gauze in the cavity some two weeks earlier, which was interfering with the healing process and was the source of the foetid smell. Freud went on to say that leaving in the gauze was an unfortunate accident that could have happened to the most careful surgeon and he reassured Fliess of his complete confidence in him.

On 28th March 1895 he again wrote to Fliess reassuring him about Emma's condition but, by 11th April, he was writing once more telling Fliess that Emma's condition had deteriorated, that there was a further highly dangerous haemorrhage, that these were "gloomy times, unbelievably gloomy ... the demoralization resulting from the obvious medical helplessness, and the whole air of danger", and that he was "really quite shaken that such a misfortune can have arisen from this operation, which was depicted as harmless."

On 20th April Freud replied to a letter from Fliess, telling him that his (Fliess's) suggestion that they could have waited was completely impractical. Indeed, if the surgeon had sat around and waited, Emma would have "bled to death in half a minute". However, he goes on to reassure Fliess that he remains for him "the prototype of the man in whose hands one confidently entrusts one's life and that of one's family".

These traumatic events occurred just some four months prior to the Irma dream of the night of 23rd July 1895. As we can see from his letters, these were profoundly anxious times for Freud. A patient was in danger of losing her life as a result of a mistake made by a surgeon he had recommended, who also happened to be (at that time) his closest friend. Freud's confidence was badly shaken.

Indeed, we may well suspect that it was because of these traumatic events that he was so sensitive to what he felt was an implied rebuke in his old friend Rie's remark about Irma's treatment. No doubt his reaction, to stay up late to write out her case history in order to justify himself, also helped to bring back in full force to his mind these traumatic events. In fact, as Schur noted when he published Freud's letters to Fliess, there were many resemblances between the traumatic events recounted in the letters and Freud's dream of 'Irma's injection'. However, without the benefit of the theory Joe has now put forward, he was, perhaps, unlikely to make the full structural comparison necessary to show that the dream of 'Irma's injection' is actually a *precise* analogical restatement of the traumatic events of Emma's treatment. It is a re-enacted metaphorical scenario of those events, with Freud's introspected views about Fliess's blame made abundantly clear to everyone, including Fliess.

The setting for the dream is a party that was to be held the following day to celebrate his wife's birthday. Among the guests is Irma, who Freud takes aside to rebuke for not having accepted his solution. Freud tells us that Irma (a name used by Freud to protect the patient's identity) was a young widow and a friend of the family. In 1984 Jeffrey Masson produced evidence from a number of sources which identify Irma as Anna Hammerschlag, a young widow whose husband had died a year after their marriage, and who was the godmother of Freud's daughter Anna.[4] She was briefly treated by Freud at this time. This manifest dream character of Irma-Anna was an analogical replacement for Emma Eckstein, as will become clear.

Both Irma-Anna and Emma were referred by Freud to Fliess for nasal examination. Fliess, as we have seen, recommended and carried out nasal surgery on Emma Eckstein to remove the turbinate bone in her nose, with near fatal consequences. Fliess, who was at that time an inexperienced surgeon, advocated this entirely unnecessary operation on the grounds that it would help her recover from what his theory said were the harmful effects of masturbation. (Fliess's theory had rightly been dismissed by the scientific community of the day as "disgusting gobbledygook".[5] Nevertheless, Freud believed for several years that it was "a fundamental biological discovery".[6]) After the operation, Fliess returned to Berlin. No doubt Freud was irritated, as in the dream, when even after the operation she still complained of somatic symptoms. When he examined Irma in the dream, she showed signs of "recalcitrance"; in his letter to Fliess of the 4th March 1895, he told him that he had encountered from Emma "resistance to irrigation".

The throat in the dream is, of course, an analogy for the nose. This is made quite clear in the dream when Freud looked down 'Irma's' throat and saw structures similar to the turbinal bones of the nose. Freud goes on to tell us that, in the dream, his examination revealed "a big white patch" and "whitish grey scabs" upon these structures, i.e. the operation site. He at once called in Dr M [Dr Breuer], a senior colleague of his, who confirmed his examination. This parallels the events recounted to Fliess in his letter of 4th March 1895, where he said that, because of the pain and swelling, he had let himself be persuaded to call in Dr G [Dr Gersuny], who said that access to the cavity was restricted and inserted a rubber tube to help drainage.

Freud notes that, in the dream, Dr M did not have his usual appearance but possessed the physical characteristics of Freud's older half brother. In his letter of 8th March, Freud told Fliess that Dr G had behaved in a rather rejecting way towards him during his visit. This explains why the character in the dream standing for Dr G is a composite of Dr M and Freud's half brother – both of them, Freud tells us in his associations to the dream, had recently rejected a suggestion that he had put to them.

We are next told that Otto was standing beside the patient. Otto [Dr Oskar Rie] is the analogical replacement for Fliess in the dream. It's not surprising that Otto should have been Fliess's analogical substitute, as both men were friends of Freud, both were doctors, both had a professional relationship with him and his family, and both had been involved in Freud's theoretical work.

After the visit of Dr G – represented by Dr M in the dream – Freud wrote a series of letters to Fliess, making him aware of each step in the developing crisis. We can see therefore, how, in a metaphorical sense, Fliess was standing beside the patient. It is entirely in keeping with this view that Otto in the dream doesn't do anything from this point, except observe what is going on.

Next in the dream sequence, we learn that Freud's friend Leopold is examining Irma. In Freud's letter of 8th March 1895 we learn that he had to call in a Dr R to examine the patient because Dr G wasn't available. We can see that the structure of the dream is working out exactly as it did in real life. In the dream, his friend Leopold's examination indicated that a portion of the skin on the left shoulder was "infiltrated". Freud could see the infiltration in spite of Irma's dress. In the real life situation, Dr R had pulled at something like a thread and a piece of gauze was removed – an "infiltration" as it was a "foreign body" (the phrase Freud used in his letter) that should not have been left there from Fliess's operation.

The next incident in the dream is that Dr M intervenes again and gives the opinion that, "There's no doubt it's an infection ..." etc. We have already shown that Dr M (perceived by Freud in the dream as a combination of Dr Breuer and Freud's half brother) is the analogical substitute for Dr G [Dr Gersuny] and, in real life, we again know from Freud's own letter of 8th March to Fliess, that Dr Gersuny *did* come the next day and assist Dr R in attending to the patient.

Next we come to perhaps the most important element of the dream sequence. Freud says, "We were directly aware too of the origin of the infection. Not long before, when she was feeling unwell, my friend Otto had given her an injection of a preparation of propyl, propyls ... propionic acid ... trimethylamin (and I saw before me the formula for this printed in heavy type) ... injections of this sort ought not to be made so thoughtlessly ... and probably the syringe had not been clean".

Freud refers to events that have happened "not long before" – in other words, before the sequence of visits analogically represented in the dream. This, of course, corresponds exactly to the sequence in real life. Fliess had carried out his abortive operation before the sequence of other doctors' visits were set in train. Everybody in the dream, including Otto (i.e. Fliess), is aware that Otto is to blame, that he had been thoughtless and probably negligent in that the syringe wasn't clean. Freud may have felt protective towards his close friend Fliess, after the discovery of Fliess's mistake (as indicated in his letters to him), but the dream makes clear that, by the evening before the dream, Freud had come to see that Fliess had been professionally negligent, and that the other doctors who were subsequently called in were also aware of Fliess's professional incompetence. It would have been natural, on the evening before his dream, for Freud to have reviewed those events, and who was to blame, as he sat writing a defence of his own professional conduct in the case of another patient, whom he had also referred to Fliess for treatment.

The injection of "propionic acid... trimethylamin" is again an analogy. Propionic acid is described in pharmacological reference books as having a 'putrid and rancid odour'. Freud in his letter to Fliess described Emma's lesion as having a 'foetid' odour. Gauze left overly long in a wound, as medical friends have told us, gives rise to a 'particularly foul smell of rotting flesh'. Fliess had told Freud that trimethylamin was one of the products of sexual metabolism. Fliess's operation removed the turbinate bone in Emma's nose to alleviate the deleterious effects of masturbation, which he claimed gave rise to a 'nasal reflex neurosis'. We can see that by this metaphorical means Freud was pointing the finger of blame at Fliess for the foul smelling lesion in Emma's nose, which had resulted from his abortive operation.

Freud's dream of 'Irma's injection' is, therefore, a metaphorical simulation of the traumatic events of the 'Emma affair', which must have been distressing for everyone involved, and in which everybody is metaphorically made aware of where the blame really lies – with Fliess. It is also apparent that Freud's sensitivity to the assumed criticism of his professional conduct, implied by Otto's remarks of the night before, reawakened the trauma of his recent involvement in the 'Emma affair'. This patient nearly lost her life after Freud referred her to his friend Fliess for surgery that was both unnecessary and unorthodox (to say the least). Just as he wrote up the case history of Irma [Anna] that night to make clear that he was not responsible for her continuing symptoms (as mentioned, he had referred her to Fliess too), so the dream also makes clear that it is Fliess and not he himself who was responsible for the mistreatment of Emma. (In fairness to Freud it should be noted that he had complete faith, at the time of his referral, in what he thought was Fliess's unrecognised genius and that his referral of patients to Fliess was done in good faith.)

Clearly, Freud's introspections about the nearly fatal case of Emma, as he wrote up his notes about Irma's case for his mentor Dr Breuer, are metaphorically expressed in his dream exactly as Joe's expectation fulfilment theory would predict.

Another house of cards falls

The major psychodynamic alternative to Freudian psychoanalysis, and its interpretation of literature and history, is the one that his one-time pupil Carl Jung developed. His psychoanalytical practice too derived from his own theory of dreaming.

In his biography, Jung says, "One [dream] in particular was important to me for it led me to the concept of the collective unconscious."[7] The 'collective unconscious' was Jung's unique contribution to the theory of the mind. This particular dream, and his interpretation of it, was as important in the development of his theories as was Freud's interpretation of the dream of Irma's injection to Freudian psychoanalytical thought and practice. Showing that Jung's interpretation of this dream is wrong should therefore be good reason for consigning Jungian, as well as Freudian, psychoanalysis to history. Some would say, not before time!

By good fortune again, enough information is available to enable the real meaning of Jung's seminal dream to be established. The dream is as follows:

Jung's house dream

I was in a house I did not know, which had two storeys. It was "my house". I found myself in the upper storey, where there was a kind of salon furnished with fine old pieces in Rococo style. On the walls hung a number of precious old paintings. I wondered that this should be my house and thought "not bad". But then it occurred to me that I did not know what the lower floor looked like. Descending the stairs, I reached the ground floor. There everything was much older. I realised that this part of the house must date from about the fifteenth or sixteenth century. The furnishings were mediaeval, the floors were of red brick. Everywhere it was rather dark. I went from one room to another thinking "now I really must explore the whole house." I came upon a heavy door and opened it. Beyond it, I discovered a stone

> stairway that led down into a cellar. Descending again, I found myself in a beautifully vaulted room which looked exceedingly ancient. Examining the walls, I discovered layers of brick among the ordinary stone blocks, and chips of brick in the mortar. As soon as I saw this, I knew that the walls dated from Roman times. My interest by now was intense. I looked more closely at the floor. It was of stone slabs and in one of these I discovered a ring. When I pulled it, the stone slab lifted and again I saw a stairway of narrow stone steps leading down to the depths. These, too, I descended and entered a low cave cut into rock. Thick dust lay on the floor and in the dust were scattered bones and broken pottery, like remains of a primitive culture. I discovered two human skulls, obviously very old, and half disintegrated. Then I awoke.

Interestingly, when he had this dream in 1909, Jung was on a voyage to America with Freud. When Jung described it to him, Freud pressed Jung to uncover any wishes in connection with the two skulls, obviously thinking that a death wish was the key to understanding it. Jung reports that, to satisfy Freud, he lied and said that they reminded him of his wife and sister-in-law. Freud appeared relieved on hearing this – relieved, no doubt, that Jung wasn't harbouring a death wish against him.

To Jung, however, the house represented an image of his psyche. At the beginning of the dream he is on the first floor, in the salon, which represents to him normal consciousness. The remaining floors represent different levels of consciousness. The cave represents the most primitive level of all, the consciousness of primitive man, which still lies buried in our unconscious. It was but a short step for Jung to go from this analysis to his idea of a 'collective unconscious' – a common store of vague racial memories and archetypes. Jung thought that these archetypical images could surface in dreams.

Again, we are lucky to know what was preoccupying Jung in the days prior to this dream. In his biography, Jung tells us that, "certain questions had been on my mind". Those questions were, "On what premise is psychology founded? To what category of human thought does it belong? What is the relationship of its almost exclusive personalism to general historical assumptions?"

If Jung was so preoccupied with these questions, he would have introspected a lot about them, an activity that would result (according to the expectation fulfilment theory) in dreams about his imagined explorations of these questions. It will become clear that Jung's dream is actually a metaphorical exploration of the last question, namely psychology's relationship to historical assumptions.

The house, as Jung saw clearly, is a metaphor for the psyche. The dream starts off with Jung being in a house he doesn't know, yet it is his own house. The fact that the house is his own represents the 'almost exclusive personalism' aspect of the question Jung was exploring. That is, the house is his personal property, just as the psyche is also a personal attribute. Yet he doesn't know the house, just as in real life he doesn't yet know the answer to his question about the psyche.

Each floor of the house corresponds to a different historical period. At the start of the dream Jung finds himself on the first floor, corresponding to the most recent historical period. This is quite a civilised period, as can be seen from the 18th century style of "fine old pieces" of furniture together with "precious old paintings" which suggests that the contribution from the great masterpieces of the past were retained and valued in this period. The fact that the furnishings, as Jung noted, are mainly 18th century and rather old fashioned suggests that Jung saw a time lag between historical influences and their manifestation in the psyche. As Jung descends through the floors, the age of the building goes back further and further into the past. On the ground floor he finds that this part of the house must date from the 15th and 16th centuries. The furnishings are mediaeval and the floors are made of red brick. The fact that everywhere was rather "dark" reminds us that we are dealing with 'the dark ages', stretching from the mediaeval period back to the end of the Roman empire.

Jung next goes down a stone stairway that leads to the cellar. He notes that the walls date from Roman times, made as they were from "stone blocks" and mortar which had "chips of bricks" in it. The fact that the architecture of the room displays a beautifully vaulted room, suggests that Jung regarded the contribution of this period to the evolution of the psyche as a high-minded one. "The beautifully vaulted room" reminds one, of course, of a church and that we are dealing with the historical period in which Christianity – Roman Catholicism – became dominant. Jung's father was a Christian minister and Jung was well aware of the influence of the spread of Christianity (Roman Catholicism) in this period. The fact that this floor is unfurnished and no artefacts are seen, unlike on every other floor of the building, also suggests that Jung saw the contribution of this period as a non-materialistic one.

In the final sequence of the dream, Jung discovers in the floor a stone slab with a ring that can be pulled up to reveal "a narrow stone stairway" leading down to a low cave cut into the rock. This part of the building corresponds to prehistoric times. Jung has described the cave as looking rather like a "prehistoric grave" and such graves are, of course, one of our chief sources of knowledge of those times. In the dream, Jung sees two half-disintegrated human skulls and scattered bones in the thick dust of the grave, together with the remains of broken pottery. (Pottery vessels containing supplies for the journey into the next world often accompanied ancient burials.) This last floor of the house is in fact an underground stone cave, so it is the only floor of the house that is not man-made, suggesting that the psyche of primitive man is as nature constructed it – largely uninfluenced by "historical assumptions".

From this modern analysis of the dream, made in the light of the expectation fulfilment theory, it is clearly apparent that Jung's dream was not an intimation from a wise unconscious of the hitherto undiscovered existence of a 'collective unconscious'. It was simply a metaphorical representation of the question which Jung was introspectively exploring when awake, namely the relationship between personal psychology and history. Jung's idiosyncratic interpretation of the dream arises because he hasn't realised that the dream is a metaphorical representation of the relationship between *two* variables: history and psychology. By focusing on only one variable, namely the psyche, Jung almost inevitably concluded that the other variable (history) was the answer. In his own words, "my dream was giving me the answer", by showing him the many levels of historical consciousness (i.e. the collective unconscious) still operating beneath the individual's personal consciousness.

Ironically, in a contribution he made to a book that was published after he died in 1961, he offered a different explanation for the dream, this time focusing on the other variable in the dream – history.[8] He now said he saw the dream as representing a history of his intellectual development, the tomb with the skulls and bones corresponding to his palaeological interests, the ground floor dating from the Middle Ages corresponding to the influence of his parents' "mediaeval concepts" and the first floor corresponding to more recent intellectual influences. This analysis, however, misses out the basement dating from Roman times.

If Jung had related his first analysis based on the psyche and his second analysis, which focused on historical development, to the question he had been introspectively exploring prior to the dream (namely the relationship between these two variables), then his final analysis might have turned out rather differently. It might have shown, as our analysis has, that his dream was a metaphorical representation of his waking introspections concerning the relationship between personal psychology and history. It doesn't represent an answer but a preoccupation with the question.

We can now see the reason why patients of Jungian analysts tend to dream dreams that appear to confirm Jungian theory while the patients of Freudian analysts tend to dream dreams that confirm Freudian theory. The subject matter of dreams are emotionally arousing introspections that remain unmanifested in the external world. Patients will introspect about their problems in terms of the theoretical framework in which the therapist sets them. This theoretical framework will be represented metaphorically or symbolically in the patient's dreams. The analyst then takes this symbolical representation of his own theory as evidence for the correctness of that theory. In just this way Jung, introspecting about the possible relationship between the psyche and history, had a dream in which those waking thoughts were metaphorically represented ... and then used the dream images as evidence for the veracity of that same speculation. This is a bit like someone having a certain theory about human nature and commissioning the making of a film in which people act out those ideas. Subsequently, forgetting the origin of the film, the self-deluded person offers the same film as independent evidence for the correctness of the theory ... and most people don't notice!

We can see now that Freud's psychoanalytical dream interpretation ideas actually work against nature and, because they had such an enormous influence, they have acted as a brake on the development of effective psychotherapy ever since he first propounded them. Freud's notion that the unconscious is a filthy cesspit of stored-up repressed wishes and sexual desires that accumulate from childhood was hopelessly wrong. To continue the metaphor, the expectation fulfilment theory explains how, on the contrary, nature had invented an emotional 'flush toilet': unexpressed or incomplete patterns of emotional arousal are discharged every night to free the brain to deal with the new emotionally arousing concerns of each ensuing day.

The terrible consequences of ignorance

Now that Freud and Jung's dreams can be analysed in the light of modern psychobiological insights, we can see that the two most influential schools of therapy of the past 100 years were based upon theories of dreaming that were false. In recent decades, it has become clear just how far messianically proclaimed Freudian and Jungian beliefs – all unsubstantiated by scientific thought or research – have thwarted the advancement of useful and effective psychotherapy.[9,10] Freud, who once wrote, "In the depths of my heart I can't help being convinced that my dear fellow men, with few exceptions, are worthless," was a walking disaster as a therapist. He had no written up cases that were successful and frequently blamed his patients for their failure to recover.[11]

Although the popularity of dream interpretation in therapy has, along with psychoanalysis, waned in recent decades, the mistaken pattern of dream interpretation begun by Freud continues to be actively practised by nearly a third of psychotherapists in America[12] and his mistaken ideas of repressed emotion still underlie much of the psychotherapeutic practice going on in the world today.

Apart from needlessly prolonging therapy, these ideas have led many therapists to generate false memories of abuse. We can easily see how this would happen. Suppose a woman goes to see a therapist about an eating disorder. If the therapist is one who believes the commonly held but scientifically unsupported view that eating disorders are most frequently caused by sexual abuse in childhood, this belief might be conveyed to the woman by the type of history taking that is done. Questions will be asked about possible sexual abuse in childhood. Even if she has no conscious memories at all of such abuse, she will still, quite understandably, introspect about this emotionally charged suggestion, which in turn will give rise to metaphorical dreams about abuse. If she reports these dreams to the therapist, the therapist may well interpret them as providing independent evidence of abuse having taken place – a mistake with potentially tragic consequences, as the woman, initially astounded and disbelieving, may come to accept that the imagined abuse *did* take place. There are many cases where therapists have encouraged clients to stop seeing their parents and siblings after 'remembering' childhood abuse. Innocent people find themselves accused of an ancient crime they find it very hard to disprove (proving a negative is notoriously difficult); families break up; the law is involved and, if courts rely on 'expert' witnesses who share the belief in repressed memories, innocent people can find themselves in prison. Unfortunately, this has happened many times.[13] (Of course, much genuine abuse does take place. And, when people suffer the symptoms of post traumatic stress as a result, they need specific interventions to help them overcome the trauma and move on in their lives.[14] However, such interventions are very different from the psychodynamic approaches derived from Freud's ideas.)

Jung was no better as a therapist than Freud. He was much more concerned with occult ideas and developing his role as a prophet, as Jung expert Professor Richard Noll of Harvard explained, putting it somewhat passionately, during an interview on the subject, "If you were actually somebody in need, Jung basically just opened up your head to his crazy ideas and made it fuzzier. His techniques took away people's ability to focus their attention and separate out thoughts. He shot their cognitive resources to hell."[15]

Unfortunately, psychoanalytical ideas did more than damage the way therapists and counsellors attempted psychological interventions with distressed people; they also infected the liberal arts establishment throughout the western world. Their influence has extended far beyond therapy and contaminated education, politics, novels, plays, films and even the way business is run today.[16,17]

Both Freud and Jung were possessed of a supreme confidence that they were right, actively promoting the elitist cult of psychoanalysis as an initiation into mysteries. Jung was more overtly 'occult'; he vigorously promoted himself as a 'seer' and 'prophet', and attracted many wealthy lady disciples, his biggest catch being the daughter of John D. Rockefeller who, in 1916, poured more than a million dollars into his enterprises.[18] But Freud, who was just as ambitious, combative, charismatic, superstitious and intelligent as Jung, was to have the bigger impact, once his ideas became actively promoted in America by his nephew Edward Bernays.

Freud was convinced that fame was surely due him, and his 'dreams as wish fulfilment' theory was at the heart of his programme, as Edward Dolnick explained in his book *Madness on the Couch*:

> Freud rated his insights with those of Copernicus and Darwin. Both of those titans of science, Freud liked to explain, had dealt mankind enormous shocks to its self-esteem. Copernicus had demonstrated that the earth was

not the centre of the universe but a tiny speck in an undistinguished suburb. Darwin had shown that humans were not the pinnacle of creation but animals who still bore ineradicable signs of their animal ancestry. Now Freud had come along and delivered human megalomania ... its third and most wounding blow. He "had proved that humans were blind to their own motives, that the ego ... is not even master in its own house, but must content itself with scanty information of what is going on unconsciously in its mind".

Nor were Copernicus and Darwin the only greats Freud compared himself with. At one time or another, the Freud scholar John Farrell notes, Freud likened his achievement and daring to that of the most exalted figures in world history and mythology: the biblical Joseph, Moses, Oedipus, Alexander the Great, Hannibal, William the Conqueror, Columbus, Leonardo, Kepler, Cromwell, Danton, Napoleon, Garibaldi, Bismarck, and even Zeus. More impressive still, Freud noted, his triumphs belonged to him alone. Einstein, for example, "had the support of a long series of predecessors from Newton onward, while I have had to hack every step of my way through a tangled jungle alone."

This was a monumental display of self-confidence. More important, this vaunting pride on the part of a single man soon transformed itself into an overwhelming institutional pride. Freud placed total faith in his own judgments; the psychoanalysts of the next generations took these same judgments as their own, and took on Freud's utter self-confidence as well.

The source of Freud's confidence was easy to place. Each day brought new confirmations of his views. Take his theory that dreams "invariably and indisputably" represent secret wishes. Support for the theory came, first of all, from patients who agreed with Freud's interpretations of their dreams. But support came also from those who emphatically rejected Freud's insights. Freud recounted proudly

> how he had dealt with one patient whose dream seemed to run counter to his thesis. She was a woman who disliked her mother-in-law and had gone out of her way to make sure that she would not have to spend her summer vacation with her. Then she had a dream that she and her mother-in-law had spent their vacation together. "Was not this the sharpest possible contradiction of my theory that in dreams wishes are fulfilled?" Freud asked his readers, with the showmanship of Houdini showing a bewildered audience his handcuffed wrists. Then he proceeded to wriggle free. "No doubt," Freud answered his own question, "and it was only necessary to follow the dream's logical consequence in order to arrive at its interpretation. The dream showed that I was wrong. *Thus it was her wish that I might be wrong, and her dream showed that wish fulfilled.*"[19]
>
> [Italics in original.]

This was not merely hubris but ironclad hubris. Freud had invented the ultimate closed system of thought. Not only was it unlikely that the theory could be in error, but it was virtually unthinkable. The Catholic Church talks of "invincible ignorance"; here was invincible arrogance.

Little did Freud suspect that his own letters would one day provide convincing evidence that his interpretation of his 'specimen' dream of Irma's injection was completely wrong. Nor, of course, could Jung have guessed that *his* own records of what had been occupying his thoughts on the day before his all-important dream would one day reveal the correct meaning of his dream, and thus disprove the main plank of his theory.

But it cannot be denied, despite the harm these two men did, that they were highly creative people. And that brings us nicely to the subject of our next chapter.

7

SOLVING PROBLEMS: CREATIVITY AND DREAMS

"It is the function of creative men and women to perceive the relations between thoughts, or things, or forms of expression that may seem utterly different, and to be able to combine them into some new forms – the power to connect the seemingly unconnected."

WILLIAM PLOMER

The relationship between creativity and dreams has long been recognised. There are many recorded anecdotes of dreams helping people solve problems. Indeed, Joe's research into the origin of why we dream is a case in point: as we've seen, it too was inspired by a dream which eventually led to this new theory. But, although Joe's dream clearly led him towards the solution he eventually found, it is, of course, not strictly comparable with the types of dream that appear instantaneously to give rise to solutions to specific problems. In these dreams, the dream content has a direct relationship with the problem being worked on. One of the most famous dream anecdotes of all time is a perfect example of this: Kekule's discovery of the structure of the benzene ring – one of the most important discoveries in the history of chemistry. Kekule had been trying for years to solve the problem of the nature of the molecular structure of benzene.

Kekule's dream

Then, one afternoon, I turned my chair to the fire and dozed. Again the atoms were gambolling before my eyes. This time the smaller groups kept modestly in the

> background. My mental eye, rendered more acute by repeated visions of this kind, could now distinguish larger structures of manifold conformation: long rows, sometimes more closely fitted together, all twining and twisting in a snake-like motion. But look! What was this? One of the snakes had seized hold of its own tail, and the forms whirled mockingly before my eyes. As if by a flash of lightening I awoke .... Let us learn to dream, gentlemen.[1]

The snake swallowing its own tail suggested to Kekule that the structure of this organic compound might be a closed ring. So, would we be right in concluding from this that the dream solved the problem for Kekule which his waking conscious mind could not?

The expectation fulfilment theory offers an alternative interpretation of the events of the dream, as follows. Kekule had worked hard on his problem, trying out many different solutions but without success. He feels he is getting nowhere. He sits by the fire and starts to doze. The dream he then has expresses his deep frustration concerning the problem. He sees the "manifold conformation: long rows, sometimes more closely fitted together" – that is, the numerous solutions he had tried, some more closely fitting the solution than others "all twining and twisting in snake-like fashion". This suggests his continuing attempts to fashion or model the correct shape of the structure. "What was this? One of the snakes had seized hold of its own tail, and the forms whirled mockingly before my eyes" – we see here a metaphorical expression of Kekule's frustration. His attempts at a solution are just going around in circles. He feels the problem is making a fool of him – mocking him. (Feelings – emotions – are, of course, what dreams are all about because it is unacted out emotional arousal patterns that dreams deactivate by completing them.)

This interpretation is given further credence by the fact that Kekule's dream occurred just after he nodded off to sleep. This stage of sleep is not REM sleep proper but the drowsy transitional state called 'hypnogogic sleep' (described in Chapter 4). The EEG brain wave pattern in hypnogogic sleep is similar to REM sleep, but the lower brainstem is not as involved as it is in full-blown REM sleep. As we saw from Silberer's research, a current waking introspection may become metaphorically translated during hypnogogic sleep. We would therefore expect Kekule's dream to reflect his waking frustration at the lack of progress in his attempts to solve his problem. This is exactly what Joe's dream analysis shows did in fact happen.

However, although the dream represents Kekule's frustration at not being able to find the correct solution to the problem, the vivid image in it of going around in circles did break him free from his entrenched mental set of looking for a *linear* solution to the problem and opened up to him the possibility that a *circular* structure might provide the solution. Are we to assume, then, that it was pure coincidence that led to the selection of the image of the whirling circle to represent the feelings of frustration? Research by Dement suggests an answer to this problem, but first we must consider how the creative process works.

Stages in the creative process

In 1926, the British philosopher Graham Wallace, in the *The Art of Thought*, concisely described the stages of the creative process in a way that we feel hasn't been bettered.[2] He called these stages: preparation, incubation, illumination and verification.

We have probably all had experience of focusing our attention on a problem (preparation), then leaving it aside for a while, perhaps going for a walk (incubation), when suddenly a solution hits us (illumination). Then, of course, we must check that the solution is viable (verification). The characteristic way in which our cognitive unconscious works by 'incubating' the problem is nature's way of enabling us to find solutions holistically (sometimes called lateral thinking). Creative solutions do not come from logical analysis, although such an analysis is necessary in the preparatory stage, but from rearranging the elements of a problem into a new pattern, or seeing the existing pattern from a different perspective.

You can clearly see this process at work yourself by applying to your own dreams the theory of dreams presented in this book. First, note all the elements of the dream, including your feelings about it. These are the feelings that you would have felt had you been able to enact the waking introspections that gave rise to your dreams. The feelings in the dream are actually more intense than the feelings you had when you were awake. (This is because, as you did not act on the feelings when you were awake, your dreaming brain concentrates completely on the aroused expectations associated with the feelings, in order to deactivate them.) Next, compare the dream elements to your waking experience of the previous day to see if you can find a matching template to the dream scenario. Remember, of course, that the match will not be between the 'objective' waking events and the dream but rather between the dream and your introspected view of those waking events. This can be regarded as the preparation phase of the dream analysis.

The corresponding waking situation doesn't usually spring to mind immediately as the purpose of the dream in the first instance was to deactivate the feelings associated with the memory. Hence it usually requires a period of 'incubation' before the unconscious mind can trace the associative links to the waking introspection that gave rise to the dream. Ironically it is often easier, when we have adequate background information, to see the meaning of someone else's dream, if we have an idea of what was preoccupying them the previous day. This is because the waking sequence has not, of course, been deactivated in our brains. Thus Joe's wife, Liz, will often identify the meaning of one of his dreams before he does and vice versa. Once the meaning has been identified all of the elements in it can be matched up, which helps to verify it. Thus, real dream interpretation, especially interpreting our own dreams, clearly involves the four traditional phases of creative problem solving: preparation, incubation, illumination and verification.

Despite popular ideas to the contrary it appears that successful problem solving in dreams may be pretty rare. Dement has reported a research project in which 500 undergraduate students, over three consecutive classes, were given one of three problems to solve.[4] They were told to study a problem for 15 minutes before going to sleep and to record any dreams they remembered from the night. If the problem had not been solved, they were to work on it for another 15 minutes in the morning. The total number of problem-solving attempts was 1,148. It was judged that 87 dreams related to the problem but that the problem was solved in a dream on only seven occasions.

One of the problems was as follows: "The letters OTTFF... form the beginning of an infinite sequence. Find a simple rule for determining any or all successive letters. According to your rule, what would be the next two letters of the sequence?" The next two letters are SS. The letters represent the first letters used in spelling out the numerical sequence one, two, three, four, five, six, seven etc.

The following dream is one of those in which the problem was solved.

The art gallery

> I was standing in an art gallery looking at the paintings on the wall. As I walked down the hall, I began to count the paintings one, two, three, four, five. But as I came to the sixth and seventh, the paintings had been ripped from their frames! I stared at the empty frames with a peculiar feeling that some mystery was about to suddenly be solved, I realised that the sixth and seventh spaces were the solution to the problem.

A second problem the students were given was to consider the letters HIJKLMNO. The solution to the problem was one word: water. In other words, 'H to O' or H_2O.

No dream was classified as actually solving the problem, but twelve were classified as 'mode of expression dreams'. An example of a 'mode of expression' dream is as follows:

> I had several dreams, all of which had water in them somewhere. In one dream I was hunting for sharks. In another I was riding waves at the ocean. In another I

> was confronted by a barracuda while skin-diving. In another it was raining quite heavily. In another I was sailing into the wind.

This dream, as the student reported, had water in it everywhere. Yet, as far as he was concerned, the student had solved the problem to his own satisfaction before going to bed, with the word 'alphabet'.

The type of holistic thinking required for creative problem solving is the antithesis of the everyday analytical approach. Rather than breaking a problem down, it involves looking at the entire problem from a different perspective. This is also the type of thinking required to solve the problems in Dement's study. Such creative problem solving is often facilitated by taking a break from the problem and getting into a relaxed frame of mind (incubation) after which the solution often 'hits' us (illumination). It may well be that dreaming can, in a sense, provide the relaxed frame of mind in which a solution can emerge. An individual's analogical thinking process may have arrived at a solution before dreaming, but he or she is either too tired or, more likely, too set in an analytical left-brain mode of thinking, for the solution to emerge.

The research psychologist Norman Dixon has reported experiments where a subliminal image shown to subjects appeared in the manifest content of a subsequent dream.[5] He argued that, in these cases, although the image has been perceived, the stimulus doesn't possess enough energy to get as far as waking consciousness but it can emerge in the less controlled consciousness of a dream. Perhaps a similar phenomenon exists as far as dream problem solving is concerned. A solution that doesn't possess enough energy to break through into consciousness, either because existing cognitive sets are too rigid or because the person is not in a suitably relaxed frame of mind, may become manifest in a dream sequence.

How the solution manifests depends on how people anticipate what will happen in their dream before they go to sleep. In the first example given, the subject has the solution expressed clearly in an analogous setting. He is looking at paintings in an art gallery. This is a metaphor for his anticipation that he will be looking at images in a dream. The sixth and seventh paintings, ripped from their frames, symbolise the missing two letters which had to be found in order to solve the problem. He expects the problem to be solved in a dream. He looks at the blank paintings with a feeling that some mystery is going to be solved. He realises that the sixth and seventh spaces are the solution.

This dream, then, metaphorically represented what this student anticipated would happen in a dream that night. His creative process had probably arrived at a correct solution before the dream occurred. Consequently the anticipated solution provided in the dream was an accurate metaphor of the correct solution. This is in contrast to the great majority of the dreams reported – these were about the problem and trying to solve it but the correct solution did not emerge from them.

In the second example, the student wrongly thought that he had solved the problem before going to sleep. In this case, Joe's theory of dreams would lead us to expect that, for the correct solution to appear in this student's dreams, it would have to be incorporated into the ongoing imagery of other dream themes, since he was no longer anticipating a solution in a dream. (This is what happened with the subliminally presented images in Dixon's study, they were incorporated into the ongoing dream sequences.) The student reported several dreams in which water was the main form of symbolism. However, the dreams were not about the problem, or about water as the solution to the problem, but rather water as a symbol to express a personal concern for the future – a fear that he was heading into 'dangerous waters' perhaps.

This student's creative thinking process had arrived at the correct solution, namely 'water', but, because he wrongly believed 'alphabet' to be the solution, it did not emerge into waking consciousness and, like a subliminally presented stimulus, was easily incorporated into the symbolism or metaphors of dreams that expressed different waking anticipations.

Similarly, Kekule's analogical thinking process had arrived at a correct solution but a suitable frame of mind for its emergence may not have been arrived at before he fell asleep, or else his conscious mental sets were too rigid to permit the solution to emerge. So the solution was incorporated into the symbolism in a dream which was expressing some other waking concern. In this case Kekule's fear that the problem was making a fool of him is expressed appropriately by the snake chasing its own tail, 'mockingly' going round in circles. The expectation fulfilment theory suggests that, for a person's problem to be *directly* solved in a dream, they must actively anticipate that the problem will be solved in their dreams and, secondly, the correct solution must have already occurred to them *prior* to having the dream. On the other hand, where a solution has occurred to a person's unconscious mind, but an appropriate milieu for its expression has not been found while they were awake, then the solution may be *indirectly* suggested by the surface imagery of the metaphor expressing a different waking concern – as in the examples of Kekule's dream and in the water solution dream just described.

To further demonstrate these two modes of problem solving by means of dreams, we can look at an interesting follow up to Dement's research that illustrates the first and then describe how two inventions, lead shot and the automatic sewing machine, illustrate the second.

The *New Scientist* asked its readers to use their dreams to solve a number of intellectual problems.[6] They were the kind of problems that would be expected to baffle the logical, conscious mind. Eleven people wrote to Morton Schatzman, who was conducting the research, and described how a dream had helped them solve the following mathematical problem:

Using six line segments of equal length, can you construct four equilateral triangles such that the sides of the triangles are the same length as the line segments.

One who wrote in said that, in a dream, she ran her hand along some railings and six of them came together "to form a kind of wigwam". Later she dreamt that her chemistry teacher appeared in the dream and said '109 28'. The student knew that this number was connected with tetrahedral molecules whose structures make up four equilateral triangles. Translating the metaphor she realised that the solution was a three-sided pyramid. Another student, who was not familiar with mathematics, was delighted with the help her dream provided. In her dream, she asked a scientist for help, and the scientist jumped up and down and eventually flew up on top of a cupboard. When the dreamer woke up, she was able to understand the metaphorical answer by realising that the triangles must be given lift off. She made a drawing using this idea and solved the problem.

Notice how the presence of the scientist in the dream would naturally alert her waking mind to the fact that this dream was about the problem from the *New Scientist*.

Another problem presented was to discover what was remarkable about the following sentence:

> 'I am not very happy acting pleased whenever prominent scientists overmagnify intellectual enlightenment.'

(The number of letters increases in each consecutive word by one to form a numerical sequence going from one to 13.)

One sixth-form student dreamed that he was lecturing to scientists seated at five tables with one, two, three, four and five scientists sitting at each respective table. The student was able to see that the dream was a metaphorical solution to the problem. Another student who solved the problem by means of a dream reported that, in his dream, he typed the sentence, 'The quick brown fox jumped over the lazy dog'. (This is, of course, the sentence that contains all 26 letters of the alphabet.) His supervisor tells him to type 1 2 3 4 5 6 7 8 9 instead. Again, we see the dream expressing the solution metaphorically. The words were replaced by a sentence known to contain all the letters of the alphabet, and thus it directs his attention to the letters in the words. The supervisor tells him to write a sequence of numbers that stops at 9. This is because the number of words in the replacement sentence in the dream has nine words in it, unlike the problem sentence, which has thirteen words in it. We can see, therefore, that the dream provided a metaphorical solution to the problem.

In these examples the dreamers were anticipating a solution to the problem in their dreams and then dreaming a metaphorical solution to the problem. In the next two examples a solution to a problem was not anticipated in a dream and so the solution had to follow the more indirect route of being incorporated into the surface images of a dream expressing another theme.

Invention and dreams

The development of the technique for making lead shot is a good example of a solution becoming incorporated into the surface structure of a dream metaphor which is expressing an ongoing concern of the dreamer. In 1782 William Watts invented the process that enabled lead shot to be made in regular shapes and sizes. One night, coming home from a drinking session, he decided to sleep it off in the porch of the church near his home. During the night it rained heavily and he had the following dream. He dreamed that his wife was pouring drops of molten lead on top of him from the roof of the church.[7] No doubt he was apprehensive of the scolding (scalding) his wife would give him when he got home, and this provided the metaphor of his wife (who was not actually seen in the dream) expressing her hostility by pouring molten lead on him. In other words, his dream expressed the feeling that he would get 'shot' when his wife got her hands on him.

Watts was an observant plumber who was well used to working with lead and familiar with the way molten lead behaves. He already knew that molten lead dropped through the air would form perfect spherical lead balls. He was also aware of the problems involved in making lead shot. Therefore, it is highly possible that his unconscious could have already solved the problem before he had the dream. Although the solution had 'incubated', the 'illumination' had yet to take place. The solution is incorporated into the surface structure of the dream metaphor.

When Watts woke up he immediately saw that he had a means of making lead shot of a regular shape and size. He carried out an experiment to test the illumination. With the help of his wife (who had presumably cooled down by then) he dropped molten lead from a considerable height – in fact from the very church roof he had dreamt about – and it did indeed form perfect lead shot as it fell through the air and cooled. This very same process is still used today.

A further example is the invention, in 1846, of the first practical sewing machine.[8] For years an inventor called Elias Howe had been trying to build a sewing machine but, like everyone else who was trying to do the same thing at that time, he couldn't make his designs work. But he was desperate to succeed because he was being hard pressed for money by his creditors. A solution eluded him and his struggle seemed fruitless. Then, one night, he dreamed that he was chased and captured by a savage tribe who told him they would spear him to death within 24 hours if he didn't solve the problem. They tied him to a stake and began dancing wildly round him, waving their spears and getting closer all the time. As they got closer and closer he got more and more desperate and, when they seemed on the point of killing him, he suddenly noticed that all of their spears had an eye hole near the point. He woke with a start, remembered the dream, and realised at once that this was the solution to his problem. The eye in the needle needed to be on the opposite end from that on a hand-held needle. The model of the hand-held needle may have conditioned his conscious mind, making it difficult for him to see that the functional elements of a needle would have to be rearranged if it was to work on a sewing machine.

The solution 'hitched a ride' up to consciousness, as it were, by being incorporated into the surface imagery of the dream metaphor that was expressing his frustration at being pressurised by his creditors (the savages in the dream). This one dream changed the working lives of millions.

The evidence, therefore, suggests that there are two possible ways that dreams may provide solutions to problems. Firstly, if a person has worked on a problem for which he has not yet found a solution, then goes to bed expecting to dream one, he may just dream a metaphorical solution. However, according to the expectation fulfilment theory, this requires (a) that he has an emotionally arousing expectation that the solution to the problem will be revealed in a dream, (b) that his creative mind reaches a solution to the problem *before* he dreams, (c) that the solution does not reach consciousness before dreaming, and (d) that he recalls the dream in which the solution appears. We would suggest that this could only be successful for a short time. As soon as the person has experienced not dreaming the correct solution (which is bound to happen sooner or later), then it will no longer be possible to generate the necessary emotionally-arousing expectation that a dream is going to provide the answer.

A second and perhaps more likely possibility is that the surface structure of a dream whose metaphorical content expresses a different waking concern may, on occasion, provide the vehicle to express the solution to a particular problem. But this would only occur when the creative mind has incubated a solution and is looking for an opportunity to express it – as with the discovery of the 'benzene ring' and the invention of the sewing machine.

So dreams in which problems are solved do not present a difficulty for this new theory about why we dream. Indeed, such solutions emerge in a form that is in accordance with what the theory would predict.

Consolidation of learning during sleep

Many studies have, however, shown that there is a connection between REM sleep and the effectiveness of memory recall for new learning, and some researchers believe that dreaming is primarily concerned with this. Much recently published work still reflects this stance.[9]

However, the dreaming and learning effect is most notable in types of learning that involve 'false starts', such as memory for routine procedures, as demonstrated by Professor Peretz Lavie when he set rats to learn the path through a maze.[10] More recently, Erin Wamsley and colleagues taught students to find their way through a complex computer maze. After learning to navigate the maze, half the students enjoyed a 90-minute nap while the rest watched videos. Five hours later, all tried the maze again. Those who had not slept showed no improvement; those who had slept but not reported dreaming about the maze showed slight improvement whereas those who dreamed about the maze performed 10 times better than the other sleepers. However, the dreams were not exact replays of navigating the maze – one sleeper even reported images of a bat cave he had once visited, mixed up with maze images.[11]

The expectation fulfilment theory would predict these findings. It suggests that REM sleep allows the introspected false starts that were not acted upon to be deactivated. Once the metaphorical acting out of the introspected false starts has taken place, the autonomic arousal is switched off, allowing the 'correct' memory to be consolidated – hence the improvement in memory for certain types of learning after REM sleep.

Even the finding that, when rats are in REM sleep after learning a maze, the pattern of brain activity is almost identical to that experienced while learning the maze[12] can be explained by our dream theory. Co-author of the study Matthew Wilson, based at the Massachusetts Institute of Technology's Center for Learning and Memory, infers from his findings that, during sleep, the brain reinforces skills learned during the day by repeating and consolidating memories. We, however, would suggest, that the equivalent brain patterns are likely to be indicators that the unexpressed emotional arousal (likely to be high anxiety) experienced while trying to learn a maze is now being discharged in a dream.

That dreaming is not primarily concerned with memory consolidation would seem to be evidenced by the fact that animals and humans denied REM sleep do not show deficits in task learning. As the brain is in a non-memory encoding state during sleep, consolidation at that time is unlikely.[13] Other researchers have suggested that, as the hippocampus is reactivated during sleep after a learning task, and performance on the task is improved afterwards, dreams are a side-effect of the reactivation of this area, explaining why dream content is not directly related to the learned material.[14] All this is more easily and economically explained by the expectation fulfilment theory of dreaming.

The REM state is the repository of our stored instinctive knowledge templates, and all new understandings are the result of a process of refinement and integration of our existing knowledge and new learning. That, in essence, is what the creative process is about, but we have more to say about it in the next chapter.

8

THE WAKING DREAM

"She likened the hills to ramparts, to the breasts of doves, and the flanks of kine. She compared the flowers to enamel and the turf to Turkey rugs worn thin ... Everything, in fact, was something else."

VIRGINIA WOOLF

One of the most fruitful discoveries arising from Joe's work has been the realisation that the REM state can be – and routinely is – activated outside the dream state. (Studies comparing the waking state with REM periods of sleep show much more similarity than the REM periods have with the other stages of sleep.[1]) We all flip in and out of trance states many times a day, and we will show that this is intimately connected with the REM state. A trance is a focused state of attention, a state of utter absorption. And the most absorbing type of trance state we ever enter *is* a dream. Most people do not realise that when their attention is completely held, for instance by a riveting speaker or by a problem that they are focused on solving, or by an activity that requires exact precision (such as archery), they are in a trance state. But the trance state most people are familiar with – and still mystified by – is that of hypnosis.

For centuries, people have been intrigued, amused, astonished, helped and harmed by what can happen when hypnotic trance states are deliberately induced and people are manipulated while in them. Until quite recently, for example, stage hypnotists were seen as having exotic occult powers, as though they were magicians, and in every major city in the world, in one guise or another, they have entertained audiences by demonstrating their seemingly amazing abilities to make people behave in bizarre and extraordinary ways, do baffling things, make utter fools of themselves or see and hear things that are not there.[2]

On another level, throughout the ages, remarkable individuals, from witch doctors to modern surgeons, stone-age shamans to present-day psychiatrists, have, by chance and circumstances, found out how to use this powerful phenomenon for benign educational, psychological and medical purposes. Over the last 160 years or so it has been well attested by scientific method that hypnosis can be used to accelerate recovery from severe burns and that, whilst in a hypnotic state, people can have dental work, and even major surgery carried out (as happened to Ivan when he was a schoolboy) without feeling any pain. Irritable bowel, shingles, asthma, phantom limb pain, male and female sexual dysfunctions and all sorts of psychological and psychosomatic disturbances can, when careful use of hypnosis is incorporated into treatment, be relieved in a fraction of the time that conventional therapies take.[3,4,5,6] Hypnosis is, therefore, a demonstrably powerful therapeutic tool and thousands of scientific papers document an incredible range of medical results obtained when using it. For example, the late renowned Irish surgeon Dr Jack Gibson performed more than 4,000 operations using hypnosis as the only form of anaesthesia. He also used it to help alcoholics and asthmatics, and to charm away warts and verrucas.[7]

In our private psychotherapy work and whilst carrying out therapy demonstrations in front of students, we have ourselves frequently used hypnotic techniques with patients to eliminate lifelong phobias and post traumatic stress disorder (PTSD) symptoms in as little as 40 minutes. Hypnosis can also play an important part in speeding up treatment for clinical depression, anxiety and anger disorders, and the treatment of addictions. And yet, despite the scientific evidence as to its power, and despite the fact that all mainstream churches have withdrawn opposition to it and all major orthodox medical and psychological associations around the world have legitimised its use, this proven psychological procedure has yet to find widespread acceptance among the practitioners of the medical and psychological professions.

This seems baffling at first sight, but the reason is simple – what we don't understand, we are afraid of. Without a coherent organising idea, it is impossible to distinguish between what is pure gimmickry and what is a powerful adjunct to healing. Therefore, health professionals might understandably feel uncomfortable working with it. But now, through the insights derived from the expectation fulfilment theory of dreaming, we have a scientifically convincing explanation for what hypnosis really is.[8] The explanation is found in the common denominator between dreaming and hypnotic phenomena – the REM state. This is the link that makes sense of it all. *Hypnosis is simply any artificial means of accessing the REM state whilst awake.*

All the many methods for inducing hypnosis are paralleled by aspects of how the REM state is normally induced and maintained. Shock inductions, when hypnosis is instantaneously induced through an unexpected occurrence, such as the hypnotist suddenly thumping a table or ringing a bell, fires the orientation response into action, just as happens at the start of REM sleep. And inducing deep relaxation creates the same electrical patterns in the brain as occurs in REM sleep. Guided imagery switches people into their right hemisphere and mimics daydreaming, a state associated with learning, in which new patterns of knowledge can be pattern matched metaphorically and integrated. The traditional swinging of the fob watch for people to follow with their eyes mimics the rapid eye movements that are triggered by the orientation response in REM sleep. Indeed *anything* that focuses and locks attention (e.g. "I want you to stare at that spot on the ceiling") fires the orientation response. In fact, even an unexpected event or idea induces at least a mini-trance, just through firing the orientation response and momentarily focusing attention. All the strange phenomena associated with hypnosis make perfect sense once it is understood that they are the very phenomena that occur naturally in the REM state.

Take wild 'dervish' dancing, for example: anthropologists have witnessed and filmed participants piercing their flesh with knives and nails without any apparent pain or bleeding. This practice, a staple topic of popular anthropology books, is not mysterious when we realise that the dervishes have induced deep trances in themselves by means of rhythmic repetitive activity, usually involving drumming, chanting or dancing. Although the major muscles associated with movement are paralysed when we dream during REM sleep, a rhythmic fine muscle movement can be observed in the fingers and toes. (Many people recognise that their pets are 'dreaming' when they notice the rhythmic paw movements their sleeping cats and dogs are making. In fact, as Jouvet showed, they are running through their repertoire of instinctive behaviours, perhaps ones stimulated during the day but not fulfilled – such as when a chase does not result in a catch, and so does not fulfil the hunting instinct.) Engaging in highly repetitive rhythmic activity can trigger also the REM state. Once in a REM state trance, incoming sensory information is easily switched off, just as it is when we dream. So dervishes can do all kinds of things to themselves without feeling pain or bleeding. In just the same way, tribal warriors use war dancing and chanting to whip themselves into a fighting frenzy before entering battle. This is on a continuum with women experiencing pain-free births after the induction of a guided trance by a hypnotherapist, and with the induction of hypnosis in surgical emergencies (when no anaesthetic is available) to enable injured patients to have badly damaged limbs amputated and wounds stitched up without feeling any pain.

The lack of bleeding in trance that dervishes demonstrate has also been noted by surgeons and dentists: operations carried out when patients are hypnotised cause far less bleeding than those when patients are chemically anaesthetised.[9,10] Indeed, because the REM state is also the programming state of the brain, it is possible, through hypnosis, to instruct the brain to redirect blood flow, and so enhance the healing process after surgery. This phenomenon is also well documented and has been filmed in laboratory conditions – less dramatic, perhaps, than exotic dervish dancing, but no less impressive. One film showed a woman, who had agreed to have scratches made on her arm, bleeding from them in turn, in accordance with the instructions of the scientist who had hypnotised her. In another film a haemophiliac is seen having a lower premolar tooth surgically removed, with hypnosis as the only anaesthetic and with no transfusion or plasma concentrates being needed. There is also film of the late American psychiatrist and pioneer of modern hypnotherapy, Dr Milton H. Erickson, putting his colleague, Dr Kay Thompson, into trance – she then bleeds and stops bleeding (from a cannula inserted in her hand) on Erickson's command.[11]

Equally mystifying to the general public is the ability of stage hypnotists to persuade people to see things that are not actually there. But the mystery disappears once we reflect that, in our dreams in the REM state at night, we all vividly see or sense things that are not there. Dreaming is a psychotic state in which we are unable to read context and therefore cannot challenge the dream content we are experiencing, however surreal it is. Once the hypnotist has induced the REM state (trance), it is, therefore, strikingly easy to get people to see leprechauns, or absent friends, or mysterious objects, or to summon up intense emotions in a moment, because that is no different from what happens in dreams every night, when we are context blind.

Stage hypnotists, therefore, have no magic powers. They merely have the confidence and showmanship to do what is necessary to replicate aspects of the machinery of the REM state, so as to put people into trance and make them suggestible. Instead of memory and instinctive drives providing the dream script, the hypnotist does it, (although he or she probably doesn't know why it happens). The REM state is like a theatre where the dream takes place, but the dream script is *separate* from the theatre. The REM state is our own 'reality generator' and the dream script is acted out, or made real, *within* that reality generator. The audience of a stage hypnotist is simply watching the enactment of dream scripts suggested by the hypnotist to the volunteers who have been put into a REM state trance. (Anyone who has seen a stage hypnotist suggest to a hypnotised member of the audience that, for example, an onion is a delicious apple and watched the victim contentedly eating it, or that a broom is a beautiful woman and then watched a hypnotised male dance sensuously with it, perhaps even getting sexually aroused in the process, will have little doubt of the reality for that person of the sensory impression thus created. This theatrical situation is almost identical to how a waking thought is metaphorically transformed into a sensory reality in a dream.)

If it is accepted that hypnosis is a direct means of accessing the REM state theatre which, as a reality generator, clothes our introspections in metaphorical sensory garb and acts them out as dreams, we have a new organising idea of immense power. For the first time, we have a theory that can separate the *content* of the dream from *the state of mind* in which a dream occurs.

There are other similarities between dreaming and hypnosis. A hypnotised subject can be given a story and asked to dream a dream there and then about it, for instance. The subject will invariably report a *metaphorical* version of the story – just as occurs in dreaming. Also, hypnotised subjects often show an uncanny knack of translating another person's dream back into its waking meaning. And, while we would not expect the brain pattern of a hypnotised subject to be exactly the same as the one that occurs in the REM state, since the hypnotised state is not induced by the lower brainstem, both states generate similar EEG brain patterns, and rapid eye movements similar to those that occur during REM sleep are often observed in subjects whilst they are in a hypnotic state.

Yet another similarity between dreaming and hypnosis is the odd phenomenon known as 'trance logic'. This has long been recognised as an important characteristic of the hypnotic state. It is typically defined as "an extreme tendency of subjects to rationalise any occurrence they experience, no matter how improbable or absurd it may be".[12] In one example a subject in trance, who was told to close the window in a room that was uncomfortably warm, did so whilst explaining that the room was cold and draughty.[13] Trance logic is regarded by some investigators as a sure sign that someone is hypnotised. (They say that its occurrence, or lack of it, can give an indication of whether someone is faking being hypnotised or not, because it is so unlike the way the normal conscious mind functions and impossible to fake.) But trance logic is not unique to hypnosis; it also occurs in dreams. Here are two examples. The first comes from one of Joe's dreams and is followed by a dream on a similar theme told to him by his brother.

Return to life

> I am talking to someone in a house when my sister walks in. I am surprised to see her, since I know she is dead. The thought immediately occurs to me that this must be a dream. I reflect to myself that, even if it is a dream, I can still enjoy the feeling that she is alive, since the feeling of her presence is so real. My sister goes on to give an explanation of her miraculous return to life. She tells me that she was not really buried in the grave after her death, because it was hospital policy to hold on to dead bodies for further experimentation. It was, therefore, an empty coffin that was buried. While the hospital researchers were doing further tests on her dead body, she had started to breathe again. They had had to keep these facts secret until now (some 12 months after her death) because they were waiting for her to regain strength. I accepted this explanation of her return to life as perfectly plausible.

The previous day, while looking at a photograph of his dead sister, Joe had thought that he could sense her presence as though she were still alive. The dream, therefore, can be seen as an acting out of his introspection from the previous day. His sister appears as herself in the dream because her body was changed from being dead to being alive. Her appearance in the dream triggered an awareness in Joe that he might be dreaming. Trance logic resolves the dilemma. In the dream, his sister gives a preposterous explanation to account for her improbable return to life but, because of trance logic, this explanation is fully accepted by Joe whilst asleep. When he told this dream to one of his brothers, his brother said that he too had had a similar dream only a couple of days earlier:

The brother's dream

> Our sister walks into the room. I am surprised to see her. I immediately think that I must be dreaming because our sister is dead. I then think to myself that it can't be a dream because I wouldn't question the reality of a dream. I therefore conclude that our sister is alive.

Here again we see the similarity between dream logic and trance logic. Joe's brother says to himself that, because he is able to question the reality of the dream, it therefore is not a dream, so instead he accepts the improbable reality of his dead sister being alive again.

One of the most remarked upon facts about dreaming is that, despite spending about two hours a night doing it, most of us recall very few dreams. Indeed, it is relatively unusual to do so, unless we take the trouble to train ourselves to recall them (and even then most dreams are still forgotten). Some people are so good at forgetting their dreams that they even come to believe they don't dream at all. Most people, however, have experienced remembering one on waking only to forget it a few moments later. It seems that, once the dream work is done, we have no need to remember them. And here we have another similarity: forgetting, or amnesia, is also associated with hypnosis.

Most good hypnotic subjects have the experience of coming out of a trance surprised to learn that considerably more or less time has elapsed than they thought and recalling little of what actually happened in the trance. People are much more likely to recall a dream, however, if they wake up from it gradually, paying attention to what they were dreaming as they do so. Conversely, if they wake up suddenly, as a result of an alarm clock or a door bell ringing, they are more likely to have amnesia for the dream. Similarly, with hypnosis, any sudden switch of attention will facilitate the amnesia of what took place in the trance. But even if the hypnotic subject has amnesia for what took place, any posthypnotic suggestions (such as "You will blow your nose every time you hear a clock chime"), given during the trance, will still be triggered when the appropriate circumstances are encountered later. Just as our instinctive programming (which is laid down in the REM state) will always be activated when matched with the appropriate environmental conditions: when we blink our eyes, for instance, in the face of a sudden movement or when a bright light flashes.

Dr Milton H. Erickson, recognised the phenomenon of what he called "the common everyday trance" which occurs about every ninety minutes. During this state, which itself lasts about twenty minutes, the brain switches from left-brain information processing to predominantly right-brain information processing. Erickson discovered that this was a good time to give his clients suggestions because they were more suggestible in this state. This is because, in order to counteract a suggestion, it is necessary to analyse it and form another viewpoint, which is a left-brain activity. Erickson also discovered that this light trance state could easily be deepened into a more profound hypnotic state with appropriate suggestions. (We have made use of this ourselves, for therapeutic effect, on numerous occasions.)

Dr Ernest Rossi linked this periodically occurring trance state to certain ultradian (many times a day) rhythms, which involve a switch from left-brain functioning to right-brain functioning for a period of about 20 minutes, every 90 to 120 minutes.[14] Again, dream sleep also follows this rhythm, occurring approximately every 90 to 120 minutes during sleep. (This is why a nap, if it coincides with the appropriate stage of these ultradian rhythms, can be incredibly refreshing as the sleeper drops straight into REM sleep, dearousing any currently unfulfilled expectations.)

Another observation made by people experienced in using hypnosis is that inducing trance states in patients, albeit inadvertently, is the basic therapeutic agent in many other forms of psychotherapy besides hypnotherapy – despite therapists often hotly denying that they are doing any such thing.[15] Anyone who understands the principles of hypnotic inductions and how people are influenced can recognise this. Whenever someone is encouraged to concentrate and focus their attention – such as when remembering past events – it is trance inducing. So, too, is the rousing of strong emotions such as anger, fear, depression and greed – because these also focus and lock attention. For instance, anxiety about visiting a GP to hear the results of important tests can induce trance and consequently amnesia for what the doctor has to say. Dissociation, positive hallucinations, suggestibility – all are associated with hypnosis (trance) and all can occur in the course of therapy. For instance, in gestalt therapy, therapists might ask clients to 'imagine' having a conversation with an absent person; the clients then become so absorbed that they hallucinate their mothers or some other important figure in their lives. Many GPs, psychiatrists, psychotherapists and counsellors are quite unaware that their interactions with patients can be deeply hypnotic. This is just as much the case in, say, cognitive therapy, which encourages people to focus on their thinking, as it is in therapies such as gestalt, which more obviously involve hypnotic phenomena.

If, as we suggest, the main reason for the reluctance to recognise the true value of hypnosis is the absence of a scientific theory to explain it, the expectation fulfilment theory of dreaming set out in this book could overcome this. We know that most people daydream, and about 20 per cent of the population can readily access a state of deep hypnosis, where suggested realities become as real as dream realities. Moreover, most of the rest of the population has the ability to access lighter trance states, such as we all experience as we drift off to sleep in front of the TV or become deeply absorbed in an activity such as reading. Therapeutic suggestions given to someone in the REM state can have profound effects on the mind/body system. So it is to be hoped that hypnosis will become more widely employed, and its great therapeutic potential unlocked, as confidence in our scientific understanding of this phenomenon increases.

However, we would add a word of caution. People in trance, however this is brought about (whether for therapeutic benefit, or as part of a crowd listening to an enigmatic speaker), are highly vulnerable – as are the people using it (it is very easy to go into a trance yourself when inducing one in others). This is because when we are in trance, however briefly, we are accessing the REM state, the natural state for reprogramming our brains. So, although hypnosis can be used for enormous benefit as a powerful therapeutic tool, we should also be very aware, for obvious reasons, of the dangers inherent in the process it taps into.

The dawn of daydreaming

This raises a fundamental question: if we can so easily be put into the REM state and become so vulnerable to outside influence that we can be made to do all kinds of wacky, weird or even dangerous things, why would nature have made the REM state so accessible to us? We believe that, by answering this question, we have revealed a new explanation for the development of complex language, the rise of civilisations and why humans developed self-consciousness.

It was when, by some mutation (perhaps as recently as 40,000 years ago[16]), some human beings learned how to daydream, and thus to develop and use a new psychological tool – that of imagination – to solve problems (rather than just reacting instinctively in the moment to immediate promptings from the environment, as animals do), that we became truly human. To daydream requires the ability to create illusory realities in the internal mental 'theatre' of one's mind and try out different scenarios in imagination. As we shall show, that can only be done in the REM state reality generator we have been describing. This is what marks us out as different from the rest of the animal kingdom. When we daydream, we step out of the present moment (which all mammals experience in terms of instant emotional responses to instinctive perceptions). We might imagine what other people might be thinking or feeling. Or we might visualise different ways of doing things, or invent new tools and behaviours by imagining what might be possible if we did something differently. In other words, daydreaming allows us to develop a profound concept of possible futures derived from our learnings from the past. It was only when we had evolved sufficiently to step out of the present moment and into our own personal mental theatre of alternative realities whilst awake, that we could look backwards and forwards in time. And only when we had developed a strong sense of the past and the future could we become self-conscious beings, able to use the past and future tenses as well as the present tense, and thus to evolve complex language.

We maintain that complex language, which for many years was thought to have evolved slowly and to be the most important reason for our becoming human, would have appeared as quickly as complex tool-making and art did. It must also have arisen as a consequence of getting access to the REM state whilst awake. Language is all about sound symbols standing in for complex concepts or metaphorical patterns. The most important symbolic mechanism we have is talking: talking about the past and the future; talking about people and things that are not there in front of us; talking about possible future actions and so on. But there can only be *words* for the past and the future if there are *concepts* for the past and the future. To develop such a concept, it first has to be experienced. And that must have required the evolution of the ability to step into the daydreaming state where such concepts can be experienced – in imagination. The very moment that became possible, humans could move beyond mere animality.[17]

It seems clear to us that gaining waking entry to the REM state was the prime achievement of early humans. Once that was established and stabilised within the population, there was a cultural explosion – tool-making, music, arts and crafts, animal husbandry and agriculture – which led eventually to city states, poetry, philosophy and science. All that the human race has achieved, and what we have become, flowed from our breakthrough into daydreaming – it opened up the whole universe to us. With self-consciousness and complex language, we accumulated and passed on knowledge of ever increasing subtlety at ever increasing rates, speeding up evolution by a huge factor. Society became more complex. Stimulating children's imaginations and their ability to daydream enabled their potential to be 'drawn out' of them (the Latin word from which 'educate' is derived means 'to lead out'), so that the achievements possible in one life time became magnified to an enormous degree. Now we could *consciously* evolve.

There is good evidence for when self-consciousness first secured a widespread base in humans (namely the huge range and variety of fine stone and bone tools suddenly produced throughout Europe from about 40,000 years ago, and the appearance at around the same time of beautiful drawings and paintings in deep natural caves and tunnels far underground). Perhaps the significance of what was happening was understood very early on by these same people. Indeed, those prehistoric cave drawings may have been the product of 'schools' for teaching the use of the imagination. Away from all outside distractions, those who had realised the significance of this new skill to survival could help others, including children, to access their reality generator. (We explored the ramifications of this for the evolution of creativity, mysticism and mental illness in our book *Godhead: the brain's big bang*.[18])

Culture could not have developed without humankind learning to access the REM state reality generator whilst awake and consciously daydream. The mechanism that gave rise to the explosion of creativity all those thousands of years ago is still the same mechanism we use in creative thought today. As we have seen, whenever someone gets a new idea, it comes to them after a period of effort to solve a problem. The effort is a necessary ingredient to focus the brain, but it is when the person relaxes from the struggle and dips into the REM state, perhaps daydreaming whilst taking a stroll, that the new idea comes into their mind. This is because making metaphorical connections is a right brain activity, but the *right* brain needs direction from the analytical *left* brain.

In just the same way, when children are educated, the point at which the real learning takes place is when he or she goes into the REM state, however briefly, and links new incoming information from the teacher to a pattern of meaning they already have in their mind. Education is a process of enriching the patterns that are already there to expand the context in which the pupil experiences life. When a teacher fails to engage a new pattern in this way, as when a mathematics teacher writes symbols on the board that are totally meaningless to a child, no progress is made. Both parties end up frustrated. Such a teacher does not understand that to educate means to 'lead out' existing patterns of knowledge in the child, in order to connect them up to new patterns to increase the pupil's understanding. And the channel through which this process occurs is, we maintain, the REM state.

Education is best achieved by surrounding children with competent, knowledgeable people of all ages, giving them the chance to enlarge their experience, and the space to observe, think, daydream and pattern match what they are learning to what they already know, as well as stretching them through the disciplines required by whatever they are learning. This effort makes them more intelligent very rapidly.[18] And adults who continue to do this, even right into old age, become the wisest among us. It is exactly the same in psychotherapy. We have seen countless times that, when therapeutic change occurs, it takes place when, overtly or inadvertently, the therapist has put the patient into the REM state and somehow enriched the patterns in their mind – expanding the context – so that they can deal with the realities of life more effectively.

We have set out to make the case that understanding the REM state and dreams really is "the royal road to a knowledge of the unconscious". (This remark of Freud's was perhaps one of the truly insightful statements he made.) We have seen that accessing the REM state outside of dreaming is the mechanism that we use for the transmission of culture, which in turn means that anybody who teaches us is focusing our attention and putting us into a hypnotic state. This type of focused trance is our natural learning state because in it we make sense of reality by pattern matching the incoming information to existing patterns already in our heads. In other words, to make sense of any new information, we have to go on an 'inner search' to look for something a bit 'like' what we are learning to match it to, so that the new material can be put into context. This is therefore a metaphorical process.

How we learn through metaphor

As we discussed in an earlier chapter, the function of REM sleep explains our ability to think in metaphorical terms. It is in REM sleep that all mammals are programmed in the womb with the templates of species-specific instinctive behaviours. If we are to make a connection between these innate genetic patterns and the myriad of patterns in our environment, we have to be able to read the analogy between them. This requires a subtle, metaphorical thinking process – which is exactly what we have.

Throughout the ages people have known this. Charles Spearman, in his major work, *The Abilities of Man*, identified two fundamental processes which he called 'education of correlates', or analogical thinking, and 'education of relationships', or abstract thinking.[19] The measurement of analogical thinking ability in some form is now a standard part of almost all intelligence tests (for example, "kitten is to cat as foal is to .....?"). We use analogical thinking to understand and make sense of our world. When we encounter a new experience, we try to find something from our past experience that is analogous to the new one.

Metaphor is an essential component of creativity. What appears on the canvas is the artist's metaphor for some aspect of reality. The novelist, in evoking situations and experiences and observing the relationship of this to that, creates circumstances the reader can empathise with and sometimes learn to view from a new perspective. Metaphor is just as key to scientific invention as it is to artistic creations (we have already seen the process at work when we looked at inventions and dreams). As physicist Dr Kevin Byron has elegantly described it, "Without the metaphors of nature and the culture in which he or she lives, the scientist would lack the imagination to create scientific hypotheses".[20] As he demonstrates in his monograph, *Inventions and Inventing: finding solutions to practical problems*, "Thinking by analogy is a powerful problem solving technique by which unknown solutions to problems may be imported from other knowledge domains where the solutions exist. The most abundant source of analogical solutions is to be found ready-made in the natural world."[21] He describes how Velcro was invented after George de Mestraal noticed that cockleburr seeds attach themselves with small hooks to the fur of passing animals, in this way ensuring spread. Alistair Pilkington invented float glass after he observed that small droplets of oil form a thin, flat film when floating on water. And the making of paper from wood pulp is credited to Rene-Antoine Reaumur's observations of wasps making pulp from tree bark to construct their nests.

Scientists also use metaphor when trying to make sense of their scientific observations. For example, the metaphor of 'waves' is used to make sense of one of the properties of light. And there was a time, not so long ago, when scientists thought the model of the 'atom' was analogous to planets orbiting the sun. A special ability of the creative scientist is to make sense of a hitherto puzzling phenomenon by seeing metaphorical relationships across a wider range of experiences – that is, to make analogies between experiences that most people would regard as disparate. Jerome Bruner gave us a beautiful example of how the great physicist Niels Bohr demonstrated just this ability.[22] Apparently Bohr told Bruner that his idea of complementarity in physics arose from his observation that it was impossible to consider his son simultaneously in the light of love and in the light of justice. He found himself in this predicament because his son had just confessed that he had stolen a pipe from a local shop. The predicament brought to his mind the trick figure of the vase and the faces often used to illustrate texts on the psychology of perception. (Depending on which aspect you view first, the white shape or the ground, you can see a vase or two faces but not both simultaneously, however quickly you flick between them.) He at once saw an analogy between this situation and the impossibility of thinking simultaneously about the position and velocity of a particle. This led him to formulate his complementary

principle which says that measuring the velocity of a particle precludes measurement of its position at the same time, and vice versa. In this example, we can see that an emotionally arousing introspection enabled Bohr to make sense of this paradox. He saw that the dilemma with his son – love versus justice – was an analogue of his physics dilemma. The analogue still left him with a dilemma because he couldn't see a resolution to it. He was then able, however, to shift the dilemma on to a different plane, which brought to mind the analogy of the vase/faces paradox. This analogy did suggest a resolution, in that it provided a sensory analogue, or model, to show that we can have mutually exclusive but complementary perceptions of the same object.

What Bohr did reflects a process that we all use to make our experience of the world comprehensible. Our brains are constantly searching for analogies between new experiences and the existing patterns of information stored in our instincts and memories. We also use metaphors or analogies to try to convey the subjective quality of our own experience to others. We use metaphorical thinking as a basic tool for understanding and flexibly communicating all the meanings we discern in our experiences. We *educate* through metaphor.

This extract from *A House is a House for Me*, a charming children's book by Mary Ann Hoberman, provides a perfect example of how a simple metaphor can identify meaningful related patterns across a wide domain of human experience.

> A glove is a house for a hand, a hand.
> A stocking's a house for a knee.
> A shoe or a boot is a house for a foot
> And a house is a house for me!
>
> A box is a house for a teabag.
> A teapot's a house for some tea.
> If you pour me a cup and I drink it all up,
> Then the teahouse will turn into me!

Cartons are houses for crackers.
Castles are houses for kings.
The more that I think about houses,
The more things are houses for things.

And if *you* get started in thinking,
I think you will find it is true
That the more that you think about houses for things,
The more things are houses to you.

Barrels are houses for pickles
And bottles are houses for jam.
A pot is a spot for potatoes.
A sandwich is home for some ham.

The cookie jar's home to the cookies.
The breadbox is home to the bread.
My coat is a house for my body.
My hat is a house for my head.

...

And once you get started in thinking this way,
It seems that whatever you see
Is either a house or it lives in a house,
And a house is a house for me!

A book is a house for a story.
A rose is a house for a smell.
My head is a house for a secret,
A secret I never will tell.

A flower's at home in a garden.
A donkey's at home in a stall.
Each creature that's known has a house of its own
And the earth is a house for us all.[23]

"May the force (me-ta-phors) be with you"

Metaphorical communication is an intrinsic part of the way we understand and share our experiences and the metaphorical expression we find in dreams is actually more widespread in waking life than is generally realised. A sudden burst of song, for example, is often a metaphorical expression of how a person is feeling about a certain matter. A woman who didn't want to get pregnant, though her husband wanted her to, was frequently heard to sing, "What do you get when you fall in love, you get enough germs to fill an ocean, that's what you get for your devotion". As a nurse, this woman was well aware that the average male ejaculation contains millions of sperm, i.e. "enough germs to fill an ocean".

A friend of Joe's was once worried about losing his job. When his wife read out a number of suitable job vacancies from the paper, he found himself spontaneously singing, "Through the eyes of love, you can see a thousand stars" and they both suddenly saw the metaphorical connection between stars and job opportunities and burst out laughing.

Another time, Joe had just congratulated a relative on finding a job. The relative, who had found himself in the position of needing to stay at Joe's home for an unspecified period, suddenly burst out singing, "What would you do if I sang out of tune? Would you stand up and walk out on me?" The song metaphorically expressed his worry about how Joe might react towards him if his new job didn't work out. On a somewhat similar theme, an Australian woman acquaintance, who had moved to England because of the demands of her husband's job, was often to be heard singing, "I like to be in America ...", the song from the musical *West Side Story*, in which the Puerto Rican girls point out all the good things about life in New York, while their Puerto Rican boyfriends counter by emphasising the downside. Another friend, who was known to be worrying about his business overdraft, was frequently heard singing, "I owe my soul to the company store".

Once you are sensitised to the prevalence of metaphor in everyday communications, you may be surprised to discover that an apparently irrelevant anecdote or joke that a friend or relative suddenly feels inspired to tell may actually be a metaphor for how they feel about an aspect of your relationship with them, which they are consciously reluctant to communicate. We often notice this happening.

Joe once conducted a weekend workshop at a small residential college. A couple he knew quite well were also spending the weekend at the college, at the invitation of one of the workshop participants who lived there. As the weekend progressed it was evident that the mutual friends felt somewhat excluded from what was going on, yet Joe and his student felt it was inappropriate to invite them to participate in the workshop. At the end of the weekend, as Joe was speaking to one of the couple, she suddenly felt impelled to tell the following anecdote:

A metaphorical rebuke

We recently visited some old friends, John and Julia Clare, whom we hadn't seen for some time. We hadn't been invited to see them; we just decided to call on the spur of the moment. But they were very cool. John said that he was expecting friends who had been invited. I didn't know why he should have treated us like this, especially when you consider how often he has visited us and brought his friends around to our house.

Joe's friend looked at him intently as she told him this and seemed satisfied to note his perplexity about why anyone should behave so unreasonably. Her anecdote is a perfect metaphorical description of her frustration at not being invited to participate in the weekend workshop. It may well be that this unconscious communication of her frustration at being excluded obviated the need for her to have a dream that night to deactivate the activated introspection underlying her frustration.

People also commonly use metaphors to explain something unknown to the listener. One evening we went out to dinner at a restaurant that neither of us had been to before, even though it was close to where Ivan lives. Whilst we waited for our table we were given the menu to study. Ostrich meat was one of the dishes on offer that night. Neither of us had ever eaten it and we were discussing whether we would try it. Another customer, who was also waiting for a table, interrupted and said, "I've tried it. It's a very interesting dish". When we asked him what it tasted like, after a moment's thought he said, "Well, it has the texture of liver and it tastes like venison *ought* to taste like." So we ordered the ostrich dish. Whilst eating it, we both agreed that the analogy he had given for what ostrich meat might taste like was accurate. It really did have a texture like liver and a more gamey flavour than one usually associates with venison.

Even young children have the ability to use metaphor and analogy creatively. At breakfast one morning, when Joe's youngest daughter, Liley-Beth, was four years old, she asked for a glass of milk. After a few sips she put the glass down and started to leave the table. Joe looked at her rather sternly, since she had the inclination, if allowed, to eat only a little at meal times and then declare an hour later that she was hungry again. Seeing his stern look she said calmly, "Daddy, doesn't Mammy sometimes make you a cup of tea, and you don't drink it all?" He had to admit to himself that this was something that happened not infrequently. (His wife, Liz, gives him a cup of tea and, after a couple of sips, he gets so engrossed in what he is reading or writing that he forgets all about the tea. Next thing he knows, it's cold!) In all honesty he could not deny that her analogy was accurate and consequently said nothing as she imperiously got down from the table with her milk unfinished.

Why we all love stories

It is often said that all the wisdom of the world that can be spoken is found in its stories.[24] And stories don't just provide nutrition for the mind; they are a medium through which knowledge is passed on to others, children and adults alike. This can only be because stories work in alignment with how the brain works. They, too, are about interconnected associations that involve fulfilling or frustrating anticipations through a metaphorical framework. And the best of them have the potential to reveal greater richness of meaning – whatever they are superficially addressing. As a Punjabi proverb has it: *The stories parents tell can make good children.*

The following version of an ancient story, about the perils of imagination, is from Georgia, but variations of it are found all over the world.

The poor man and the pot of butter

A poor man was going along the road when he found a pot of butter lying by the wayside. He picked it up, hung it on his stick, and carried it off over his shoulder. As he went on his way he said to himself:

"The butter left in my path for me to find is an indication that it is God's will that I should grow rich. I will go into the city and sell this butter for half a piece of silver; with that I will buy a cockerel and a dozen hens and take them home with me, rear them, sell some of the eggs, breed more chickens, fatten up some of them and sell those ones for a silver piece each. I will spend that money on piglets which I will fatten, and sell for two pieces each. Then I will buy steers and rear them for the plough, till the land – and maybe buy a bit of forest and a healthy young ox. I shall make my fortune."

Deep in exciting thoughts, he saw himself taking a large load of wood on a great ox-cart to the city to sell. When he came to the old humpbacked bridge on the outskirts of the city, so absorbed was he that he said to himself:

"The ox will not cross it – I must urge it on," and he shouted out loud: "Hey-up!" and waved his stick at the imaginary ox.

At this the pot of butter was tossed in the air. It fell on the bridge and broke, and the butter was spilled and spoiled in the dirt. All the riches of his daydream van-

> *ished in a single moment and, in destroying that which might have led to success by the thought of that success itself, he was as cast down as he had previously been excited.*[25]

This story, in all its myriad forms, has survived the rise and fall of empires, changes of language, and the perishing of great buildings, works of art and civil engineering. It is also the origin of what is perhaps the world's best-known proverb: *Don't count your chickens before they are hatched.*

Any good story can broaden our perspective like this, giving us new ways of understanding our life situations. And this is the remarkable thing – the reason that stories are so satisfying and illuminating is that they tap into the same process that nature uses for the transmission of knowledge. As we explained earlier, nature, through the REM state, lays down a pattern but it is only a *partial* pattern, one that hasn't yet found a corresponding 'story' in the environment to complete it. What we do to make sense of the culture we are born into, for example, is use nature's incomplete patterns inside us, such as the drive to learn language, and find something to match to in the environment to complete them. (We contend, in fact, that all living things, and all inanimate matter, require this to occur – but that's another story.[26])

Real education is always about enriching existing patterns of knowledge. And that is why all good teachers are natural storytellers, using the imagery and language of metaphor to convey new meanings. The use of metaphor in teaching stories was brought to perfection as a communication instrument many thousands of years ago.[27,28] As part of ancient teaching traditions, such stories are highly nutritious, containing as they do sophisticated, multiple levels of meaning. They were deliberately designed and used to bypass the limitations of the conditioned mind in order to allow a more objective assessment of the message contained in the story. The information in these stories acts like a blueprint stored in the mind, until the appropriate moment when it enables the recognition of a pattern in events which hadn't been identified before, thus enriching the understanding of those events.

The following well-known Zen teaching story has several layers of meaning in it and works in the way described above.

The seeker of wisdom

A man spent many years travelling the world in search of wisdom. He visited numerous famous teachers, sat at the feet of gurus with a reputation for sanctity, listened to the discourses of philosophers and heard the preaching of religious luminaries from many traditions. One fine day he eventually arrived at the little house of an ancient Zen master who, he was assured by all and sundry, could help him in his quest. The master invited him in and the seeker immediately began to tell of his travels and adventures – whom he had met, what they had said, and what he thought he had learned from them, and so on. After a while, the master asked him if he would partake of some tea. The traveller nodded and carried on talking. When it came time to pour the tea, the master placed a cup in front of his earnest guest, who was still speaking, tilted the teapot, and slowly poured out the golden liquid. He poured until the cup overflowed ... and still he poured. Eventually the self absorbed traveller noticed and, thinking the master was absent minded or senile, burst out saying, "Stop! The vessel is too full. It's overflowing."

"Exactly my point," said the old man, who stood up and vanished out of the seeker's life.

This story, on one level, can amuse, but it also serves to pass on several vital teachings, including the fact that we have to make an *appropriate* effort if we are not to waste our time on this planet. It does so in a way that the ordinary intellect, using language, could never do.

All new learning occurs through pattern matching. The brain is, perhaps above all, a metaphorical pattern-matching organ. All the new knowledge it adds to its existing innate knowledge derives from the process of connecting up an existing pattern of understanding to a richer one, one which reveals more to us. This is the moment when 'the penny drops' and is why stories and jokes are so intrinsically satisfying and universally popular. They focus our attention and set up a complex pattern of anticipation which then needs to be completed. (When you laugh before a joke is finished it is because you have already seen how the pattern is most likely to be completed.)

The increasing use of metaphor and story in modern psychotherapy and counselling owes much to the work of Dr Milton H. Erickson, whose brilliant psychotherapeutic work developed outside the psychoanalytical orthodoxy that so dominated the field from the 1920s to the 1960s. He is now widely acknowledged as the most effective psychotherapist of his generation. He was a supreme storyteller and frequently showed that appropriate metaphors can bypass the limitations of conscious mental sets and mobilise the resources of the unconscious mind for therapeutic change.[29,30] Just as all good teachers are great storytellers, so are all good psychotherapists, because stories that are appropriate will contain patterns of metaphorical significance that can reframe events in a person's life and place them in a larger, more helpful framework.

As already mentioned, scientific discoveries are also dependent on this process – finding a new metaphor, a new pattern that throws light on a phenomenon that hitherto has been a mystery. In mathematics, for instance, a set of symbols contains a 'story' or a 'rule' that incorporates a 'pattern'. Mathematicians can, for example, examine the pattern of an equation about the nature of matter and argue back, or think themselves back, to new properties that that matter itself might contain. As Philip Mirowski said, "Mathematics does not come to us written indelibly on 'Nature's Tablets', but rather is the product of a controlled search governed by metaphorical considerations ..."[31] It seems that all knowledge is both discovered and transmitted through this powerful metaphorical pattern-matching process.

So our brains are programmed by nature to take part in an endless quest for metaphor. Recognising how something is 'like' something else is how the brain, moment by moment, tries to predict its best course of action. We can now begin to see why our amazing faculty to develop knowledge (even as far as penetrating the mysteries of the formation of the Universe and grasping its ultimate meaning) is on a continuum with both the metaphorical nature of programming instincts in the REM state and with dreaming.

The limits of metaphor

Just as we have the potential to identify *appropriate* metaphors we can also, of course, make *inappropriate* matches between two patterns. In fact, the expectation fulfilment theory implies that this will inevitably happen on some occasions, as the capacity for analogy or metaphor derives from the programming of instinctive behaviour. Instinctive templates only partly specify the pattern to be identified in order to allow an animal maximum flexibility in its response to the particular environment it finds itself in. It is this fact that makes mismatches unavoidable sometimes.

There is, for instance, a fish called the cleaner fish, which has a symbiotic relationship with the grouper fish: it picks bits out of its mouth. The cleaner fish does a kind of dance that puts the grouper fish into a trance. In this state, it opens its mouth and remains paralysed for the length of the trance. The cleaner fish then gets on with its business. Unfortunately for the grouper fish, there is another type of fish, called the blenny fish, which has cottoned on to the potential benefits for itself of such a performance. It copies the dance of the cleaner fish; the grouper fish responds as it would to the cleaner fish, and opens its mouth in trance. The blenny fish then proceeds to take a bite out of it.

You may recall seeing pictures of the famous ethologist Konrad Lorenz being followed by a family of young goslings. Goslings are programmed whilst still in the egg to become attached to the first large moving object they encounter after hatching. The instinct programme rule must be something like, "When you get out of your shell the first large moving object you see will be the creature that is going to look after you". Now, if that large moving object is not the goslings' mother but Lorenz in his wellington boots, and they bond with him and his boots (as actually happened), then clearly the wrong pattern has been matched to. The goslings followed Lorenz persistently; they became distressed when he left them and ran to him for support when they felt frightened – a perversion of what nature intended, as goslings are obviously not supposed to bond with boots. Sexual perversions in humans come about in the same way, when sexual arousal at a formative moment inappropriately connects with, and becomes perpetually associated with, an 'unnatural' stimulus. Indeed, a great many mental problems may be caused by this emotional process.

The same process that stops the goslings from *looking* any further for their mother, can also stop humans from *thinking* any further. This is because, once a pattern has been matched, even if the match is not a particularly good one, the brain is satisfied and stops searching. (Just as with dreaming, as long as a match is made, it will switch off the search and dearouse the original pattern.) This is why so many children tend to automatically hold the same cultural, political or religious allegiances as their parents. It is also why many people can stay loyal to products, foods or places rather than try something new or different. A poor pattern match (metaphor) can stop thought. As an illustration of this, think of the sentimental idea that a kind person working in a social setting is like a 'good shepherd'. Most people don't make the connection that a shepherd is the agent of the butcher and that a good shepherd makes the sheep ready for slaughter! Or think of the metaphors of 'inner child' and 'Oedipus complex', which some psychotherapists use as if they are concrete reality, with the serious consequence of being harmful to patients.[32] And how about 'collateral damage', a term that politicians euphemistically use as a metaphor in an attempt to head off criticism and stop people questioning their tyrannical policies when they initiate bombing raids on other countries and kill innocent civilians.

Unless we are aware of the limits of metaphor and the possibility of mismatches occurring, we are at best vulnerable to making stupid mistakes and, at worst, to being conditioned with deeply harmful ideas and behaviours. People can be just as dogmatic, cruel and blinded by prejudice from an inappropriate metaphorical pattern match as by wrong factual information.

Metaphors should not be 'over interpreted' either. They are a delicate network of allusions to similarities that lose their ability to function holistically if pursued too far. If you explain a joke or story it flops. Metaphors are also only useful if appropriate for the audience they are told to. One about milk and cows is useless if told to someone who doesn't know that milk comes from cows. (A recent survey showed that large numbers of young people are unaware of the connection and are puzzled by pictures of cows on milk cartons.)

The brain's REM state, then, is a crucial and highly successful mechanism for the transmission of innate knowledge, amassed by the genome of our species over millions of years, and for gathering and transmitting newly acquired (that is, in one's own lifetime), culturally generated knowledge. However, there are great risks attendant on having access to this most powerful of all tools, because it means we have access to both our own and others people's programming states. As well as being taught or programmed with socially and personally useful ideas and behaviours, we can just as easily be programmed with destructive ideas and thus create a sick society. If we misuse our daydream faculty – our imagination – we can condition ourselves into horrendous, neurotic reaction patterns. As we shall shortly see, the misuse of our imagination is fundamentally involved in the generation of clinical depression, anxiety disorders, anger problems, psychosis, greed, cruelty and addiction.

The following everyday example from Joe's own personal experience shows how easily the metaphorical process can lead to mental problems. It was the sort of situation anyone could find themselves in. One day his family television set broke down. It was a large and heavy TV and, together, he and his wife carried it through the main square of the town where they live to the repair shop. Suddenly Joe felt acutely self-conscious. He felt as though people knew something intimate and embarrassing about his domestic situation. Driving back home after leaving the TV at the repair shop, he found himself making many negative comments about life such as, "Maybe it would have been better not to have been born; then one wouldn't have to go through all this hassle". He was surprised at himself for saying this.

A little while later, sitting at home, his mood slumped even further. This had nothing directly to do with the absence of the television since he was looking forward to having a break from it. But the feeling of depression was real and strong and he wondered where it was coming from. He reflected that his circumstances were as good as they had ever been, so he deliberately focused his mind on the *feeling* of depression for a moment, to see what thoughts or memories might be recalled.

He found himself back in a childhood memory from when he was 14 years old and escorting his mother through the local town to the doctor's surgery. He had gone with his mother because she needed assistance in keeping her balance. She was also in a disturbing and uncharacteristically flippant mood. What is more, she had been in this childish, laughing and girlish frame of mind ever since taking medicine prescribed by the doctor to relieve her menopausal symptoms. When Joe and his mother got to the surgery, the doctor said, "Mrs Griffin, you're drunk!" It turned out that she, who rarely drank alcohol, had reacted to the alcohol content of the medicine by becoming highly inebriated.

As Joe held her arm and walked her home down the High Street, he felt acutely self-conscious. It seemed as though his very survival depended on none of his school mates seeing him in this situation. As a 14-year-old boy, it would be bad enough to be seen holding your mother's arm going down the street, but for her to be giggling and staggering about drunk as well would have meant endless ridicule. He was also aware that he was totally without control over the outcome; he couldn't abandon his mother in this state and yet he also had to walk past the top of the very road that led to his school.

All young men and women are, of course, acutely aware of the need for peer approval and compete for individual status in their peer group. This need is programmed into us from ancient, prehuman times. In the wild, animals that are rejected by their social group are highly vulnerable because, without the protection of the herd or pack, they can easily be picked off by predators – their immediate survival is at stake. (This is the origin of why the pain of rejection is so hard to bear.) Therefore we could certainly expect an instinctive sensitivity on the part of a young man to the danger of peer group rejection. During our teenage years we are driven by an innate force to maintain peer group acceptability whilst, at the same time, struggling to find our individual identity. So the feelings Joe had then, as he escorted his 'inebriated' mother to the doctor, were entirely natural. But it was not at all appropriate to have these feelings as he accompanied his wife with a broken-down television set, up a side street from the main square of a different town, more than 30 years later. We can see this situation as a mismatch of patterns arising from the fact that the patterns have some elements in common. As we have seen when considering programmed instincts, the brain is a metaphorical pattern-matching organ and there was a metaphorical connection between the events, but struggling down a street with a broken television set is not the same as struggling down a street with a mother who has a problem, and a middle-aged man is not the same as a young man. As with the case of Lorenz's goslings, the metaphorical pattern match was not accurate enough.

Nevertheless the consequences of this mismatch were a sudden feeling of hopelessness, which released a cascade of chemical compounds into the system that prolonged the depressed state. Having identified the mismatch of patterns and reflected on how well his life was actually going, it still took Joe about an hour to shake off the depressed mood. What if he had continued to think negative thoughts and prolonged that misery? And what if he had then gone to a psychotherapist who was inclined to explore 'emotional issues' from his past while in that state of mind? He quite possibly would have begun to look for everything that had ever gone wrong in his life. Clearly such a process would reinforce the depressive state rather than extinguish it. Which is why research shows that the type of psychotherapy and counselling that encourage introspection about emotionally arousing past events in people's lives tends to deepen depression and prolong anxieties.[33,34]

To take another example, suppose a woman had been sexually abused when she was young and now finds she is having difficulty in a new relationship, even though she loves her partner. What often happens in such cases is that she is wrongly identifying sex with her current partner as being similar to the experience of the sexual abuse she was subjected to as a child. Consciously she knows the two situations are different, but her metaphorical mind has made the connection, tagged it with strong emotions, and is not letting it go. In this situation a therapist with a psychodynamic perspective might encourage the woman to get in touch with her past feelings resulting from the abuse and to explore her childhood memories of it in greater detail. The danger here is that such an exploration gives the 'abuse' template even greater prominence and exacerbates the problem even further.

A therapist who understands this, by contrast, would help the client to distance herself from the traumatic memories, place a boundary around them and thus limit the influence of the past abuse on her life today. (One helpful way to do this would be to ask her to list a hundred ways her new relationship differed from the abusive relationship. This exercise would help her to uncouple the different, wrongly matched, patterns and enable her to relax and enjoy her new partner.)

The failure to recognise that emotional problems often occur because of such faulty mismatches – the perception of *false* analogies between past and present experiences (which are often easily corrected) – has held back the development of effective psychotherapy for decades. Conversely, the ability to perceive *useful* analogies and metaphors can have a very positive effect on psychotherapy. This has always been appreciated by the traditional psychologies of the east and by some western psychotherapists.

Our conscious mind's preferred mode of action is the slow one of logical thought, whilst our unconscious mind's preferred mode is metaphor – or 'association of ideas', as it is sometimes called – the fast way. If we are to be effective human beings, both these faculties have to work well together. We believe this needs to be better recognised in education and social work as well as in psychology and psychotherapy. This is what we are going to look at next.

9

PRACTICAL APPLICATIONS OF THE EXPECTATION FULFILMENT THEORY

"Learn how much knowledge is needed before we can see how ignorant we are."

PROVERB

The history of scientific discovery tells us that, whenever an accurate idea about the way things work in the natural world is discovered, sooner or later it has practical applications. For example, for a number of years after the laser beam was first discovered, it was thought of as nothing more than an amusing curiosity. Then people began to realise what else lasers could do. Now they are used in a wide variety of ways, from basic scientific research to medical procedures that improve the quality of life of countless patients (through minimally invasive surgery), and in many industrial processes, including welding and high-volume manufacture of microelectronic products. This pattern is echoed in the history of countless other scientific discoveries – it often takes a while for new findings to be appreciated, accepted and used.[1]

Our colleague, Pat Williams, noted this when writing about a well-known discovery that saved millions of lives – eventually:

> Remember what revolutionised the treatment of puerperal fever, which in the nineteenth century produced mortality rates as high as 30 per cent? The Hungarian obstetrician Ignaz Semmelweis (1818-1865) noticed something his colleagues couldn't see, and would rage around the wards shouting at them: 'Wash your hands! Wash them when you come into the ward! Wash them in between examining each patient. Wash your hands!'

> All his colleagues ignored what Semmelweis saw because they had prejudged the situation, and knew the disease was unpreventable. So they sneered at and patronised him, embarrassed by his antics, comfortably wrapped in their certainty that the cure for deaths from 'childbed fever', if it ever could be found, would be more interestingly complex, more sophisticated, than ... mere hand washing.
>
> But we know now who was right.
>
> Semmelweis influenced the development of the knowledge and control of infection, and thus the history of antisepsis, because his mind was not preoccupied with the idea that the illness could not be cured, did not prejudge it, and so had no pre-existing requirement for 'complicated' treatment. He could see what would actually be 'effective' treatment.[2]

It follows, therefore, that, if Joe's key dream experiment, and the findings that arose from it, really are a genuine breakthrough, we should see his theory producing significant practical applications in the world, just as Semmelweis's eventually did. Equally, of course, had Freud's and Jung's theories, and the other dream theories we have mentioned, been correct then we ought by now to have seen them having practical applications in the real world. But this has not happened. In fact, it is now well established that attempting to work with depressed and anxious people using Freudian and Jungian ideas tends to delay recovery from psychological and emotional problems by, in some cases, decades.[3] So, is Joe's expectation fulfilment theory of dreaming any different in this regard? Has it shone the light of explanation on other scientific enquiries, and made a useful difference to the lives of people in the real world?

The answer is a resounding "yes" – particularly in the fields of medicine, psychology, psychotherapy and education.

To become accepted, any theory must be testable to see if it is plausible and in tune with reality, which is why scientists work to falsify theories. This was eloquently summed up by the physicist Richard

Feynman when he said, "To develop working ideas efficiently, I try to fail as fast as I can."

In the case of the expectation fulfilment theory of dreaming, for example, a useful test would be to see if it had implications for how depression occurs. The theory would predict that depressed people have proportionately more prolonged, or intensive, periods of REM sleep (because they tend to worry and catastrophise more than non-depressed people and therefore have far more emotionally-arousing, unacted out thoughts). As described in Chapter 4, the amount of REM sleep depressed people experience was investigated in sleep laboratories and, indeed, the results were as the expectation fulfilment theory predicts. Depressed people do have, proportionately, more prolonged and/or intensive REM sleep.

The theory would also predict that the dreams that depressed people have are not happy ones. Dreams do not just derive from *negative* unexpressed emotional arousal. People who are not depressed will experience many *positive* anticipations during their day which will, naturally, generate positive emotions. Happy, upbeat, unfulfilled expectations are the source of enjoyable dreams, as when unexpressed sexual attraction results in a sexual dream, or when imaginings about some eagerly awaited forthcoming trip generate excitement, and the pleasant journey is metaphorically completed in a dream. But if depressed people were found to have lots of happy dreams, that would disprove the expectation fulfilment theory, as it predicts that the excess REM sleep time is needed in order to discharge the arousal caused by overly high amounts of negative introspection.

And, indeed, it has been shown in sleep laboratory studies that, when depressed people are woken during REM sleep and asked what they were dreaming about, they typically describe unhappy, worrying dream content, often accompanied by anxiety nightmares.

The verification of both of these facts – depressed people's excessive REM sleep and the unhappy content of their dreams – provides substantial support for the theory. It would have been equally easy to prove the theory false (which, as said, is how every good scientific theory has to be tested), purely by a finding that depressed people have normal amounts of REM sleep and happy dreams. But this is absolutely not the case. So far, each time it has been put to the test, the theory has been verified. No one, to our knowledge, has managed to disprove it since it was first presented. Another hallmark of a good theory is that it serves to make sense of disparate, existing data and this seems to be the case with the expectation fulfilment theory too: it has brought together a large number of anomalous findings, and makes sense of a much wider range of data than any dream theory put forward previously.

Dreams and clinical depression

It is not surprising, then, that the practical application of Joe's dream findings that has received most attention so far is more effective treatment for clinical depression. Since 1999, thousands of professionals from many countries have heard us talk about this specific topic at seminars and workshops held in the United Kingdom and Ireland.[4] This is because Joe's work had answered a question that had puzzled scientists for decades; why do depressed people have proportionally more REM sleep and more intensive REM sleep than non-depressed people. Our book, *Human Givens: the new approach to emotional health and clear thinking* (first published in 2003 and enlarged and updated in a revised edition published in 2013) clearly set out and expanded upon the ideas arising from this work. It sold, mainly by word of mouth, 3,000 copies in ten weeks which was unusual for a popular science hardback that hadn't even, at that time, reached the bookshops. It had to be quickly reprinted to keep up with demand. The book contains a number of new organising ideas of relevance to psychology, psychotherapy, social work and education, as well as original thinking about the way that consciousness might have evolved, but it was the single chapter on depression that got the media excited. *New Scientist* devoted four pages to an interview with Joe about it in their series, 'Meet the people shaping the future of science',[5] and major articles appeared in *The Times*[6] and the *Irish Times*.[7] The BBC also featured the subject in several programmes, including Radio 4's 'All in the Mind'.

So why the interest? Clearly, one reason is that clinical depression, as almost everybody knows, is massively on the increase in the West. Nearly every family is affected, directly or indirectly, by members whose mood has sunk so low that all meaning and pleasure has drained from their lives. Figures released by the UK government, for example, suggest that 50 per cent of the female population and 25 per cent of males will, at some point in their lives, experience a serious bout of depression.[8] Furthermore, epidemiological studies have shown that the rate of increase in depression has grown in all age groups, but fastest in young people.[9] And suicide rates have increased in all countries, especially among the young.[10] The population born since 1945 has seen depression increase by a factor of nearly ten since their grandparents' time.[11] And even this rate is accelerating. Prescriptions for antidepressants rose by more than 40 per cent between 2006 and 2010, according to figures obtained in 2011 from NHS Prescription Services under the Freedom of Information Act (although some of the rise may be accounted for by increased awareness of the condition).

As countries become westernised, their rates of depression (or emotionalised neurasthenia, as the Chinese like to call it, because they focus more on the physical symptoms of tiredness, etc.), increase even more. The World Health Organization (WHO), in its report *The Global Burden of Disease*, estimates that, by the year 2020, depression will be second only to ischaemic heart disease as a leading cause of injury and disease worldwide.[12] All this is very odd because, on the face of it, we have never had it so good materially – as anyone over the age of 60 will confirm. In Britain, for example, there has been no threat of invasion since the 1940s; we have universal education, health services and housing for all; and, on display in every high street, is a cornucopia of luxuries to indulge every whim (unimaginable to most people 50 years ago) – cars, affordable fashionable clothes, an unbelievable variety of foodstuffs from all over the world, cheap foreign travel, books, TV and computers offering ubiquitous entertainment in every home and smart phones offering instant access to information to the internet, wherever you happen to be. And yet the rate of depression, and most other forms of mental disorder, continues to rise. What can possibly lie behind this?

We suggest that the answer is to do with the misuse of imagination, our most recently evolved mental faculty. Consideration of known facts about depression in the light of the theory we have set out here, and the ease with which, using human givens therapy, we can usually lift depressed people out of their low mood and quickly re-engage them with life, shows that this is highly likely to be so.

As we've said, it has been known for a long time, since the 1960s, that depressed people have pathological amounts of REM sleep relative to non-REM sleep.[13,14,15] In order to understand the significance of this, we need to remind ourselves of what the last 60 years of sleep research has discovered about normal sleep patterns.

The electrical activity in the brain that we call brainwaves can be measured by electrodes. This enabled scientists to identify different stages of sleep. They found that we usually pass through five phases known as Stages 1, 2, 3, 4, and REM. These stages progress in a cycle from Stage 1 through to REM, then start over again. In normal health, we spend almost 50 per cent of our total sleep time in Stage 2 sleep, about 20 percent in REM sleep, and the remaining 30 per cent in the other stages. (Babies, by contrast, spend about half of their sleep time in REM sleep because of the programming of instinctive behaviours, which is still taking place.)

In Stage 1 sleep, which is light, we drift in and out of sleep and can be awakened easily. Our eyes move slowly and muscle activity slows. People woken up from Stage 1 sleep often remember fragmented visual images. Many also experience sudden muscle contractions called hypnic myoclonia, often preceded by a sensation of starting to fall. These 'sudden jerk' movements, caused by the firing of the orientation response, are similar to the 'jumps' we make when startled. When we enter Stage 2 sleep, our eye movements stop and our brain waves become slower, interspersed with occasional bursts of rapid waves called sleep spindles. In Stage 3, extremely slow brain waves called delta waves begin to appear, interspersed with smaller, faster waves. By Stage 4, the brain produces delta waves almost exclusively. It is very difficult to wake someone during Stages 3 and 4, which is why this period is often called deep sleep. There is no eye movement or muscle activity. People woken up during deep sleep do not adjust to their environment immediately and often feel groggy and disoriented for several minutes. ("Where am I?") There is also considerable evidence that it is during these slow wave stages of sleep that glucose is restored to the glial cells, replenishing the brain with energy.[16] It is also during this stage that the body is believed to carry out most of its physical repair work. The growth hormone is secreted which, in children, encourages growth and, in adults, assists with the healing of muscles and repair of general wear and tear in tissues. In contrast, in the final stage of sleep, REM sleep, large amounts of the brain's energy reserves are expended on dreaming.

When we switch into REM sleep, breathing becomes more rapid, irregular, and shallow; the eyes jerk rapidly in various directions, and limb muscles become temporarily paralysed. Heart rate increases, blood pressure rises, and genital engorgement occurs. And, as we know, when people are woken up during REM sleep, they often describe dreams.

The first REM sleep period usually occurs about seventy to ninety minutes after we fall asleep. A complete sleep cycle takes on average ninety to a hundred and ten minutes to complete. The first sleep cycles each night contain relatively short REM periods and long periods of deep sleep. As the night progresses, the REM sleep periods increase in length while deep sleep decreases. By morning, we spend nearly all of our sleep time in Stages 1, 2, and REM.

But the pattern of sleeping described above is not what was found when depressed people were studied in sleep laboratories. Rather than ninety minutes elapsing before entering into the REM state and dreaming for a short while, depressed people usually fall into REM sleep quickly, a trait known as 'short REM latency'. Their dreams are also more intense. And as the night progresses things do not change significantly. The unfortunate depressed person continues to spend a far higher proportion of sleep time in REM sleep than the non-depressed person.[17] As a consequence, the deepest forms of recuperative slow-wave sleep are dramatically curtailed. This results in a weakening of their immune system, which leads to a propensity for minor illnesses, colds etc.

So there is a double-whammy, so to speak, for people who are depressed. Firstly, the energy levels in their brain are not being adequately maintained because of insufficient slow-wave sleep and, secondly, they are further exhausting their brains through excessive amounts of arousal discharge through worry-induced dream pressure. So it is not surprising that depressed people almost universally describe the experience of waking up early, feeling miserable, drained and exhausted. If people have pathological amounts of REM sleep, and bring their arousal level down too far, they will inevitably wake up feeling exhausted, as though, to use a metaphor, their battery is flat.

The significance of the connection between depression and disproportionate REM sleep has lain unrecognised in the psychiatric literature for nearly forty years. This was because the real function of dreaming was not understood. We believe we have made the case that the missing piece of the jigsaw came to light as a result of the findings of Joe's key experiment.

The cycle of depression

These insights mean we can now describe the cycle of depression – a description which has been recognised and confirmed by thousands of people from their personal experience. This is how it goes:

- Something happens in a person's life that impacts on their ability to get their basic needs met, needs that we are all given at birth by nature. Emotional and physical needs are what we call 'human givens', because we all inherited them in our genes. Physical needs include a wholesome diet, exercise, good air to breathe and clean water to drink. Emotional needs include the need for security, to feel one has some control over events, to give and receive attention, to be emotionally connected to others, to have intimate closeness to at least one other person, to have status within one's family and peer groups, to feel autonomous and competent, and to be 'stretched' in what we do (because being physically and/or mentally stretched is what gives meaning and purpose to our lives – a healthy brain is a busy problem-solving brain).

- The person, particularly if they are of a pessimistic disposition, begins to introspect (worry) about their difficulties, misusing their imagination by allowing emotionally arousing thoughts and fantasies to go round and round in their heads all day long, making them feel hopelessly stuck in their situation. The imagination is, of course, also a human given. But it is not a need, it is a resource, built in to help us get our needs met more effectively. When people worry excessively, they are misusing this powerful resource.
- As the emotional arousal becomes more extreme, it simplifies their thinking style until they can see their situation only in black or white, all or nothing, catastrophic terms. (This occurs because emotional arousal repeatedly switches on the 'fight or flight' response, one of the most ancient survival mechanisms to evolve in living creatures. Its effect is to make us angry or anxious, originally so that we would be ready to fight or flee, if the situation demanded it. In the interests of survival, this response retains the power to inhibit activity in the neocortex and override more subtle forms of thought so that, when under threat, we can act instantly to 'save' ourselves.)
- Depression is a strong emotion. Like all strong emotions, it focuses and locks attention. The excessive amount of emotional worrying that depressed people do puts enormous pressure on the brain's dreaming process, as it attempts to deal with the overload of autonomic arousal that this causes. This distorts the REM sleep system, causing excessive discharge of the autonomic arousal which leads, in turn, to physical exhaustion on waking and a loss of motivation to do anything. This, in turn, creates further reason to worry, because the individual knows that it is not normal to feel this way, and so they start to think that there is something fundamentally flawed and freakish about themselves. So the cycle continues until life events or the brain's own process of home-

ostasis brings them out of their depressed mindset. (Depression is generally a self-limiting phenomenon. Left untreated to run its course, in most people it will eventually peter out within four to ten months. However, between a tenth and a fifth of those given a diagnosis of depression go on to develop a chronic condition.[18])

The loss of motivation is interesting. As we have seen, it would appear that the PGO spikes that fire off continually during dreaming are part of the same alerting system that fires and focuses our attention when we are awake – our orientation response.[19,20] Without an ability to focus attention it is difficult to do anything. Even getting up in the morning, washing, and making breakfast become burdensome. Without focus we cannot act. Without action there can be no joy, meaning or purpose in life. And, indeed, depressed people commonly talk of there being no point to anything, and say that their life, work and relationships are meaningless – a state of mind that can easily lead to thoughts of suicide.

Of course, anyone who has ever tried to help a depressed person, whether formally or informally, knows that they spend hours every day engaged in an excessive amount of emotionally arousing thinking. Consequently, with this new understanding of dreams that we have put forward, we would expect them to have pathological levels of dream sleep and to wake exhausted. We would also expect that, if we brought depressed people into a sleep laboratory and woke them up every time they went into dream sleep, they would be less depressed the following day – which is exactly what research has shown happens.[21] Indeed, it is now a regular treatment in some German hospitals, when all else fails, to instigate a REM sleep deprivation programme to help shift people out of depressed states.[22]

Another interesting corollary of all this is that antidepressant medication, when it is effective, is known to normalise the amount of REM sleep that a person has.[23] This is the prime chemical mechanism by which antidepressants work, when they work. A question that we are often asked is whether, given that dream sleep is performing a useful function, using antidepressants to cut back on dream sleep is not harmful in some way? The answer to this is that, although a normal proportionate amount of REM sleep is hugely restorative to the human mind and brain, too much is damaging – just as two aspirins can take away a headache but a whole bottle can kill. Some of the older antidepressants eliminate REM sleep in its entirety, without apparently causing undue side effects as a direct result. This, we suggest, is because such antidepressants work by preventing emotional arousal, thus obviating the need for REM sleep. However, many patients on such medication report feeling like zombies, unable to make an emotional response to life at all. Clearly this is not a happy solution.

Antidepressants are an effective treatment for about a third of the people who take them and have some benefits for a further third. But there are considerable risks associated with taking them, some of which have been known for a long time.* More recently, new concerns have come to light. In a survey of 1,829 people in New Zealand who had been prescribed anti-depressants in the previous five years, more than half of people aged 18 to 25 reported suicidal feelings and, in the total sample, 62 per cent of people reported sexual difficulties and 60 per cent felt emotionally numb. Other effects included "feeling not like myself" (52 per cent of respondents), reduction in positive feelings (42 per cent), and caring less about others (39 per cent). As the researchers pointed out, such reactions appear to be alarmingly common and are extremely concerning.[24] For many people, the side effects are more unpleasant than the depression, so they stop taking the drugs. The drugs don't work at all for the remaining third

* Antidepressants, like the 'Prozac group' of modern SSRIs (selective serotonin reuptake inhibitors) are very powerful drugs that can cause dizziness, nausea, anxiety, facial and whole body tics, muscle spasms, parkinsonism (symptoms similar to those seen in Parkinson's disease), brain damage, sexual dysfunction, memory loss, neurotoxicity and debilitating withdrawal symptoms that are often mistaken for the original symptoms returning. There is also a direct link between suicide and violent behaviour in some people who have taken them.[25] They should not be given to children as children's brains are still forming – human frontal lobe connections are not fully in place until a person is about 20 years old.[26] Because of common toxic side effects, they should not be prescribed to older people who have any sign of natural brain deterioration.

for whom they are prescribed.

Despite enormous amounts of money poured into research by drug companies, there is no widely accepted agreement for why antidepressants work, although the placebo effect is known to play a part.[27] Research by drug companies (not highly publicised) has shown that there is virtually no difference in outcome between antidepressant treatment and treatment by placebos.[28] Why should a placebo, which has no active chemical component, reduce depression as effectively as an antidepressant? This is another mystery that has baffled psychiatry, but, once it is understood that dream sleep is instigated by emotionally arousing daytime thinking, the answer should become clear.

A placebo may not have a chemically active ingredient, but it does have a *psychologically* active ingredient: a well-delivered placebo generates hope. And hope will focus attention elsewhere. With realistic hope in place, individuals are less likely to misuse imagination and catastrophise. They can begin to entertain positive expectations of the future and thus reduce their excessive amounts of REM sleep. And when they find themselves waking up more refreshed each morning, they know the depression is lifting, which in turn engenders more hope.

From the practical psychotherapeutic point of view this has massive implications. Encouraging people to do less negative worrying today means that they will have less REM sleep tonight and will wake up tomorrow with a more refreshed, energised brain because today's worry brings on tomorrow's depression. By concentrating on means of lowering the depressed person's emotional arousal, stopping them misusing their imagination (worrying), helping them to focus outwards (to get their needs met) and to accommodate themselves to insoluble problems or to find a practical solution to soluble ones – the problems that caused them to worry in the first place – and then using guided imagery, rehearsing success in all these areas, we know that we can have an impact upon the depression within 24 hours. We demonstrate this regularly and have often had severely depressed people completely out of their depression in two sessions of human givens counselling. (Many such sessions have been filmed for teaching purposes, to take students step-by-step through the skills involved when working with a seriously depressed patient.)

People often ask, if antidepressants reduce or cut out dreaming, does that lead to a harmful level of reduction of REM sleep? As we have mentioned, however, what actually happens is that antidepressants don't just reduce REM sleep, they also reduce the *need* for it because they prevent the patient getting emotionally stressed when they are awake; consequently the reduction in REM sleep is not harmful. It returns to normal levels.

Sometimes people who have recovered from depression, and who had been told about the connection between depression and dreaming, are puzzled by the fact that they seem to be dreaming more after emerging from depression than when they were depressed. The reason for this is that, when we come out of depression, the dream cycle returns to normal, with most dreaming occurring towards morning, when it is more likely to be recalled.

Over the past seventeen years, we and our colleagues, and the thousands of people we have now taught, have applied this human givens perspective on dreaming and depression in the therapy and counselling they offer. Between us all, we have helped tens of thousands of depressed people to lift themselves out of their low mood in a fraction of the time that either antidepressants or more conventional psychotherapies take – two thirds quicker. Human givens therapy for depression is in marked contrast to some of the more conventional psychotherapy models, which frequently encourage depressed people to ruminate on what has gone wrong in their lives and to relive trauma from the past. In one meta-analysis of hundreds of studies, for example, it was found that depressed people given psychodynamic, 'insight' orientated therapy (such as psychoanalysis and gestalt therapy) had a poorer outcome than control groups of depressed people who received no treatment of any kind.[29] In other words, psychodynamic forms of therapy can make depression worse. And since, as we have seen, emotionally arousing negative rumination is the very mechanism that drives up the frequency and duration of REM sleep, which in turn leads to brain exhaustion and depression, this would be predicted by the expectation fulfilment theory.

Therapists who practise psychodynamic therapy often justify their methods and poor results by saying that, to be effective, therapy has to be painful – 'no pain, no gain' – as if the pain suffered by a depressed or anxious person was not already bad enough. This is clearly misguided and unintentionally cruel, but it is said so often and with such confidence by some sections of the intelligentsia that the idea has permeated our culture – it is what many people believe therapy is about. So, many depressed patients go along with it, denying the evidence of their own experience – that very often they feel worse and worse and worse, and never better at all.

In fact, it is so well established that the wrong type of counselling can prolong clinical depression (an important implication of the research we are reporting here) that we cannot urge people too much to be cautious, very cautious, about the type of counselling or psychotherapy they opt to undergo. It is axiomatic to us that effective therapy must be of a kind that generates hope immediately (otherwise the depressed person might not come back – they might even go away and kill themselves). Effective therapy targets what needs to be done with great precision. The first requirement is to reduce stress levels (because agitation causes the autonomic nervous system to become hyperactive, overriding the rational part of the brain and exacerbating emotional black and white thinking). When a depressed person is calmed down and less stressed, there is the possibility of a good night's sleep – nothing looks so bad when you have slept well and re-energised your brain. Effective therapy also concentrates on stopping negative rumination (worrying), focuses imagination outwards (as opposed to focusing it inwards on an individual's emotional state, causing them to catastrophise), gets them physically active and encourages them to put pleasure back into living. It helps them to look at their lifestyles in a positive, practical way, giving them the tools to improve their relationships, solve problems and challenges, and rethink the way they live, so they can get their needs met more effectively.

We would go so far as to say that, however difficult the circumstances of a person's life, depression is simply an unnecessary extra layer of suffering on top. Two people could be dying in a hospice of the same cancer. Both have a short life expectancy and both could be facing the same concerns about the wellbeing of their families and the same fears of the unknown – but the way they handle these circumstances determines whether they generate depression or not. The person still actively engaged in making the most of the time that they have left, by setting projects to accomplish day by day, by enjoying engaging with the environment moment by moment, by openly expressing their concerns and acknowledging the concerns others have for them, and by playing their part in planning their families' future, will be the one who does not fall into clinical depression. There is always something that we can do to impact positively upon our circumstances, however small that something is. The moving true story recounted in the book, *Tuesdays with Morrie*, is a testament to that fact. It describes the last months in the life of Morrie, a former university lecturer, who developed motor neurone disease. Even as he became almost completely physically incapacitated, unable eventually to move any part of his body unaided, he remained mentally alert and eager, keen to appreciate the world from his window and the stories of the world brought to him by his friends. The wisdom he dispensed and the optimism he displayed, even when in constant pain and discomfort, serve as an all too salutary reminder that depression is never a necessary recourse, even when times are exceptionally hard.[30]

Two of Joe's case histories will serve to illustrate some of the points we have covered before we move on to consider the possibility of a connection between stress, depression, dreaming and psychosis.

The young woman

Susan came to see me, accompanied by her mother. Her eyes were downcast; she sat miserably in her chair, quite unwilling to engage with me. Her mother explained to me what a brilliant student she had been, what a creative and dynamic person she really was, but that, in the last six months, during her first year in college, she had slipped into a depressed state and had spent three months in a mental hospital on a high drug dosage. No improvement took place, so she discharged herself. Of her own volition she stopped taking all the medication because she realised that it was worsening her symptoms, rather than relieving them (this can happen in some cases). But, nonetheless, she was still severely depressed.

When I asked her mother how Susan spent her time, she said she stayed up half the night watching television, spent as much time as she possibly could on her own and no longer had contact with her friends or took part in any physical activity at all. I asked Susan what she wanted from therapy, and she said, "I want to be left alone. I want my parents off my back. I want to stop being nagged. I want to be allowed to sleep in as long as I want to, and I want to watch as much television as I want." Indeed, Susan was spending practically her whole waking life just watching television.

Now this was a pretty hopeless case on first appearances: the patient wouldn't engage; she was severely depressed; the mental hospital and antidepressants had failed to help her. The situation seemed quite hopeless. I said to her, "Look Susan, you must be feeling quite stressed out, because I know from helping many other depressed people that, although by outward appearance, they seem to have totally switched off, inside themselves there is usually a very high level of tension." She nodded quickly and said, "Yes". So I then asked her, "Would you like me to show you how to get those stress levels down?" She shook her shoulders nonchalantly but readily engaged with some relaxation exercises and guided imagery. In her imagination I revivified some of the positive aspects of her life, as gleaned from her mother, pointing out what an attractive, intelligent, creative and dynamic person she really was. I also told her in technical detail about the dangers of watching too much television and how, if she made some simple life changes, she could improve her mood really rapidly. I recorded all this on audiotape so she could relax and listen to these positive, affirming messages and allow them to sink in.

When I saw her the second week she was more willing to smile at me and engage with me, but she was still quite depressed. It took a total of three visits, over three weeks, before she completely 'clicked out' of her depressed state and became animated, bright and energetic, just as her mother had described her as being. Susan decided for herself that watching television was an addictive behaviour. She started going to the gym again, mixing with friends and going out walking. With her emotional levels lowered, she had been able to think about her situation more clearly and had realised that the course she had been doing at college really didn't suit her. In fact, that was a major part of what she had been worrying about, instigating her depression. She realised that she wanted to refashion her life quite differently. She had decided that she was not going to go back to college but was going to go directly into business, and so she began looking round for a job.

This treatment took place about twelve months ago and, since then, I have seen Susan about every two months – at her insistence; she just wants to come back to check in with me that everything is OK. All we ever do is have a pleasant conversation, in which I praise her for the achievements she tells me about. Indeed, she now has a job in marketing, which is working out highly successfully. She has also referred several of her friends to me because, like most of us, she knows people who are depressed. This story is by no means unique; it is a routine one for me and fellow colleagues who base their therapy approach on human givens principles.

The middle-aged man

Tom had worked with horses all his life and came to see me when he was in his mid to late forties. He sat in my therapy room deeply miserable, accompanied by his wife, who was desperately worried about him. He looked exhausted and was clearly severely depressed. As with Susan, antidepressant medication hadn't worked for him. (We know that medication tends not to work so well for those with powerful imaginations. The emotional arousal caused by their negative fantasies and catastrophising can override the serotonin boost delivered by the drugs, to reduce REM sleep, and so the excessive REM sleep continues. In some cases, even when they do experience some improvement from medication, they still feel helpless in the face of what they perceive as the enormity of their problems. They can't think straight and see how to deal with them, so they still need help to chart their way through their current difficulties.)

Tom despaired of his situation. He had given up all hope in life. Three years earlier he had had a heart attack and, as a consequence, had to give up his job working with horses. All his life he had loved and lived for horses but, as part of the health insurance settlement after his illness, he had signed a document that committed him never to work with or have anything to do with horses again. Yet, without contact with horses, his life seemed utterly meaningless to him.

He had two young children and his wife described how his young son would come in from the garden and beg his daddy to play football in the garden with him. But Tom would not budge from his chair. His daughter would sometimes ask for help with her homework; his wife said she needed his support in managing family life, but because Tom felt life was so meaningless and because he had become so absorbed in his own feelings, he didn't help her. This type of behaviour is typical of what happens when the high emotional arousal associated with depression leads to a simplified, narrow focus – the all or nothing, black or white thinking of the emotional brain. Tom told me he felt unloved and uncared for, that he was a burden on other people and everyone really wished he were no longer around. Only two days earlier he had attempted suicide.

Following exactly the same approach previously described, I talked to him about his high stress levels, helped him to bring down his arousal and, when he was relaxed and in the REM state, reminded him just how much he really had going for him: how much his wife loved and cared for him, how much his children needed him, and why children need a father (research evidence shows that children benefit hugely from having a father actively engaged in their lives). I explained that it was possible to shift out of this depression quickly and that all he needed to do was to become physically active again, get off the rumination circuit, say, "No!" to negative thoughts, when they occurred, start behaving positively, and to connect and engage with life around him once more.

I also found out that it wasn't an absolute that he could never, ever, be involved with horses again. There was some wriggle room. After some lateral thinking, as we explored the possibilities over the next couple of therapy sessions, Tom agreed to allow me to write to the insurance company with which he had made this agreement. I pointed out to them that, as his mental health practitioner, I regarded that it was essential for his mental health that he be allowed to re-engage with horses again. They readily agreed that he could be involved with horses again, on a part-time basis, providing that the remuneration remained low and that his involvement was largely a therapeutic hobby. Tom contacted his old employers and they were thrilled to have him back on those terms. Tom then came out of his depression completely and is actively involved with his family again and enjoying life to the full. In all I saw him five times.

These cases show how, in our clinical work, we can transform the treatment of depression by using the insights generated from the dream research we have reported in this book. We have demonstrated it over and over again. Our aim now is that there should be enough health service workers trained in the human givens approach so that the numbers of people suffering from depression, desperate often even to the point of suicide, can be significantly reduced. When that happens, the results should be dramatic, as some doctors are already finding with the treatment of pain.

Pain and dreaming

The discovery of why we dream, and how excessive time spent in the dream state affects the brain, has important implications for the treatment of certain types of chronic pain: fibromyalgia, for instance, a condition in which there is widespread pain in the muscles throughout the body. 'Fibro' means fibrous tissues, 'myo' means muscle, and 'algia' means pain. It is a condition for which there is no known medical cause. It has been estimated that up to 20 per cent of patients attending general rheumatology clinics are suffering from symptoms of fibromyalgia, with ten female sufferers for every male. As well as widespread pain, patients with this disorder report feeling tired, having disturbed sleep and a lot of dreams. In addition, they often experience irritable bowel, migraine, bladder and eye symptoms. This range of symptoms points to a problem with the autonomic nervous system.

An important clue as to what may be going on here is the consistent finding that fibromyalgia sufferers have excessive levels of REM sleep and consequently insufficient physically restorative Stage 4 slow-wave sleep. It is in Stage 4 slow-wave sleep that growth hormones are released, which is thought to repair the damage caused to body tissues by the wear and tear of everyday activities. And we have already shown that too much REM sleep can be caused by too much worry about oneself, often exacerbated by withdrawal from social activities and other active pleasures because of the pain. In the words of musculoskeletal pain consultant Dr Grahame Brown, "It is part of the pain cycle". In his article on this subject in the journal *Human Givens*,[31] he wrote of an experiment carried out in Canada in which the pain symptoms of fibromyalgia were induced in a group of healthy university student volunteers by means of waking them every time they went into slow-wave sleep and only allowing them to have REM sleep.[32] Within a few days of slow-wave sleep deprivation, the students started to complain of aches and pains and within two weeks they had pain all over their bodies. As soon as their sleep pattern was corrected, their symptoms disappeared. Dr Brown concluded that, "Too much REM sleep precludes sufficient restorative sleep, and insufficient tissue healing may take place, leading to widespread pain". By making use of this insight he has been able to treat this patient group much more successfully – encouraging them to take up activities and hobbies which they used to enjoy, but feared would add to their pain, and teaching them how to calm themselves and relax (anxiety and tension exacerbate pain; activity and outward focus serve as distraction). By becoming more active and involved with life again, they had less to worry about and less reason for excessive REM sleep.

When the mental theatre crumbles – madness

Over a number of years, as we worked on the therapeutic application of these ideas about the REM state and dreaming, and taught them to other health professionals, Ivan became increasingly convinced that Joe's findings should throw some light on psychotic symptoms and schizophrenia. When he checked the scientific literature he found that, although it is much studied and there are numerous competing theories, there is no generally accepted understanding of the causes of the symptoms of psychotic breakdown and schizophrenia. And that remains the situation.[33] Almost everywhere he looked the emphasis was on diagnosis, but diagnostic observations, however subtle, do not in themselves explain anything, unless there is also an organising idea for making sense of them. It became clear to Ivan, from reading the literature, that psychotic breakdowns are invariably preceded by periods of extreme stress, anxiety and/or depression or use of mood-altering drugs.[34,35,36] Could it be, he wondered, that anxious worrying, due to stress overload (caused by a person's needs not being met), the consequent depression, and then the development of psychotic symptoms, are on a continuum? And could Joe's theory about the REM state being a reality generator provide the link that makes sense of the huge variety of psychotic symptoms?

Shortly after we reviewed these thoughts together, Ivan, by chance, was given permission to videotape an emergency therapy session with a teacher and highly creative musician who had become so distressed that, in desperation, she had cut her own throat six months earlier. He had been told that she was still depressed but not that she had been hearing voices and was exhibiting other psychotic symptoms. In fact, when she arrived, she was very agitated and in an active psychotic state. The more we studied the video, the more it became clear to us that the teacher was exhibiting REM state phenomena. These included rapid eye movements with eyes open, dissociation, instant emotional responses to metaphors, reliving the intensity of remembered emotions, trance logic, hallucinating frightening faces on surfaces, hearing voices, and losing touch with normal bodily sensations (she used the metaphorical explanation that there was just air in her arms and legs). As we have seen, all these phenomena can also be experienced in the dream state and hypnosis. Indeed, seeing the presence of so many signs of REM state activity (the way she responded instantly to a metaphor, for example), was like watching a hypnotised subject responding to being given a suggestion; we could directly observe her flipping into the REM state as she was hearing, feeling and seeing things that weren't there – something that normally only occurs when we dream or are hypnotised. We also found her psychotic statement that "there is just air in my arms and legs" easily understandable as a metaphor for what it feels like when we lose normal contact with bodily sensations – just as when, during dreaming, we are cut off from all our bodily senses. (In hypnosis the same thing happens. Hypnotised subjects, when relaxed, often can't move because of the characteristic muscle paralysis in the REM state – and, when they come out of trance, they typically say that their body felt as light as air or, conversely, so heavy they felt stuck to the chair.) The only way her right hemisphere (the hemisphere most active in the REM state) could explain this frightening disconnection from sensation was with a metaphor. (Some psychotic patients put a 'religious' interpretation on such experiences, saying, "I can't feel any more. I've lost my soul!") The more we considered our observations, the more it seemed as if somehow the normal operation of the REM state mechanism had broken down for her. When psychotic, she was perceiving reality through the REM state.

This gave us the possibility of a new organising idea: schizophrenia is waking reality processed through the dreaming brain.

We asked ourselves, how could this happen? What process would lead a person's brain to do this? And how could we understand the likely consequences of the pure metaphorical mind becoming dominant outside of its normal confinement within the REM state 'theatre' of dreams or other trance states?

As we observed in *Human Givens: A new approach to emotional health and clear thinking*, the REM state is the mechanism that connects us with reality; it is constantly running in the background, searching out at lightning speed the codes needed to match metaphorically to whatever is meaningful in the environment, and thus creating our perception of reality.[37] It is a reality generator, accessing the templates that are the basis of meaning. (This is easily seen when people access memories that evoke strong emotions: rapid eye movements occur even when their eyes are open. We have much evidence of this on film.)

In the dream state, when REM is at its most obviously active and sensory information from the outside world is 'shut off', the templates searching for their completion scan the brain and make metaphorical images from whatever they call up from memory. The dream contains these images and, while we are in it, becomes the reality we are conscious of. This is why the reality in dreams so often feels profoundly richer than waking reality – each particular metaphorical dream image can contain multiple levels of meaning, because the job of the dream is to deactivate emotional arousals and it can do that with several streams of arousals through the same image at the same time (as we saw in the dream of the 'chocolate' aunts described on page 84). Our waking reality is quite different – it is dramatically toned down. It has to be because, if we always saw multiple levels of meaning in everything, we wouldn't be able to make sense of, or operate within, our environment. We would end up totally confused and in a psychotic state. To deal with this problem, the neocortex of the brain, the rational part of our awake mind, inhibits multi-meaning.

Our observations of hundreds of depressed patients had confirmed that excessive worry puts huge stress on the REM sleep mechanism. So, we hypothesised, schizophrenia develops in those particularly imaginative, highly sensitive people who become so stressed that the REM sleep discharge mechanism cannot take the strain, and so their ability to separate waking reality from the metaphorical reality of the dream world (where the metaphors themselves seem totally real), becomes impaired. When they wake up, they cannot properly switch out of the REM state and become stuck in it. Naturally their thinking is then predominantly driven from the right hemisphere, the part of the brain most active in metaphorical pattern matching and dreaming. Many of their bodily behaviours could be expected to derive from those found in normal dreaming. In other words, the left hemisphere's role, which is normally to analyse and organise reality in a rational way, and is predominantly in charge during wakefulness, has been usurped. The delicate working partnership of the brain's hemispheres has shattered.

This, to our minds, provides a plausible way of explaining the wide variety of psychotic symptoms. The phenomenon of 'word salad' – the loosening of meaningful associations between words and phrases that results in people talking in a stream of apparent nonsense – is just what one might expect if the left hemisphere of the brain were to be out of sync with the metaphorical mind of the right hemisphere, as the latter would continue to generate associations without waiting for the left hemisphere to check them out and articulate them.

Catatonia, where patients can stand, sit or lie motionless for long periods in strange postures, oblivious to pain, is what the body also does during REM state dreaming, when the anti-gravity muscles are paralysed. Indeed, resistance to pain is often observed among schizophrenic patients and is even more marked during severe episodes. This is easily understood when we realise that, in dreaming also, cut off from all sensation, we experience no physical pain. That, too, is a REM state phenomenon (and is why hypnotised people can have major surgery painlessly without anaesthetic, as we have discussed).

Hearing voices is entirely predictable from our theory too. Talking is primarily a left hemisphere activity, whereas right hemisphere activity is mainly concerned with processing pattern matching and tagging emotions to those patterns to prompt action. We don't talk when the right hemisphere is dominant during dreaming in REM sleep, although talking whilst in slow-wave sleep is common (but the content rarely seems to make sense to the awake mind.) However, during a psychotic episode, if the person is in the REM state awake, there would still be some logical activity and thinking taking place in the left hemisphere. But, because the REM state is not anticipating any input from the left hemisphere, it has to interpret those thoughts metaphorically and comes up with the image of alien voices, which can seem to be commenting on the person's every move, or haranguing them or giving 'instructions'. (It might be expected that such thoughts would often be critical because the left hemisphere would, to some degree, still be able to analyse what was going on and 'logically' know that the behaviour is not normal.) This could further be interpreted metaphorically by the right hemisphere as being spied upon, or being persecuted, or that aliens are inside their head or that they are being followed everywhere by strange 'rays' that know everything they are doing. (Neurophysiological evidence confirms that, when schizophrenic people are hearing voices, the speech centres in the left neocortex are activated.[38] And other researchers have observed and filmed REM activity when patients hear voices.[39])

The visual hallucinations or delusions associated with psychosis are also totally characteristic of the dream state, the function of which is to generate such hallucinatory realities. Whilst dreaming we all believe completely in the reality of our dreams, just as the schizophrenic person believes in their reality.

Right now, the human race is experiencing another great period of creativity, one that is transforming life on this planet in spectacular fashion, and this burst of productivity is coinciding with an equally dramatic increase in mental disorders. We have already discussed the rise in depression but the prevalence of psychosis, which was once considerably less than one case per 1,000, has also risen. For many years it has now been higher than five cases per 1,000.[40] It has long been suggested that there is a connection between creativity and mental illness. Certainly, people prone to schizophrenia tend to come from creative families.[41] And even if they themselves are not productively creative, then high rates of creativity are found among their siblings and other relatives.[42]

Furthermore, creative people tend to be more sensitive to the emotional environment around them and are less robust in withstanding hostility, intolerance or criticism. Indeed, the higher the level of emotional criticism within the family context, the higher the rate of schizophrenic and depressive relapse.[43] When people go into a psychotic REM trance due to emotional arousal any criticism may well be acting like a post-hypnotic suggestion, compounding the condition.

So again, we come back to the idea we mooted that, by giving us access to the daydreaming faculty, nature also opened up the route to mental illness. Being creative always requires the ability to daydream, in other words, to have a more direct involvement with the REM state 'theatre' but this inevitably also means that creative and highly imaginative people are more vulnerable to negative suggestions and to misuse of the power of imagination. They may endlessly worry about possible life scenarios (thereby overstressing the REM state mechanism, resulting in a roller coaster ride of emotionally disturbing days and disturbed nights) – and end up saturated with anxiety and depression, and, in the case of some, prey to the experience of frightening psychotic symptoms which further aggravate their situation.

Of course, some of what we are saying here is speculation, but it is speculation that derives from a new organising idea which we feel has considerable explanatory power. As we said before, what people don't understand, they are afraid of – and people suffering psychosis commit suicide at alarming rates because they are afraid of what they are experiencing.[44] They also sense that the medical profession has no confident understanding of what they are going through or of how to treat psychosis effectively. Indeed, they sense that some of the people treating them may also be afraid of madness, just as members of their families and the general public are. But we have found that, when we explain the ideas outlined above to people who have suffered, or are still suffering at times, from psychosis, they respond with tremendous interest and relief and enthusiastically endorse the validity of our description of what has happened to them: that psychotic symptoms are what develop in highly stressed people when the REM state of our dreams is activated whilst they are awake. And how, in extreme cases, they can become totally trapped in that state.

If we are right, it follows, as we pointed out in our previous book,[45] that if psychotherapy were more effective at treating stress overload, anxiety problems and depression (as therapy from the human givens perspective indeed is), then patients' own natural homeostatic processes would rebalance them, depression would lift in most cases and fewer people would degenerate into psychosis. Because psychotic people are so hypersensitive to metaphor, mental health professionals need to be trained how to reduce their patients' arousal levels with calming metaphors. Conversely, they need to consciously avoid metaphors that may remind patients of their predicament, flipping them back into right hemisphere dominance and psychosis. And, when working with these patients, use metaphorical language that encourages left hemisphere activity. These are teachable skills. Health professionals also need to consider that psychotic patients' language and behaviour may be clear metaphorical representations of their emotional needs and concerns, which they can express no other way if processing waking reality directly through the REM state. In addition to this, whenever possible, the families of psychotic patients should be helped to make sure that their behaviour and attitudes expressed towards the patient are supportive rather than hostile.

We would also suggest, perhaps surprisingly to some, that the skills of occupational therapists could be of especial benefit in the treatment of patients with psychosis. It would make sense that people who are psychotic need help to connect to ordinary life in disciplined, purposeful, but unstressful ways: gardening, cooking, making things, or any other meaningful way (such as caring for it) of interacting with their environment. Interesting studies from WHO show that flourishing rural communities in third world countries, using these sorts of naturally supportive approaches, have a much higher success rate in curing psychotic illness than developed western countries that have come to rely on 'antipsychotic' medication.[46] (Drugs, it should be obvious, are not the only way to lower the emotional arousal that puts pressure on the dreaming brain. Indeed, recent research has shown that people whose medication was discontinued after they achieved remission from first-episode psychosis experienced twice the recovery rate of those kept on antipsychotic drugs after remission of symptoms.[47]) Experiments with this more naturalistic approach in the West, too, going back to the early 19th century and including some in the present day, have shown that patients 'treated' simply by being offered friendship and a regular routine of purposeful, practical activity, meals and sleep, had equally as good recovery rates as the people being given the right type of social support in a drug-free environment in third world countries today.[48, 49]

Above all, if we are right, as a society we need to ensure that vulnerable people receive effective psychotherapy more quickly – before stress, anxiety and depression completely overload the REM discharge mechanism and too much damage is done. As always, prevention is the better course wherever possible. Enormous savings could be made if those engaged in ineffective forms of counselling and psychotherapy were retrained so that they could act quickly to deal with stress, anxiety and depression and prevent the triggering of major breakdowns in those genetically predisposed to developing psychosis. In other words, therapists need to work from the givens of human nature, not ideology, profit motives or bureaucratic convenience. We predict that, if such an approach were adopted, people would have fewer psychotic breakdowns and higher recovery rates from schizophrenia.

Over many years, as we have explained these ideas to professionals who work with psychotic people, and to sufferers themselves, we have had more and more positive feedback. Support workers who have studied our methods found they were able to help patients more effectively when they didn't give too much attention to the voices, hallucinations and other strange behaviours patients exhibited, but concentrated instead on focusing them on activity, getting them engaged in the environment, helping them to keep down their stress levels etc. Those who have tried these methods have reported that often the voices fade away and an individual shifts out of their psychotic state.

Discussing a dream in a psychotherapy session with a therapist who understands the role dreams play in metaphorically completing unacted out emotional arousals from the previous day, may provide the sense of distance needed for an emotional, anxious or depressed person to stand back and see their situation with a new clarity and objectivity. Reported dreams, through the language of metaphor, can further provide a therapist with an insight into what patients are really worrying about, which ordinary verbal language may not convey. (Nightmares are often a gift in this regard.) A dream can also provide powerful, ready-made metaphors (that the patient is the more likely to relate to, as they are their own!) that the therapist can adapt to use in therapeutic interventions, by reframing the implications of the metaphors towards a positive outcome. The sense of wonder at previously unrecognised personal resources, which can be evoked by an individual's discovery that they have the ability to create in their dreams powerful metaphorical visions concerning their problems, should also be capitalised on.

It may well be that, whilst mainstream psychiatry believes that antipsychotic medication makes difficult clinical cases easier to handle, it may not provide the most successful outcome for the unfortunate sufferer (antipsychotic medication helps only about half who are prescribed it and has miserable side effects, physical and mental[50]), whereas a better understanding of the role of dreaming in all our lives could make a huge difference to the effectiveness of treatment.

10

DREAMING REALITY

"The universe is real but you can't see it.
You have to imagine it."

ALEXANDER CALDER

"If one drop falls, why not two?"

SAYING

One warm, pine-perfumed summer night, many years ago, Ivan sat on a quayside on a small Mediterranean island waiting for a ferry to take him and his family back to the mainland on the start of their journey home from a holiday. It was three in the morning and he held his sleeping three year old daughter, Eleanor, in his arms whilst his wife cradled their baby Kim. There was no wind and apart from the slight rushing sounds of collapsing wavelets all was quiet, so much so that it was easy to fancy one could hear shooting stars 'wooshing' as they flashed in quick arcs high above.

There were a few dim lights visible from the houses surrounding the tiny port but up on the mountainside stood a castle, dramatically floodlit. All else was deepest darkness. There was no moon and dawn was still an hour away. Little Eleanor stirred herself and looked around. After a while her sleepy young voice posed a wonderful question: "Daddy, why is that castle up in the sky?"

Ivan looked up and saw the scene through her eyes. Eleanor's uninformed young mind, unaware of the art of floodlighting, and lacking the certain adult knowledge that the ancient building stood on solid rock, described what she saw directly. And in the blackness the floodlit castle *did* look as if it were floating in space, for all the world like a magical fairytale palace, majestically flying through the night against a background of a million stars. They both gazed upwards in wonder for a while until Eleanor drifted back to sleep as the faint sound of the ferry could just be heard making its way across the sea to pick them up and take them away from this beautiful place.

This delightful incident illustrates the fundamental fact that what we see *always* depends on what we know. A perception occurs to us when a pattern already inside our brain matches up to a pattern in the world outside that it corresponds to in some way, or a pattern in one part of the brain comes together with a different pattern in another part of the brain to create a new understanding. As we have already seen, the innate patterns passed on to us through our genes and programmed into us in the REM state, are necessarily incomplete, and nature's instruction to the brain is to seek to match them up to other patterns in the outside world, thereby making them more 'complete'. Food would have no meaning for us unless we had an *inner* pattern – the feeling of hunger – driving us to seek it in the *outside* world. In the same way visual information has no meaning for people born blind due to cataracts. If such people have the cataracts removed later in life, all they see is chaos. For them it is a painful, slow process to gradually learn to make sense of images they see (although their vision can never be the same as that of someone born with sight, as neuronal brain cells concerned with vision wither if not 'switched on' by a certain age). People released from blindness have to connect the existing patterns in their brain for the things they previously recognised, by touch or sound, to the new visual stimuli. In other words, they must build up meaningful inner visual patterns in order to connect them to the outer world through sight.

Perception, therefore, is always about meaning. We do not see an objectively real world; we only see what is meaningful to us. When we see a chair, we perceive it as a chair because we already have a meaningful pattern in our brain that corresponds to what we see –which is that it is something specially devised to sit upon. In effect, what we see in the outside world are meanings that relate to patterns inside us to which our brains give significance. We would maintain that all perceptions of the outside world are the result of pattern matching, and our awareness of a reality outside of ourselves derives from the patterns originally programmed into us in the REM state – whether as innate knowledge or subsequently acquired new knowledge.

In fact, it seems to us that the whole basis for our perception of reality, for even knowing that external reality exists, comes from the REM state. Without the fundamental patterns (core templates) that were first programmed into the brain in the fetal stage in the REM state, consciousness of reality could not exist for us. The REM state generates our reality for us; it is truly our reality generator. We have explored some of the implications of this both here and in our previous book *Human Givens*. We have looked, for example, at how understanding this can explain why dreams are so important for deactivating our arousal. We have shown how dreams serve the additional function of maintaining the integrity of the templates through which we interact with external reality. And we have also made the case for the vital role played by the REM state in all educational processes – indeed, from this view, without humans at some point learning how to access the REM reality generator whilst awake and consciously daydream (the remarkable development that occurred only about 40,000 years ago,[1]), culture itself could never have developed. As we explored in Chapter 8, it would make sense that it was this process of learning how to use imagination through the conscious act of daydreaming, and thereby accessing the REM state whilst awake, that enabled real creativity to emerge in humans and distance us from animal kind.

Why has it taken so long for this discovery to be made?

It is curious that this intuitively sensible and easily verifiable finding, that our dreams are a metaphorical acting out of our unfulfilled expectations, should have taken so long to be discovered. After all, humans have been fascinated and intrigued by dreams since earliest times. The answer to this puzzle is supplied by the theory itself because, since dreams deactivate the emotionally arousing thought pattern behind the dream, this very process makes it difficult to recall the waking experience on which the dream is based. It was because of Joe's serendipitous rediscovery of the autosymbolic effect – that a waking thought could be translated into a visual metaphor at sleep onset – that he actively looked for the connections between dreams and waking experiences. It was the repeated searching through his memories every day, looking for the metaphorical connections, that brought the waking experiences back to mind. But even that was only sufficient to reveal a metaphorical connection between his waking experiences and dreams. It wasn't obvious to him at that stage that it was our *unfulfilled* expectations that were metaphorically acted out, not the experiences themselves. It was only by setting up an experiment to predict his dreams, basing his predictions on the emotionally arousing experiences of the day, that showed that it wasn't the most emotionally arousing experiences themselves that predicted the brain's basis for selecting specific dream themes. As we now know, his findings showed that some powerful emotionally arousing experiences did not become dreams, whilst other rather minor emotionally arousing experiences did. And it was only by comparing the predictions that did become dreams with those that didn't, that it was possible for him to discover that our unfulfilled expectations, rather than emotionally arousing experiences *per se*, become the subject matter of our dreams.

It was, therefore, a combination of serendipity, knowledge of scientific method, and the setting up, for the first time, of an experiment to predict his own dreams (who else but the researcher can recall their own introspections of the previous day?) which enabled this discovery to be made. This is a perfect example of why it is important in any scientific endeavour to include the 'knower' in the 'known'. Anyone wishing to check the findings described in this book can set up the same experiment and confirm it for themselves. The final requirement, however, was the ability to make a creative leap. Without this, Joe could not have arrived at the insight made possible by his findings, and the many more that are still emerging from them.

Relating it all to reality

A book is nothing if it does not connect with its readers. When you dream tonight, as you will, even if afterwards you don't remember doing so, your brain, like a magic mirror in a dark cave, throwing up images whether light falls on it or not, will act out in metaphorical sensory form the unmanifested hopes, fears and reflections that occupied your introspective life today. By deactivating the leftover patterns of arousal in your autonomic system, your dreams will refresh your emotional brain, leaving it better prepared to deal with tomorrow's emotionally arousing experiences. Yet the astonishing diversity and richness, the profundity and the beauty to which human dreaming has given expression, is derived from a process which evolved in the first instance just to program basic instinctive behaviours.

Most dreams are routine productions, whose goal is usefully accomplished without our needing consciously to recall them. But this need not blind us to the potential insights that can be gained from those dreams whose metaphorical expression is so beautiful, bizarre or dramatic that they are propelled across the threshold of sleep into waking consciousness for us to examine.

We hope that this work is of such compass that you are convinced by the expectation fulfilment theory; that you can see it integrates all of the apparently disparate facts, psychological and biological, that till now have made up our incomplete knowledge about dreaming; and that it provides the crucial missing understanding that makes sense of it all. In addition, the theory has led to the development of the first scientific explanation for hypnosis and all of its weird and wonderful manifestations. From the practical point of view, the theory has also already underpinned a significant advance in psychotherapy (the human givens approach), particularly for the treatment of depression and anxiety disorders. It also holds promise for improving the treatment of people suffering from psychotic breakdown, and changing our understanding of their needs.

We are quite convinced that, for our understanding of human

psychology to progress – and even for our future survival as a thriving species to be ensured (as far as human effort and interventions can influence such a possibility) – it will be vital to understand more about the REM state and its role in our evolution and mental health. Our hunch, however, is that this book only scratches the surface of what this new understanding of the dream process could mean for humanity. While convinced that the REM state plays a central role in how we each develop a knowledge of who we are, we are also equally certain that the most profound implications of this new theory are yet to be uncovered. The REM state clearly brings us to the threshold of our relationship with reality. But it is just a vehicle. The true nature of that reality, and our relationship to it, will always be the most important question that we can explore. As the ancient Greeks advised us in the inscription over the Temple of Delphi: 'Man, know thyself and thou shalt know the universe'.

APPENDIX

LOOSE ENDS

A question we are frequently asked when we lecture on why we evolved to dream and the role dreams play in mental health is, *can dreams predict the future*? Out of an audience of several hundred people, dozens will, if we ask, put their hands up to say they have experienced this. Such a finding, if true, would certainly lead to a questioning of the fundamentalist, reductionist view about how nature works. Our personal view is coloured by the fact that scientists are struggling to make sense of a very strange universe indeed.

Modern-day experiments in physics have forced many scientists to develop an open-minded approach to the way they look at the basic nature of reality. Nothing is obviously simple in the physical world. Quantum mechanics, for instance, does not permit a separation between the observer and the observed. It has been shown that, if an atomic particle, an electron or a photon, for example, is connected to another particle to form a system, they never separate. The two particles can physically split up and move to different parts of the universe, but if one changes its direction of spin, the other also *instantaneously* changes its direction of spin. Various experiments have produced findings to confirm the idea that, in spite of the local appearances of phenomena, the universe is actually supported by an invisible reality which is unmediated by any detectable links and that somehow this reality allows instantaneous, or at least faster than light, communication. This is known as the property of nonlocality.[1] Quantum nonlocality proves that "particles that were once together in an interaction remain in some sense parts of a single system which responds together to further interactions"[2]. Since the entire universe is deemed to have originated in a flash of light known as the Big Bang, the existence of quantum nonlocality points towards a profound cosmological holism and this suggests that, "If everything that ever interacted in the Big Bang maintains its connection with everything it interacted with, then every particle in every star and galaxy that we can see 'knows' about the existence of every other particle."[3]

If such mind-boggling concepts are being grappled with by scientists working in the field of modern quantum physics, it behoves us psychologists to have an equally open-minded view as to how the universe may function, which means not shying away from facing equally mind-boggling questions about how the mind works and how it might be connected to wider reality – to consider, for instance, the possibility of precognition and telepathy.

In the Afterword that appeared in the first edition of, *Human Givens*, we introduced an idea we termed the 'relaton' theory because, although it derived from our interest in psychology and brain functioning, it nevertheless seemed to throw light on how modern physicists view the nature of reality and the possibility that knowledge can exist *outside* of the human mind.[4] We suggested that the knowledge accessed from our genes by the REM state, and programmed in to us so that we can develop into beings who can survive on this planet, is not the only knowledge available to us: the whole universe consists of encoded knowledge and it is possible that a fully 'complete' human being can tap into it directly. Furthermore, we suggested that the REM state is the biological mechanism for doing so. These ideas are now explained fully in our book *Godhead: the brain's big bang*.

This would explain the undoubted achievements of the shamanistic traditions that arose in all hunting societies. Gifted individuals were selected and taught how to enter trance (REM) states – through prolonged dancing, some form of self-mortification, or the use of hallucinogenic plants – and in that state they were able to access valuable information, such as the whereabouts of animals to hunt, how to cure a sick person or where to find somebody who was lost, and bring the information back to use in ordinary life. According to anthropologists who have studied this, and shamans themselves, many shamans work directly through dreams.[5]

The anthropologist Jeremy Narby, in his book, *The Cosmic Serpent: DNA and the Origins of Knowledge*, describes his work among the Ashaninca people who lived in the Peruvian part of the Amazonian rain forest. They told him that their extensive knowledge of plants and the plants' uses was given to them *by the plants themselves* in trances induced by drinking 'ayahuasca'. He wrote that, "The main enigma I encountered during my research on Ashaninca ecology was that these extremely practical and frank people, living almost autonomously in the Amazonian forest, insisted that their extensive botanical knowledge came from plant induced hallucinations. How could this be true?

"The enigma was all the more intriguing because the botanical knowledge of indigenous Amazonians has long astonished scientists. The chemical composition of ayahuasca is a case in point. Amazonian shamans have been preparing ayahuasca for millennia. The brew is a necessary combination of two plants, which must be boiled together for hours. The first contains a hallucinogenic substance, dimethyl-tryptamine, which also seems to be secreted by the human brain; but this hallucinogen has no effect when swallowed, because a stomach enzyme called monoamine oxidase blocks it. The second plant, however, contains several substances that inactivate this precise stomach enzyme, allowing the hallucinogen to reach the brain. The sophistication of this recipe has prompted Richard Evans Schultes, the most renowned ethnobotanist of the twentieth century, to comment: One wonders how peoples in primitive societies, with no knowledge of chemistry or physiology, ever hit upon a solution to the activation of an alkaloid by a monoamine oxidase inhibitor. Pure experimentation? Perhaps not. The examples are too numerous and may become even more numerous with future research.'

"So here are people without electron microscopes who choose, among some 80,000 Amazonian plant species, the leaves of a bush containing a hallucinogenic brain hormone, which they combine with a vine containing substances that inactivate an enzyme of the digestive tract, which would otherwise block the hallucinogenic effect. And they do this to modify their consciousness.

"It is as if they knew about the molecular properties of plants and the art of combining them, and when one asks them how they know these things, they say their knowledge comes directly from hallucinogenic plants.

"Not many anthropologists have looked into this enigma, but the failure of academics to consider this kind of mystery is not limited to the Amazon. Over the course of the 20th century, anthropologists have examined shamanic practices around the world without fully grasping them."[6]

The idea that knowledge can directly flow into people is ancient, almost certainly stretching back 35,000 years when artifacts and cave drawings were redolent of shamanistic trance practices.[7] A mere 2,400 years ago, Plato, generally recognised as the pre-eminent architect of western culture, held the fundamental belief that knowledge is intuitively accessed; that a world of ideas exists beyond the physical reality of human beings; and that human beings can access that knowledge. The whole basis of western culture, which is widely acknowledged as deriving from the philosophy of ancient Greece, can therefore be said to derive from this notion. Indeed, the philosopher Alfred North Whitehead once famously said that, "The safest general characterization of the European philosophical tradition is that it consists of a series of footnotes to Plato".[8]

In *Human Givens* we quoted the example of Plato's description of how Socrates drew out from a young slave boy the answer to a complex geometric question and remarked afterwards that this process was connected to the dream state. He said that the boy had always held the knowledge but it had to be recovered from him, when his brain was enabled to be in a receptive state. Plato was not the only Greek philosopher to believe in nonlocality. Plotinus also taught that the metaphysical principle of mind is nonlocal, and explained that, because it is not limited by time and space, it can be present everywhere.[9] But it was not just the ancient Greeks who used questioning, dreams and rituals to induce trance states to access knowledge. All cultures older than our modern one, throughout recorded history, saw that somehow we have to train ourselves to recover knowledge which is always available to us and that this is central to becoming truly human. It could be that, in artificially limiting the field of enquiry, western science is missing something vital.

If knowledge is available beyond the conventionally accepted confines of space and time, which many millions believe, is there any evidence for it? Can people have intimations – precognition – about future events, as so many say they do? Is this so-called psychic phenomenon worth giving attention to? Now, it must be admitted at once that this is an area full of chicanery. But, as this question always comes up at every seminar where we talk about dreams, we feel it would leave the readers of this book somewhat dissatisfied if we didn't have the courage to comment on the issue. And, as we have seen, such ideas are not precluded by a modern understanding of physics.

The occurrence of precognitive dreams is a controversial issue amongst sleep researchers. But we can see how, if dreams are caused by our expectations of the future expressed metaphorically, they might come to seem to be prophetic. For example, if a woman is afraid that her mother might die because she is old and fragile, the mother is likely to be replaced in a dream by someone else the daughter knows who is also old and fragile. The daughter dreams that it is that person who dies, and so completes the arousal pattern of worry that had been set in train about her mother. Not surprisingly, on some occasions, such a dream may actually come true and the old person who died in the dream does actually die shortly afterwards. This dream clearly would not require a precognitive explanation, in the sense of the dreamer having access to paranormal information. So a number of dreams will inevitably, and not just coincidentally, predict the future, because it is in the nature of dreams that they are about emotionally arousing expectations that we anticipate might happen.

But over and above that, is there any evidence that dreams actually predict the future? What's certain is that there is strong anecdotal evidence from all around the world, in all times, that people have had dramatic dreams that appear to predict the future. And there is a great deal of anecdotal evidence of people dreaming future events that do not concern them personally. Such accounts, although not scientifically collected, can be impressive. They have been reported from times as early as the ancient civilisations of Assyria, Babylonia, Egypt and India, and continue right up to the present. Cicero, in Roman times, gave many examples of precognitive dreams that warned of impending danger. One of these was a dream experienced by a man called Simonides, who had recently found the body of a stranger on the shore and had it buried. At the time Simonides was planning to go on a sea voyage but in his dream the buried man warned him not to go, because the ship would be lost. Simonides did not make the journey and later it was discovered that the ship had sunk, drowning all on board.

Here is a modern example, collected by Rupert Sheldrake, in which a man called Keith Vass tells of a dream he had on the morning of 11th September, 2001, before the World Trade Center in New York was attacked:

> Across the way from me was an identical building to the Mellon Bank Center. In reality there is no such building, but this one was identical in every way. It was dusk, and there was a major storm whirling. My building was shaking, as was the one across the street. I did not know whether to vacate or not. Then I noticed the building across the way began to break and crumble at the top. Chunks of the grey granite facing started to break away and fall to the street. Then the entire building imploded and went down, visually appearing much like the WTC when it went down. I was horrified and hurried to the exit staircase and walked briskly about thirty floors to the first floor and left the building. When I got outside, I noticed that it was not a hurricane or storm at all. It was a war and there were bombs falling everywhere.[10]

Clearly this is a metaphorical dream version of what happened a few hours later to the twin towers in New York.

Reports of psychic premonitions are not, of course, confined to dreams; they are also reported from waking states. There is no inherent reason why, if such phenomena exist, they should also not occur during dream sleep. One's reaction to this evidence is inevitably going to be decided in part by one's view of psychic phenomena in general. The only dream experience that Joe can personally recall that may have some psychic connection is the following dream.

The coffin nightmare

I am visiting friends of mine in their home. The husband is at work. I am talking to his wife when the phone rings. Putting the phone down, she informs me rather casually that she has just learned that her husband has died at work. His body would be arriving at the house shortly. Sure enough, moments later, her husband's body arrives in a van and is carried into the house in a cardboard coffin. I am horrified, since it seems likely that the coffin may burst open at any moment.

The dream occurred following a meal with friends in a restaurant the previous evening. Joe had just finished teaching a seminar in England and was enjoying a relaxing conversation over dinner. One of his friends mentioned casually that a mutual friend was dying. He was rather surprised at the casual way this shocking news was given. The first part of the dream can be seen as a metaphorical acting out of that surprise. But Joe was puzzled by the second part of the dream involving the cardboard coffin. Later, on returning to Ireland, he told his wife the dream. "That's rather odd," she said, "because that day I had been rather appalled to hear a news item on the radio about cardboard coffins." Was there, they both wondered, a telepathic element to his dream? And, if there were, why was the cardboard coffin not metaphorically represented? Presumably this didn't happen because the information about the cardboard coffins hadn't reached Joe's own sensory consciousness beforehand, and therefore couldn't be metaphorically pattern matched.

In modern times, the book that did most to arouse public interest in the possibility of dreams foretelling the future was John Dunne's,

An Experiment With Time.[11] Dunne kept a dream diary and noted many dreams that appeared to foretell future events. Perhaps the most curious aspect of his research was that the glimpses of the future that he appeared to see in his dreams were for the most part concerned with insignificant details. (In one dream, for example, he saw an umbrella, unsupported, standing upside down on its handle outside the Piccadilly Hotel. The next day he saw an old lady walking towards the same Piccadilly Hotel, holding a similar umbrella upside down, pounding its handle on the pavement.) But Dunne recorded so many of these events that he felt that chance coincidence was an unlikely explanation.

One possible explanation for the insignificance of the details could be this: because a waking concern has to find metaphorical clothing for the dream, some detail from the future, if it is indeed true that the mind can have access to knowledge about the future, might well be incorporated into the manifest structure of the dream, if it can play a part in expressing the concern analogically. (As the dreamer wouldn't be consciously aware of such details they can appear as they are, untransformed.)

A researcher who has taken an experimental, scientific approach to psychic phenomena in dreams is Professor Montague Ullman, the founder of the dream laboratory at the Maimonides Medical centre in New York.[12,13] In a series of scientifically controlled experiments he produced significant evidence that telepathy can take place in dreams. In a typical experiment, a subject would concentrate on a randomly selected painting and try to get another subject, who was asleep in an adjoining room, to dream about it. On some occasions, the experiments succeeded and, on some occasions, they failed. Over a series of fifteen trials the number of hits exceeded misses such that the odds of the results being due to chance were calculated at a thousand to one. However, whilst most scientists are willing to concede the possibility of extrasensory perception, they feel that insufficient scientific evidence exists, as yet, to validate it.

If we were to entertain the possibility that such phenomena do occur, how might we explain them? One possibility might be that the brain *can* communicate with reality beyond time and space, a form of subtle direct perception. In that case, indications of such possibilities may arise somehow in dream states. But that does not necessarily mean that they have to be concerned with anything of significance in themselves. Such details from the future could simply be used by the brain to represent metaphorically a waking concern of the recent past.

On the face of it, the following example of a vivid dream Ivan had seems, because of its unlikely nature, impossible to explain other than by precognition. It occurred one bitterly cold winter in southern England.

The lizards in winter

> Our house was invaded by lizards. They seemed to be everywhere, wherever we looked, under chairs, under the sofa, behind cupboards. Some were alive, slowly creeping around, but some were dead. It was very disturbing.

The dream was so vivid that Ivan talked about it on waking and mentioned it later to the rest of his family and to colleagues at work. He had seen lizards on holiday around the Mediterranean but never in England and experienced the dream as a very odd one indeed.

One week later, his family awoke and found, to their amazement, the dream had come true. There *were* lizards, and bits of lizards, in the kitchen, on the stairs and in several rooms. Some were moving slowly; some had tails missing; some seemed dead. They were all over the place and it took a while to find them all. The only explanation for it seemed to be that the two family cats had found a nest of hibernating lizards and, throughout the night, had brought them into the house through the cat flap. But why had Ivan dreamed this a week before? And why did the dream appear to represent fairly closely what actually happened a week later, rather than the event being transposed into metaphor? (Presumably, as in Joe's dream of the cardboard coffin, the information had not reached Ivan's sensory consciousness beforehand, so a substitute pattern match was impossible.)

We might expect this kind of precognition experience (if it does occur) to be more likely to occur in the REM state than in other states of consciousness. This is because the orientation response, in alerting an organism to a change in the environment, is signalling to the brain that it needs to gather quickly as much information as is necessary in order to predict what is most likely to happen. (Is the sudden bang a car backfiring, which can be ignored, or a gunshot, indicating a dangerous situation that needs either to be escaped or else investigated, if someone else is the intended victim?) Since, when dreaming, no information comes through to the brain from the sense organs or consciousness, the emotional brain has to release its as yet incomplete expectations about what it expects to happen. If paranormal information about the future were indeed available to the limbic system, it would be natural for it to be released at this point.

There are many examples of this type of precognition in dreams collected by serious researchers, which seem to confirm that this is what might be happening. The following three precognitive dreams, just a small sample of the many collected by Dr Keith Hearne, are typical:

The undertaker

I dreamed that a local undertaker came to our cottage door in Essex. He had a plank of wood with him and gave me a bill with a date on it. A month later my husband died on the date given in the dream and the bill for the funeral was the amount previously shown.[14]

The rose bush

My eldest son lost his signet ring while throwing snowballs in the front garden. He was very upset because his fiancée had given it to him. During that night I had a dream that I could see the snow had melted under a rose bush by the front gate and there was his ring shining in

> the sunlight. Next morning I hurriedly went to the rose bush by the gate and there was the ring just as I had seen it in my dream. I have also dreamed of the names of racehorses winning big races prior to the event, not even knowing the horses even existed. Last year I dreamed the winner of the Grand National. My family were very grateful and cashed in on my dream![15]
>
> **Wild duck**
>
> When I was 12 I dreamed of seeing a cousin shoot himself accidentally while going over a stone wall when hunting wild duck. In the morning I told my mother and she said it was only a dream. I was frightened though, and also told my teacher when I got to school; but nobody took any notice of me. On going home from school I was met by my father and realized something was wrong. He said my young cousin had accidentally shot and killed himself today out after wild duck. I was frightened of my dreams for a long time afterwards."[16]

By and large these types of dreams are not regarded by scientists as proof of anything. J. Allan Hobson's attitude is typical. "There is absolutely no scientific evidence ... It is simply coincidental correspondence between a situation about which one has legitimate and intense concern and the occurrence of the event one fears."[17]

Apart from the examples we've given, we can't say that we have had any experience of such paranormal dreams. Nonetheless, we are impressed by the strength of the anecdotal evidence. We also recognise that, since ancient times, many people widely acknowledged to be wise have derived knowledge that was substantiated by science only many centuries later.[18] We are also impressed by the fact that modern physics does not preclude such possibilities. So, what we would say at this stage is that it is important to stay open-minded about these subjects. The history of science is littered with the embarrassing pronouncements of expert commentators, declaring that only minor details of a particular subject remain to be settled, only to find their views totally overthrown and disproved by subsequent discoveries.

To coin a saying: premature closure in our account of reality is the daughter of conceit. There is one more topic to mention, and that is lucid dreams.

Lucid dreaming

This is a subject on which we can be more definite. Throughout history there have been reports of people becoming conscious of being in a dream. During such dreams, they can reason, remember to some extent the conditions of waking life, and act upon reflection or in accordance with plans decided upon before sleep. Outside of laboratory conditions, becoming aware of dreaming seems most likely to occur when dreaming about something that, at an elemental level, is known not to be at all likely, such as flying. Flying dreams are usually very enjoyable and people can begin consciously to engage in exploring the feeling of flight, steering, gliding and so on, once the dream is underway, all the while knowing that it is a dream. (Incidently, when we have asked people for further details about their flying dreams, they may say that the flying sensation was like moving through water, but with greater ease. They describe their limbs as pulling or propelling them through the air, as though swimming. It's as if an ancient premammalian template for swimming, left over from a time when our far distant ancestors lived in the oceans, is still able to be co-opted by the brain for a metaphor.)

Lucid dreaming was studied under laboratory conditions by Keith Hearne and also Stephen La Berge. They devised ingenious ways by which subjects could give researchers predetermined signals when they were dreaming. The signals took the form of deliberately scrunching their eyes up tight, since other muscles are paralysed during REM sleep. He observed that, at the onset of lucid dreams, there is an increased tendency to awaken, probably because lucid dreamers are thinking at that point, which withdraws attention from the dream.[19] Having a firm intention, prior to going to sleep, to become aware of dreaming can increase the chances of a lucid dream, as can practising certain forms of self-suggestion over time.

Theories of dreaming that do not allow for occasional lucidity are, necessarily, incorrect or incomplete, because lucid dreaming is an acknowledged phenomenon. Our view of the REM state and the function of dreaming does not exclude lucidity in dreams. Some dream researchers had hoped to make lucid dreaming more accessible, with the aim of providing not only a means of creating exciting fantasies but also therapeutic benefits. However, lucid dreaming is a fairly volatile and rare phenomenon, even for those who have experienced it, and so such hopes have not been realised. Perhaps those thwarted researchers have overlooked the fact that a means of achieving this outcome has already been around for thousands of years – hypnosis.

REFERENCES AND NOTES

Chapter 1: An ancient puzzle

1. Foulkes, D. (1985) *Dreaming: A cognitive-psychological analysis*. Lawrence Erlbaum Associates.
2. Bortoft, H. (1996) *The Wholeness of Nature*. Lindisfarne Books.
3. Griffin, J. (1997) *The Origin of Dreams*. The Therapist Ltd. The first appearance of this new solution to the problem of why we dream was published in a series of articles, the first of which appeared in 1993 in *The Therapist*, the journal of the European Therapy Studies Institute (ETSI). The interest was so great that an academic monograph in book form was published by the same organisation.
4. Aserinsky, E. & Kleitman, N. (1953) Regularly occurring periods of eye mobility and concomitant phenomena during sleep. *Science*, 18, 273–274.
5. Hudson, L. (1985) *Night Life: The interpretation of dreams*. Weidenfeld and Nicholson.

Chapter 2: Earlier explanations examined

1. Highbarger, E. L. (1940) *The Gates of Dreams*. The Johns Hopkins Press.
2. De Becker, R. (1968) *The Understanding of Dreams and their Influence on the History of Man*. Hawthorn.
3. Khaldûn, Ibn (1974) *The Muqaddimah*. Translated from the Arabic by Franz Rosenthal and abridged and edited by Dawood, N. J. Princeton University Press.
4. Maury, A. (1853) Nouvelle observations sur les analogies des phénomènes du rêve et de l'aliénation mentale, *Ann. Med-Psychol.*, 5, 404.
5. Strumpell, L. (1877) *Die Natur und Enstehung der Traume*. Leipzig.
6. Freud, S. (1953) *The Interpretation of Dreams*. In the standard edition of the complete psychological works of Sigmund Freud, Strackey, J. (Ed.). Hogarth Press.
7. Jung, C. (1964) *Man and His Symbols*. Dell Publishing.
8. Noll, R. (1995) *The Jung Cult: origins of a charismatic movement*. Princeton University Press.
9. French, T. (1954) *The Integration of Behavior, 11: the integrative process in dreams*. University of Chicago Press.
10. French, T. & Fromm, E. (1964) *Dream Interpretation*. Basic Books.
11. Hall, C. S. (1953) A cognitive theory of dreams. *Journal of General Psychology*, 49, 277–282.
12. Hall, C. & Van de Castle, R. (1966) *The Content Analysis of Dreams*. Appleton-Century-Crofts.
13. Hobson, J. A. & McCarley, R. W. (1977) The brain as a dream-state generator: an activation-synthesis hypothesis of dream process. *American Journal of Psychiatry*, 134, 1335–1368.

14. Hobson, J. A. (1988) *The Dreaming Brain*. Basic Books.

15. Macquet, P, Peters, J. et al. (1996) Functional neuroanatomy of human rapid eye movement sleep and dreaming. *Nature*, 383, 6596, 163–166.

16. Ibid.

17. Berger, M., Lund, R. et al. (1983) REM latency in neurotic and endogenous depression and the cholinergic REM induction test. *Psychiatry Research*, 10, 113–123.

18. Hobson, J. A. (2005) *Dreams Freud Never Had*. Pi Press.

19. Solms, M. (2000) Dreaming and REM sleep are controlled by different brain mechanisms. *Behaviour and Brain Sciences*, 26, 6, 843–850.

20. Crick, F. & Mitchison, G. (1983) The function of dream sleep. *Nature*, 304, 111–114.

21. Hudson, L. (1985) *Night Life: the interpretation of dreams*. Weidenfeld and Nicholson.

22. Domhoff, G. W. (2000) Needed: a new theory. *Behavioural and Brain Sciences*, 23, 6, 928–930.

23. Evans, C. & Newman, E. A. (1964) Dreaming, an analogy from computers. *New Scientist*, 419, 577–579.

24. Evans, C. & Evans, P. (1983) *Landscapes of the Night*. Victor Gollancz.

25. Jouvet, M. (1978) Does a genetic programming of the brain occur during paradoxical sleep? In Buser, P. A. & Rougel-Buser, A. (Eds.) *Cerebral Correlates of Conscious Experience*. Elsevier.

26. Cartwright, R. (2012) *The Twenty-four Hour Mind: the role of sleep and dreaming in our emotional lives*. Oxford University Press.

27. Hartmann, E. (1995) Making connections in a safe place: is dreaming psychotherapy? *Dreaming*, 5, 213–228.

28. Domhoff, G. W. (2008) The awesome lawfulness of your nightly dreams. Lecture given at University of California Santa Cruz, April 9.

29. Revonsuo, A. & Valli, K. (2000) Dreaming and consciousness: testing the threat simulation function of dreaming. *Psyche*, 6, 8. http://psyche.cs.monash.edu.au/v6/psyche-6-08-revonsuo.html

30. Winson, J. (2002) The meaning of dreams. *Scientific American*, 12, 1, 54–61.

31. Jouvet, M. (2001) *The Paradox of Sleep*. MIT Press.

32. Antrobus, J. (1993) Characteristics of dreams. In M. A. Carskadon (Ed), *Encyclopedia of Sleep and Dreaming*. Macmillan.

33. Domhoff, G. W. (2008) The awesome lawfulness of your nightly dreams. Lecture given at University of California Santa Cruz, April 9.

34. Domhoff, G. W. (2001) A new neurocognitive theory of dreams. Dreaming, 11, 13-33.

35. Lawton, G. (2003) To sleep, perchance to dream. *New Scientist,* 178, 2401.

36. Griffin, J. (1993) The origin of dreams. *The Therapist*, 1, 1.

37. Shah, I. (1970) *The Dermis Probe*. Jonathan Cape.

Chapter 3: An experimental adventure

1. Ebbinghaus, H. (1885) *Memory: A contribution to experimental psychology.* (Roger, H. A. & Bussenius, C. E. trans). Columbia University Press.
2. Domhoff, G. W. (2000) Methods and measures for the study of dream content. In M. Kryger, T. Roth and W. Dement (Eds.), *Principles and Practices of Sleep Medicine*, 3 (pp. 463–471). W. B. Saunders.
3. Wamsley, E.J. & Stickgold, R. (2011) Memory, sleep and dreaming: experiencing consolidation. *Sleep Medicine Clinics*, 6, 1, 97–108.
4. Snyder, F. (1966) Toward an evolutionary theory of dreaming. *American Journal of Psychiatry*, 123, 121–142.
5. Ullman, M. (1959) The adaptive significance of the dream. *Journal of Nervous Mental Disorder*, 129, 144–149.
6. Silberer, H. (1909) Bericht uber eine Methode, gewisse symbolische Halluzinations – erscheinungen hervozurufen und zu beobachten, *Jahrbuch psychoanalyt. psychopath. Forsch.*, 513. (114, 176, 460–61, 499, 645–8).
7. Silberer, H. (1951) Report on a method of eliciting and observing certain symbolic hallucination phenomena. *Organization and Pathology of Thought*, translation and commentary by Rapaport, D. Columbia University Press, 195–233.
8. Freud, S. (1953) *The Interpretation of Dreams*. Page 647 of the standard edition of the complete psychological works of Sigmund Freud. Strackey, J. (Ed.). Hogarth Press.
9. Domhoff, G. W. (2001) A new neurocognitive theory of dreams. *Dreaming*, 11, 13–33.
10. Domhoff, G. W. (2008) The awesome lawfulness of your nightly dreams. Lecture given at University of California Santa Cruz, April 9.
11. Farr, R. (1993) A device is not a paradigm. *The Psychologist*, 6, 261–262.

Chapter 4: Our sleeping brains

1. Aserinsky, E. & Kleitman, N. (1953) Regularly occurring periods of eye mobility and concomitant phenomena during sleep. *Science*, 18, 273–274.
2. Dement, W. & Kleitman, N. (1957) Cyclic variations in E.E.G. during sleep and their relation to eye movements, body motility and dreaming. *Electro-encephalography and Clinical Neurophysiology*, 9, 673–690.
3. Foulkes, D. (1962) Dream reports from different states of sleep. *Journal of Abnormal Social Psychology*, 65, 14–25.
4. Foulkes, D. (1985) *Dreaming: a cognitive psychological analysis*. Erlbaum Associates.
5. Griffin, J. & Tyrrell, I. (2003) *Human Givens: the new approach to emotional health and clear thinking*. HG Publishing Ltd.
6. Jouvet, M. & Michel, F. (1959) Correlations électromyographiques du sommeil chez le chat décortiqué et mésencéphalique, *Comptes Rendus de la Societé Biologie*, 154: 422–425.
7. Mourizzi, G. (1963) Active processes in the brainstem during sleep. *Harvey Lectures Series,* 58, 233–297.

8. Hartmann, E. (1967) *The Biology of Dreaming*. C. C. Thomas.
9. Dement, W. (1968) The biological role of REM sleep. In Kales, A. (Ed.) *Sleep: Physiology & Pathology*. Lippincott, 1969, 245–265.
10. Jouvet, M. (1967) Mechanisms of the states of sleep; A neuro-pharmacological approach. Presented at the 45th annual meeting of, and published by, the Association for Research in Nervous and Mental Disease. 45, 86–126.
11. Dement, W. (1968) The biological role of REM sleep. In Kales, A. (Ed.) *Sleep: Physiology & Pathology*. Lippincott, 1969, 245–265.
12. Domhoff, G. W. The purpose of dreams. Dreamresearch.net http://www2.ucsc.edu/dreams/Articles/purpose.html
13. Dement, W. (1960) The effect of dream deprivation. *Science*, 131, 1705–1707.
14. Ferguson, J. & Dement, W. (1968) Changes in the intensity of REM sleep with deprivation. *Psychophysiology*, 4, 380.
15. Dement, W. et al (1967) Studies on the effects of REM deprivation in humans and in animals. In Kety, S. S., Ewarts, E. V. & Williams, H. L. (Eds.), *Sleep and Altered States of Consciousness*, Proceedings of the Association for Research in Nervous and Mental Disease, 45, 456–468.
16. Vogel, G. W. (1979) A motivational function of REM sleep. In Drucker-Colin, R., Shkurovich, M. & Sterman, M. B. (Eds.) *The Function of Sleep*. Academic Press, 233–250.
17. Roffwarg, H. P., Muzio, J. & Dement, W. (1966) The ontogenetic development of the human sleep-dream cycle. *Science*, 152, 604–618.
18. Jouvet, M. (1965) Paradoxical sleep – a study of its nature and mechanisms. *Progress in Brain Research*, 18, 20–57.
19. Jouvet, M. (1967) Mechanisms of the states of sleep; A neuro-pharmacological approach. Presented at the 45th annual meeting of, and published by, the Association for Research in Nervous and Mental Disease. 45, 86–126.
20. Roffwarg, H. P., Muzio, J. & Dement, W. (1966) The ontogenetic development of the human sleep-dream cycle. *Science*, 152, 604–618.
21. Hunt, T. H. (1989) *The Multiplicity of Dreams, Memory, Imagination and Consciousness*, 28–30. Yale University Press.
22. Hobson, J. A. (1989) *Sleep*. Scientific American Library, a division of HPHLP.
23. Piaget, J. (1971) *Biology and Knowledge*. Edinburgh University Press.
24. Walker, S. (1983) *Animal Thought*. Routledge & Kegan Paul.
25. Jouvet, M. (1999) *The Paradox of Sleep*. MIT Press.
26. Vygotsky, L. S. (1934) *Thought and Language*, Izd. AKAD. Pedagog. Also translation Kozulin, A. (1988) MIT Press.
27. Chomsky, N. (1957) *Syntactic Structures*. Mouton.
28. Bruner, J. (1986) *Actual Minds, Possible Worlds*. Harvard University Press.
29. Ornitz, E. M. & Ritvo, E. R. (1976). In Freeman, B. J., Ornitz, E. M. & Tanguay, P. E. (Eds.) *Autism*. Spectrum Books.
30. Morrison, A. R. (1983) A window on the sleeping brain. *Scientific American*, 248, 86–94.

31. Morrison, A. R. & Reiner, P. B. (1985) A dissection of paradoxical sleep. In McGinty, D. J., Drucken, C., Morrison, A. R. & Parmeggiani, P. (Eds.), *Brain Mechanisms of Sleep*. Raven Press, 97–110.

32. Hunt, T. H. (1989) *The Multiplicity of Dreams, Memory, Imagination and Consciousness*, 28–30. Yale University Press.

33. Hobson, J. A. (1988) *The Dreaming Brain*. Basic Books.

34. Cartwright, R.D., Berniche, N., Borowitz, G. & Kling, G. (1969) Effect of an erotic movie on sleep and dreams of young men. *Archives of General Psychiatry*, 20, 163-271.

35. Foulkes, D. & Rechtschaffen, A. (1964) Presleep determination of dream content: effects of two films. *Perceptual and Motor Skills*, 19, 983-1005.

36. Busáki, G. (1995) The hippocampo–neurocortical dialogue. *Cerebral Cortex*, 6, 81–92.

37. Jouvet, M. (1978) Does a genetic programming of the brain occur during paradoxical sleep? In Buser, P. A. & Rougel-Buser, A. (Eds.) *Cerebral Correlates of Conscious Experience*. Elsevier.

38. Karasov, W. H. & Diamond, J. (1985) Digestive adaptations for fuelling the cost of endothermy. *Science*, 228, 202–204.

39. MacLean, P. D. (1982) *Primate Brain Evolution: methods and concepts*. Armstrong, E. & Folk, D. (Eds.) Plenum Publishing, 309.

40. Rechtschaffen, A., Gilliland, M. A., Bergmann, B. M. & Winter, J. B. (1983) Physiological correlates of prolonged sleep deprivation in rats. *Science*, 221, 182.

41. Rechtschaffen, A. & Bergmann, B. M. (1995) Sleep deprivation in rats by the disk-over-water method. *Behavioural Brain Research*, 69, 55–63.

42. Hobson, J. A. (1994) *The Chemistry of Conscious States: how the brain changes its mind*. Little, Brown.

43. Jouvet, M. (1965) Paradoxical sleep – a study of its nature and mechanisms. *Progress in Brain Research*, 18, 20–57.

44. Cohen, H. & Dement, W. (1965) Sleep: changes in threshold to electroconvulsive shock in rats after deprivation of 'paradoxical' phase. *Science*, 150, 1318.

45. Dewson, J., Dement, W., Wagener, T. & Nobel, K. (1967) REM sleep deprivation: a central-neural change during wakefulness. *Science*, 156, 403–406.

46. Dement,W., Henry, P., Cohen, H. & Ferguson, J. (1967) Studies on the effects of REM deprivation in humans and in animals. In Kety, S. S., Ewarts, E. V. & Williams, H. L. (Eds.), *Sleep and Altered States of Consciousness,* Proceedings of the Association for Research in Nervous and Mental Disease, 45, 456–468.

47. Dement, W. (1972) *Some Must Watch While Some Must Sleep*. Stanford Alumni, Stanford & Freeman, W. H.

48. Horne, J. (1988) *Why We Sleep: the functions of sleep in humans and other mammals*. Oxford University Press.

49. Vogel, G. W. (1979) A motivational function of REM sleep. In Drucker-Colin, R., Shkurovich, M. & Sterman, M.B. (Eds.) *The Function of Sleep*. Academic Press. 233–250.

50. Lavie, P. (1996) *The Enchanted World of Sleep*. Yale University Press.

51. Lyamin, O. I., Manger, P. R., Mukhametov, L. M., Siegel, J. M. & Shpak, O. V. (2000) Rest and activity states in a gray whale. *Journal of Sleep Research*, 9, 3, 261–267.

52. Siegel, J. M., Manger, P. R., Nienhuis, R., Fahringer, H. M. & Pettigrew, J. D. (1999) Sleep in the platypus. *Neuroscience*, 91, 392.

53. Ibid.

54. Crick, F. & Mitchison, G. (1983) The function of dream sleep. *Nature*, 304, 111–114.

55. Domhoff, G. W. (2001) A new neurocognitive theory of dreams. *Dreaming*, 11, 13-33.

56. van der Helm, E., Yao, J., Dutt, S., Rao, V., Saletin, J.M. & Walker, M.P. (2011) REM sleep depotentiates amygdala activity to previous emotional experience. *Current Biology*, 21, 23, 2029–2032.

57. Gujar, N., McDonald, S., Nishida, M., & Walker, M. (2010) A role for REM sleep in recalibrating the sensitivity of the human brain to specific emotions. *Cerebral Cortex*, 21, 1, 115-123.

58. Selterman, D.F., Apetroaia, A. I., Riela, S. & Aron, A. (2014) Dreaming of You: behavior and emotion in dreams of significant others predict subsequent relational behavior. *Social Psychological and Personality Science*, 5, 1, 111–118.

59. Revonsuo, A. & Valli, K. (2000) Dreaming and consciousness: testing the threat simulation function of dreaming. *Psyche*, 6, 8. http://psyche.cs.monash.edu.au/v6/psyche-6-08-revonsuo.html)

60. See, for overview, Domhoff, G. W. (2008) The awesome lawfulness of your nightly dreams. Lecture given at University of California Santa Cruz, April 9.

61. Saurat, M., Agbakou, M., Attigui, P., Golmard, J. & Arnulf, I.(2011) Walking dreams in congenital and acquired paraplegia. *Consciousness and Cognition*, 20, 4, 1425–32.

62. Fosse, M. J., Fosse, R., Hobson, A. J. & Stickgold, R. J. (2003). Dreaming and episodic memory: a functional dissociation? *Journal of Cognitive Neuroscience*, 15, 1, 1–9.

63. Wamsley, E. J. & Stickgold, R. (2011) Memory, sleep and dreaming: experiencing consolidation. *Sleep Medicine Clinics*, 2011, 6, 1, 97–108.

Chapter 5: The psychology of dreaming

1. Blakeslee, T. R. (1980) *The Right Brain*. Macmillan.

2. Ornstein, R. (1997) *The Right Mind: making sense of the hemispheres*. Harcourt Brace.

3. Hoppe, K. D. (1977) Split brains and psychoanalysis. *The Psycho-Analytic Quarterly*, 46, 220–224.

4. Bogen, J. E. (1969) The other side of the brain, 11: an appositional mind. *Bulletin of the Los Angeles Neurological Society* 34, 135–162.

5. Watzlawick, P. (1978) *The Language of Change*. Basic Books.

6. For a more up-to-date account of brain hemisphere differences, see McGilchrist, I. (2009) *The Master and his Emissary: the divided brain and the making of the Western world*. Yale University Press.
7. Griffin, J. and Tyrrell, I. (2003, 2013) *Human Givens: the new approach to emotional health and clear thinking*. HG Publishing.

Chapter 6:
Two houses of cards collapse: the seminal dreams of Freud and Jung

1. Freud, S. (1953) *The Interpretation of Dreams*. Page 647 of the standard edition of the complete psychological works of Sigmund Freud. Strackey, J. (Ed.). Hogarth Press.
2. Masson, J. M. (1985) (Ed.) *The Complete Letters of Sigmund Freud to Wilhelm Fliess*, 1887–1904. Harvard University Press.
3. Schur, M. (1966) Some additional 'day residues' of the specimen dream of psychoanalysis. Lowenstein, R. M., Newman, L. M., Schur, M. & Solnit A. J., (Eds.), *Psychoanalysis: A General Psychology – Essays in Honour of Hartmann, H.* International Universities Press, 45–85.
4. Masson, J. M. (1984) *Freud: The Assault on Truth*. Faber & Faber.
5. Ry, B. (1897) in a review of Fliess's book, *The Relationship between the Nose and the Female Sexual Organs*, published in *Wiener Klinische Rundschau*. Dr Benjamin Ry's words are quoted in a footnote in Masson's *The Complete Letters of Sigmund Freud to Wilhelm Fliess* (see ref. 2 above).
6. Sulloway, F. J. (1979) *Freud, Biologist of the Mind: Beyond the Psychoanalytic Legend*. André Deutsch.
7. Jung, C. (1965) *Memories, Dreams, Reflections*. Vintage Books, 158–159. Strictly speaking this is not an autobiography. Jung only wrote the first three chapters, about his early life himself and a final section called 'Late Thoughts'. The rest of it is the work of many hands and so it has been called "a product of discipleship" rather than of autobiographical history. See: *The Jung Cult: Origins of a Charismatic Movement* by Richard Noll (1995) Princeton University Press.
8. Jung, C. (1964) *Man and His Symbols*. Dell Publishing, 42–44.
9. Dolnick, E. (1998) *Madness on the Couch*. Simon & Schuster.
10. Webster, R. (1995) *Why Freud Was Wrong*. Harper Collins.
11. Dewdney, A. K. (1997) *Yes, We Have No Neutrons – an eye-opening tour through the twists and turns of bad science*. John Wiley & Sons.
12. Lilienfeld, S. O., Lynn, S. J. and Lohr, J. M. Eds. (2003) *Science and Pseudoscience in Clinical Psychology*. Guilford Press.
13. Pendergrast, M. (1995) *Victims of Memory: incest accusations and shattered lives*. Harper Collins.
14. Griffin, J. & Tyrrell, I. (2003, 2013) *Human Givens: the new approach to emotional health and clear thinking*. HG Publishing Ltd.
15. Noll, R. & Tyrrell, I. (1997) The Mysterious Jung – psychotherapy and the occult. *The Therapist*, 4, 2, 24–30.
16. Curtis, A. & Tyrrell, I. (2002) A seething mass of desires: Freud's hold over history. *Human Givens*, 9, 3, 24–31.

17. Furedi, F. (2003) *Therapy Culture: cultivating vulnerability in an uncertain age*. Routledge.
18. Noll, R. (1995) *The Jung Cult: origins of a charismatic movement*. Princeton University Press.
19. Dolnick, E. (1998) *Madness on the Couch*. Simon & Schuster.

Chapter 7: Solving problems: creativity and dreams

1. Koestler, A. (1964) *The Act of Creation*. Hutchinson.
2. Wallace, G. (1926) *The Art of Thought*. Jonathan Cape.
3. Lavie, P. (1996) *The Enchanted World of Sleep*. Yale University Press.
4. Dement, W. (1972) *Some Must Watch While Some Must Sleep*. Stanford Alumni, Stanford & Freeman, W. H.
5. Dixon, N. (1981) *Preconscious Processing*. John Wiley & Sons.
6. Schatzman, M. (1983) Solving problems in your sleep. *New Scientist*, 98, 692.
7. Inglis, B. (1987) *The Power of Dreams*. Grafton Books.
8. Ibid.
9. See, for instance, Wamsley, E. J., Tucker, T., Payne, J. D., Benavides, J. A. & Stickgold, R. (2010) Dreaming of a learning task is associated with enhanced sleep-dependent memory consolidation. *Current Biology*, 20, 9, 850–55; Wamsley, E. J. & Stickgold, R. (2013) The Psychology of Dreams. *Encyclopedia of Sleep*, 132–138; Wamsley, E. J. (2014) Dreaming and offline memory consolidation. *Current Neurology and Neuroscience Reports*, 14, 3, 433–5.
10. Lavie, P. (1996). *The Enchanted World of Sleep*. Yale University Press.
11. Wamsley, E. J., Tucker, T., Payne, J. D., Benavides, J. A. & Stickgold, R.(2010) Dreaming of a learning task is associated with enhanced sleep-dependent memory consolidation. *Current Biology*, 20, 9, 850–55.
12. Kenway, L. & Wilson, M. A. (2001) Temporally structured replay of awake hippocampal ensemble activity during rapid eye movement sleep. *Neuron*, 29, 1, 145–156.
13. Vertes, R. P. (2004) Memory consolidation in sleep. *Neuron* 44, 1, 135-148.
14. Wamsley, E. J.; Tucker, M.; Payne, J. D.; Benavides, J. A. & Stickgold, R. (2010) Dreaming of a learning task is associated with enhanced sleep-dependent memory consolidation. *Current Biology*, 20, 9, 850–855.

Chapter 8: The waking dream

1. Weitzman, E. D. & Kremen, H. (1965) Auditory responses during different stages of sleep in man. *Electroencephalography and Clinical Neurophysiology*, 18, 65–70.
2. Waterfield, R. (2002) *Hidden Depths: the story of hypnosis*. Macmillan.
3. Kroger, W. S. (1977) *Clinical and Experimental Hypnosis*. Lippincott.
4. Rossi, E. R. (1993) *The psychobiology of mind-body healing*. Norton.

5. Erickson, M. H. (1992) *The Seminars, Workshops and Lectures of Milton H. Erickson (Vols I–IV)*. Free Association Books.
6. Griffin, J. & Tyrrell, I. (2003, 2013) *Human Givens: the new approach to emotional health and clear thinking*. HG Publishing Ltd.
7. Tyrrell, I. (Ed.) (1997) *Therapia: new insights into therapy and human behaviour*. The Therapist Ltd.
8. Griffin, J. & Tyrrell, I. (1998) *Hypnosis and Trance States: a new psycho-biological explanation*. European Therapy Studies Institute.
9. Barber, J. (1996) *Hypnosis and Suggestion in the Treatment of Pain*. Norton.
10. Hartland, J. (1989) *Medical and Dental Hypnosis and its Clinical Application*. Baillière Tindall.
11. Battino, R. and South, T. L. (1999) *Ericksonian Approaches*. Crown House Publishing.
12. Weitzenhoffer, A. M. (1989) *The Practice of Hypnotism*. John Wiley & Sons.
13. Ibid.
14. Rossi, E. R. (1991) *Twenty Minute Break: the new science of ultradian rhythms*. Palisades Gateway Publishing.
15. Yapko, M. D. (1990) *Trancework: an introduction to the practice of clinical hypnosis*. Brunner Mazel.
16. Lewis-Williams, D. (2002) *The Mind in the Cave*. Thames & Hudson.
17. Bromhall, C. (2003) *The Eternal Child*. Ebury Press. Clive Bromhall has reached the same conclusion by a different road. He wrote in his hugely insightful book *The Eternal Child* that, "For our ancestors to become truly human – to be conscious of their own existence and actions – they had to be able to daydream... Without simultaneously experiencing an internal world – through daydreaming – and an external world, then there is no concept of 'inside' and 'outside', and thus no concept of 'me' and 'not me'." He has also realised that daydreaming was an essential prerequisite for the explosion in human creativity and the origin of complex language.
18. Griffin, J. & Tyrrell, I. (2011) *Godhead: the brain's big bang – the explosive origin of creativity, mysticism and mental illness*. HG Publishing Ltd.
19. Spearman, C. E. (1927) *The Abilities of Man, their Nature and Development*. Macmillan.
20. Byron, K. (1999) *Inventions and Inventing: finding solutions to practical problems*. Institute for Cultural Research, London.
21. Ibid.
22. Bruner, J. (1986) *Actual Minds, Possible Worlds*. Harvard University Press.
23. Hoberman, M. A. (1978) *A House Is a House for Me*. Viking. We would like to thank Pat Williams for drawing this delightful book to our attention.
24. Shah, I. (1979) *World Tales*. Allen Lane.
25. Retold from *A Book of Wisdom and Lies* by Sulkhan-Saba Orbeliani. Translated by Katharine Vivian (1982). The Octagon Press.
26. Griffin, J. & Tyrrell, I. (2003, 2013) *Human Givens: the new approach to emotional health and clear thinking*. HG Publishing Ltd.

27. Rosen, S. (1982) *My Voice Will Go With You: the teaching tales of Milton H. Erickson*. Norton.
28. Gafner, G. & Benson, S. (2003) *Hypnotic Techniques*. Norton.
29. Rosen, S. (1982) *My Voice Will Go With You: The teaching tales of Milton H. Erickson*. Norton.
30. Gafner, G. & Benson, S. (2003) *Hypnotic Techniques*. Norton.
31. Mirowski, P. (1989) *More Heat Than Light*. Cambridge University Press
32. Pendergrast, M. (1997) Bradshaw: the evangelists of dysfunction. *The Therapist*, 4, 2, 4–5.
33. Danton, W., Antonuccio, D. & DeNelsky, G. (1995) Depression: psychotherapy is the best medicine. *Professional Psychology Research and Practice*, 26, 574.
34. Danton, W., Antonuccio, D. & Rosenthal, Z. (1997) No need to panic. *The Therapist*, 4, 4, 38–41.

Chapter 9:
Practical applications of the new expectation fulfilment theory

1. Dyson, J. & Uhlig, R. (Ed.) (2001) *A History of Great Inventions*. Constable & Robinson.
2. Williams, P. (1997) How simplicities could help the NHS. *The Therapist*. Vol 4, 2, 8–9.
3. Danton, W., Antonuccio, D. & DeNelsky, G. (1995) Depression: psychotherapy is the best medicine. *Professional Psychology Research and Practice*, 26, 574.
4. See the Human Givens College website: www.humangivenscollege.com
5. Kiser, B. (2003) The dreamcatcher. *New Scientist*, 178, 2390.
6. Woodham, A. (2002) Depressed? Look on the bright side. *The Times*, 6 August.
7. Thompson, T. (2003) Is too much dreaming bad for you? *Irish Times*, 23 June.
8. NHS National Services Framework for Mental Health.
9. Lane, R. E. (2000) *The Loss of Happiness in Market Democracies*. Yale University Press.
10. Wasserman, D., Cheng, Q. & Jiang, G-X. (2005) Global suicide rates among young people aged 15–19. *World Psychiatry*, 4, 2, 114–120.
11. Seligman in James Buie (1988) *'Me' Decades Generate Depression: individualism erodes commitment to others*. APA Monitor 19:18. "People born after 1945 were ten times more likely to suffer from depression than people born 50 years earlier."
12. World Health Organization (2008) *The Global Burden of Disease* 2004 update. http://www.who.int/healthinfo/global_burden_disease/GBD_ report_2004update
13. Coble, P. A., Kupfer, D. J. & Shaw, D. H. (1981) Distribution of REM latency in depression. *Biological Psychiatry*, 1981, 16, 453–466.
14. Kupfer, D. J., Ulrich, R. F., Coble, P. A., Jarrett, D. B., Grochocinski, V. J., Doman, J., Matthews, G. & Borbely, A. A. (1984) The application of automated REM and slow-wave sleep analysis (normal and depressives). *Psychiatric Research*, 13, 325–334.

15. Reynolds, C. F. III & Kupfer. D. (1988) Sleep in depression. In Williams, R.Z., Karacan I. & Moore C. A., (Eds.) *Sleep disorders, diagnosis and treatment.* John Wiley.

16. Karnovsky, M. L., Reich, P., Anchors, J. M. & Burrows B. L. (1983) Changes in brain glycogen during slow-wave sleep in the rat. *Journal of Neurochemistry*, 41, 1498–1501.

17. Berger, M., van Calker, D. & Riemann, D. (2003) Sleep and manipulations of the sleep-wake rhythm in depression. *Acta Psychiatrica Scandinavica,* 108 (s418), 83–91.

18. Yapko, M. (1994) *When Living Hurts*. Brunner Mazel.

19. Morrison, A. (1983). A window on the sleeping brain. *Scientific American*, 248, 8694.

20. Morrison, A. & Reiner, P. (1985). A dissection of paradoxical sleep. In McGinty, D. J., Drucker-Colin, R., Morrison, A. & Parmeggiani P. L. (Eds.) *Brain Mechanisms of Sleep.*

21. Vogel, G. W., Buffenstein, A., Minter, K. & Hennessey A. (1990) Drug effects on REM sleep and on endogenous depression. *Neuroscience Biobehavioral Review.* 1990, 14, 49–63.

22. Riemann, D., Voderholzer, U. & Berger M. (2002) Sleep and sleep-wake manipulations in bipolar depression. *Neuropsychobiology*. 2002, 45, Suppl 1: 7–12.

23. Vogel, G. W. (1979) A motivational function of REM sleep. In Drucker-Colin, R., Shkurovich, M. & Sterman, M. B. (Eds.) *The Function of Sleep*. Academic Press, 233–250.

24. Read, J., Cartwright, C. & Gibson, K.(2014) Adverse emotional and interpersonal effects reported by 1829 New Zealanders while taking antidepressants. *Psychiatry Research,* doi: 10.1016/j.psychres.2014.01.042

25. Glenmullen, J. (2000) P*rozac Backlash: Overcoming the dangers of Prozac, Zoloft, Paxil and other antidepressants with safe, effective alternatives.* Simon & Schuster.

26. Robinson, I. (1999) *Mind Sculpture*. Bantam Press.

27. Dubovsky, S. L. (1997) *Mind-Body Deceptions: the psychosomatics of everyday life*. Norton; Kirsch, I. (2009) The Emperor's New Drugs: exploding the antidepressant myth. Bodley Head.

28. Kirch, I. & Moore, T. (2002) Data from 47 placebo controlled trials of six SSRI antidepressant drugs, run by pharmaceutical companies themselves, were examined in a meta-analysis. It showed virtually no difference in effectiveness between the active drugs and placebos. The meta-analysis and nine commentaries on it can be viewed on the American Psychological Association's electronic journal *Prevention and Treatment* (www.journals.apa.org/prevention)

29. Danton, W., Antonuccio, D. & DeNelsky, G. (1995). Depression: psychotherapy is the best medicine. *Professional Psychology Research and Practice*, 26, 574.

30. Albom, M. (1997) *Tuesdays with Morrie*. Doubleday.

31. Brown, G. (2001) Talking to the person with pain. *Human Givens*, 8, 2, 36–41.

32. Moldofsky, H., Scarisbrick, P., England, R. & Smythe, H. (1975) Musculoskeletal symptoms and non-REM sleep disturbance in patients with fibrositis syndrome and healthy subjects. *Psychosomatic Medicine*, 371, 341–351.

33. Bentall, R. P. (2003) *Madness Explained: psychosis and human nature.* Penguin/Allen Lane.

34. Siris, S. G. (1995) Depression and schizophrenia. In Hirsch, S. R. & Weinberger, D. R. (Eds.) *Schizophrenia.* Blackwell.

35. Huppert, J. D. & Smith, T. E. (2001) Longitudinal analysis of subjective quality of life in schizophrenia: anxiety as the best symptom predictor. *Journal of Nervous and Mental Disease*, 189, 669–75.

36. Emsley, R., Oosthuizen, P., Niehaus, D. & Stein, D. (2001) Anxiety symptoms in schizophrenia: the need for heightened clinical awareness. *Primary Care Psychiatry*, 7, 25–9.

37. Llinas, R. & Pare, D. (1991) On dreaming and wakefulness. *Neuroscience,* 44, 3, 521–535. According to neuroscientists Denis Pare and Rodolfo Llinas, the brain's simultaneous 40 Hz 'neural oscillations', which are associated with consciousness, also occur during REM sleep. Given this, Pare and Llinas were led to the conclusion that the only difference between our dreaming and waking states is that in waking states, the "closed system that generates oscillatory states" is modulated by incoming stimuli from the outside world. In other words, what we call our "waking state" is really a REM dream state, with a sensory topping. Or, as P. D. Ouspensky put it, we shouldn't speak of being either asleep or awake, but of "sleep plus waking state."

38. Frith, C. T. (1995) Functional imaging and cognitive abnormality, *Lancet*, 346, 8975, 615–620.

39. Leff, J. (2002) *The Unbalanced Mind.* Phoenix.

40. Torrey, E. F. and Miller, M. (2001) *The Invisible Plague: the rise of mental illness from 1750 to the present.* Rutgers University Press.

41. Nettle, D. (2000) *Strong Imagination: madness, creativity and human nature.* Oxford University Press.

42. Ibid.

43. Leff, J. (2002) *The Unbalanced Mind.* Phoenix.

44. Drake, R. & Cotton, P. G. ((1986) Depression, hopelessness and suicide in chronic schizophrenia. *British Journal of Psychiatry*, 148, 554–9

45. Griffin, J. & Tyrrell, I. (2003, 2013) *Human Givens: the new approach to emotional health and clear thinking.* HG Publishing Ltd.

46. Sartorius, N., Jablensky, A., Korten, A., Ernberg, G., Anker, M., Cooper, J. E. & Day, R. (1986) Early manifestations and first-contact incidence of schizophrenia in different cultures. *Psychological Medicine*, 16, 909–928.

47. Wunderink, L., Nieboer, R. M., Wiersma, D., Sytema, S. & Nienhuis, F. J. (2013). Recovery in remitted first-episode psychosis at 7 years of follow-up of an early dose reduction/discontinuation or maintenance treatment strategy: long-term follow-up of a 2-year randomised clinical trial. *Journal of the American Medical Association Psychiatry*, 1,70, 9, 913-920.

48. Whitaker, R. (2002) *Mad in America: bad science, bad medicine and the enduring mistreatment of the mentally ill.* Perseus Publishing.

49. Traditional community resources for mental health: a report of temple healing from India. (2002) *British Medical Journal*, 325, 38–40.

50. Tyrrell, I. & Bentall, R. (2003) "What was that you said, again?" A new look at psychosis. *Human Givens*, 10, 3, 24–31.

Chapter 10: Dreaming Reality

1. Lewis-Williams, D. (2002) *The Mind in the Cave*. Thames & Hudson.

Appendix: Loose ends

1. Gribbin, J. (1984) *In Search of Schrodinger's Cat: quantum physics and reality*. Bantam.

2. ibid.

3. ibid.

4. Griffin, J. & Tyrrell, I. (2003, 2013) *Human Givens: the new approach to emotional health and clear thinking*. HG Publishing Ltd.

5. Vitebsky, P. (1995) *The Shaman: voyages of the soul, trance, ecstasy and healing from Siberia to the Amazon*. Macmillan.

6. Narby, J. (1998) *The Cosmic Serpent: DNA and the origins of knowledge*. Victor Gollancz.

7. Lewis-Williams, D. (2002) *The Mind in the Cave*. Thames & Hudson.

8. Whitehead, A. N. (1929) *Process and Reality*. Macmillan.

9. Translated by Kenneth Guthrie. Introduction by Michael Hornum. (1977) *Porphyry's Launching-Points to the Realm of Mind: an introduction to the neoplatonic philosophy of Plotinus*. Phanes Press.

10. Sheldrake, R. (2003) *The Sense of Being Stared At*. Hutchinson

11. Dunne, J. W. (1927) *An experiment with time*. Faber & Faber. [1969].

12. Ullman, M. (1961) Dreaming, altered states of consciousness and the problem of vigilance. *Journal of Nervous Mental Diseases*, 133, 529–535.

13. Ullman, M. & Krippner, S. with Vaughan, A. (1988) *Dream Telepathy* (2nd Ed.). McFarland, Jefferson.

14. Hearne, K. (1989) *Visions of the Future*. Thorsons.

15. Ibid.

16. Ibid.

17. Hobson, J. A. (2002) *Dreaming: An introduction to the science of sleep*. Oxford University Press.

18. Shah, I. (1964) *The Sufis*. Octagon Press.

19. La Berge, S. (1985) *Lucid Dreaming*. Ballantine Books. [1998].

INDEX

L

M

Q

R

U

V

W

Z

Compiled by Indexing Specialists (UK) Ltd, Indexing House, 306A Portland Road, Hove, East Sussex, BN3 6LP
Tel: 01273 416777 | Email: indexers@indexinghouse.co.uk | Website: www.indexing.co.uk

ABOUT THE AUTHORS

Joe Griffin is a social psychologist with graduate and postgraduate degrees from the LSE. He has had many years experience both in psychotherapeutic practice and in training psychotherapists.

Scientific reviewers around the world have described his research on dreaming with such phrases as, "The bridge between neurophysiology and psychology... rigorously scientific... an important milestone... moves our understanding on significantly... a watershed in our exploration of the evolution of mental processes... a major key to the nature of all psychic states." He is co-author with Ivan Tyrrell of five landmark monographs about advances in psychological interventions for emotional disturbances and numerous best-selling books, including *How to lift depression...fast*, *Freedom from Addiction* and *Dreaming Reality: How dreaming keeps us sane or can drive us mad.*

Joe has two daughters and lives with his wife, Liz, in a small medieval town by the river Barrow in rural Ireland.

Ivan Tyrrell's interest in psychology stems from a childhood experience of undergoing surgery under hypnosis. For twenty years he studied the comparative effectiveness of psychotherapy and counselling models, linking this to what science is discovering about the brain and mind/body/mood connections. As Editorial Director of the *Human Givens Journal* he has collaborated on many major articles with a variety of distinguished clinicians, writers and other individuals with a focus on psychology, social issues and mental health.

Ivan worked for many years as a psychotherapist and lecturer and is now joint director of Human Givens College, teaching on their diploma course. He founded the Human Givens Institute. He has one son and three daughters and lives with his wife, Véronique, in the Cotswold countryside.

ABOUT THE AUTHORS

Joe Griffin's theory of why we evolved to dream was first published in the fore-runner of the journal, *Human Givens: promoting emotional health and clear thinking.*

The official journal of the Human Givens Institute, this publication explores the relevance of the very latest knowledge about human psychology to the way we live today, focusing on practical implications across a wide range of disciplines – from psychotherapy and health and welfare, to education and even diplomacy. As such it is often at the forefront of new thinking about human biology and psychology, and proves inspiring reading. Many of its articles can be read on the archive section of the Institute's website at:

www.hgi.org.uk

* * *

For more information about the HG approach, please visit:

www.humangivenscollege.com
www.griffintyrrell.co.uk
www.humangivens.com
blog.humangivens.com
facebook.com/humangivens
twitter.com/humangivens